Mastering phpMyAdmin 3.3.x for Effective MySQL Management

A complete guide to getting started with
phpMyAdmin 3.3 and mastering its features

Marc Delisle

[PACKT] open source*

PUBLISHING

community experience distilled

BIRMINGHAM - MUMBAI

Mastering phpMyAdmin 3.3.x
for Effective MySQL Management

First published: October 2010

Production Reference: 1041010

Published by Packt Publishing Ltd.
32 Lincoln Road
Olton
Birmingham, B27 6PA, UK.

ISBN 978-1-849513-54-8

www.packtpub.com

Cover Image by Marc Delisle (marc@phpmyadmin.net)

Credits

Author
Marc Delisle

Reviewers
Michal Čihař
Ben Dodson
Kai 'Oswald' Seidler

Development Editor
Reshma Sundaresan

Technical Editor
Conrad Sardinha

Indexer
Hemangini Bari

Editorial Team Leader
Akshara Aware

Project Team Leader
Lata Basantani

Project Coordinator
Sneha Harkut

Proofreader
Dirk Manuel

Production Coordinator
Adline Swetha Jesuthas

Cover Work
Adline Swetha Jesuthas

About the Author

Marc Delisle was awarded "MySQL Community Member of the year 2009" because of his involvement with phpMyAdmin. He started to contribute to the project in December 1998, when he developed the multi-language version. He is still involved with phpMyAdmin as a developer and project administrator.

Marc is a system administrator at Cegep de Sherbrooke, Québec, Canada. He has taught networking, security, and web application development. In one of his classes, he was pleased to meet a phpMyAdmin user from Argentina. Marc lives in Sherbrooke with his wife and they enjoy spending time with their four children.

This book was Marc's first one and was quickly followed by *Creating your MySQL Database: Practical Design Tips and Techniques*, also published by Packt Publishing.

I am truly grateful to Louay Fatoohi who approached me for this book project, and to the Packt team whose sound comments were greatly appreciated during the production. My thanks also go to the excellent reviewers Kai 'Oswald' Seidler, Ben Dodson, and Michal Čihař. Their sharp eyes helped in making this book clearer and more complete.

Finally, I wish to thank all contributors to phpMyAdmin's source code, translations, and documentation; their dedication to this project continues to push me forward.

About the Reviewers

Michal Čihař was born in 1980 in Prague, the capital city of the Czech Republic, and he is still living there. He studied Software Engineering at the Czech Technical University, and during these studies he started contributing to several free software projects, with the biggest contributions being made to phpMyAdmin and Gammu, and related projects. He currently works for Novell, mostly on the SUSE Linux Enterprise platform.

Michal has been active in the phpMyAdmin project since 2001, when he started as a translator for the Czech language, later moving to a developer role (working, for example, on index manipulation, and export and import subsystems), and since 2010 he has also acted as a secondary project manager.

Ben Dodson has worked with the Internet for over 15 years, yet originally studied Politics. He trained briefly as an Air Traffic Controller for the RAF before deciding to change career paths and work as a freelance HTML/PHP developer, in Devon. He relocated to London to work for a digital agency, and was rapidly promoted to Development Manager in charge of a team of front- and back-end web developers in several countries.

After working for a few more agencies, he decided to return to freelancing but this time as an iPhone Developer. He now splits his time in Central London between working on his own applications and working on applications for brand-name clients, incorporating everything from store locators to iPad magazine concepts.

Ben still maintains a strong connection to his web development roots by working on APIs for geo-coded Wikipedia Articles (www.wikilocation.org) and the London Underground (www.tubeupdates.com). One of his main interests is in the power of location-aware applications and so he has spent a lot of time developing Gowalla Tools, a suite of applications that utilize the popular Gowalla geo-location service.

Aside from his websites and iPhone applications, Ben enjoys working on everything from browser extensions to OpenID servers. He is a keen photographer and designer, and is currently working on his first book, which discusses Machiavellian republicanism.

Ben has been invited to speak at several conferences and has appeared on BBC Television's "Working Lunch" program to discuss e-commerce, and also Channel Five's "The Gadget Show" to demonstrate iPhone Application development.

Kai 'Oswald' Seidler was born in Hamburg in 1970. He graduated from the Technical University of Berlin with a Diplom Informatiker degree (Master of Science equivalent) in Computer Science. In the '90s he created and managed Germany's biggest IRCnet server, `irc.fu-berlin.de`, and co-managed one of the world's largest anonymous FTP servers, `ftp.cs.tu-berlin.de`. He professionally set up his first public web server in 1993. From 1993 until 1998, he was a member of Projektgruppe Kulturraum Internet, a research project on net culture and network organization. In 2002, he co-founded Apache Friends and created the multi-platform Apache web server bundle XAMPP. Around 2005, XAMPP became the most popular Apache stack worldwide. In 2006, his third book, *Das XAMPP-Handbuch*, was published by Addison Wesley.

Currently he's working as a technology evangelist for web tier products at Sun Microsystems.

To Carole, André, Corinne, Annie, and Guillaume, with all my love.

Table of Contents

Preface

phpMyAdmin is an open source tool written in PHP. It handles the administration of MySQL over the World Wide Web (WWW). It can perform various tasks, such as creating, modifying, or deleting databases, tables, fields, or rows. It can also execute SQL statements and manage users and their permissions. When it comes to exploiting phpMyAdmin to its full potential, even experienced developers and system administrators search for tutorials to accomplish their tasks.

Mastering phpMyAdmin 3.3.x for Effective MySQL Management is an easy-to-read, step-by-step practical guide that walks you through every facet of this legendary tool—phpMyAdmin—and takes you a step ahead in taking full advantage of its potential. This book is filled with illustrative examples that will help you to understand every phpMyAdmin feature in detail.

This book jump starts with installing and configuring phpMyAdmin, and then looks into phpMyAdmin's features. This is followed by configuring authentication in phpMyAdmin, and setting parameters that influence the interface as a whole. You will first create two basic tables, and then edit and delete data, tables, and databases. As backups are crucial to a project, you will create up-to-date backups and take intermediary snapshots during development and production phases. Then you will look into importing the data that you have exported. You will also explore the various search mechanisms, and query across multiple tables.

Then, you will learn some advanced features, such as defining inter-table relations and installing the linked-tables infrastructure. Some queries are out of the scope of the interface; you will enter SQL commands to accomplish these tasks.

You will also learn some new features introduced in version 3.3.x, such as synchronizing databases on different servers, and managing MySQL replication in order to improve performance and data security. You will also store queries as bookmarks for their quick retrieval. Towards the end of the book you will learn to document your database, track changes made to the database, and manage user accounts using phpMyAdmin server management features.

This book is an upgrade from the previous version that covered phpMyAdmin Version 3.1. Version 3.3.x introduced features such as new import and export modules, tracking changes, synchronizing structure and data between servers, providing support for replication.

What this book covers

Chapter1, Getting Started with phpMyAdmin, gives us the reasons why we should use phpMyAdmin as a means of managing MySQL databases. It then covers the downloading and installation procedures for phpMyAdmin.

Chapter 2, Configuring Authentication and Security, provides an overview of various authentication types used in phpMyAdmin. It then covers the security issues related to the phpMyAdmin installation.

Chapter 3, Over Viewing the Interface, gives us an overview of the phpMyAdmin interface. This includes the login panel, the navigation and main panels in both Light mode and Full mode, and the Query window.

Chapter 4, Taking First Steps, is all about database creation. It teaches us how to create a table, how to insert data manually, and how to sort the data.

Chapter 5, Changing Data and Structure, covers the various aspects of data editing in phpMyAdmin. It teaches us how to handle NULL values, multi-row editing, and data deletion. Finally, it explores the subject of changing the structure of tables, focusing on editing field attributes and index management.

Chapter 6, Exporting Structure and Data (Backup), deals with backups and exports. It lists various ways to trigger an export, available export formats, the options associated with export formats, and the various places where the export files can be sent.

Chapter 7, Importing Structure and Data, tells us how to bring back exported data that was created for backup and transfer purposes. It covers the various options available in phpMyAdmin to import data, and different mechanisms involved in importing SQL and CSV files. Finally, it covers the limitations that may be faced while importing files, and the ways to overcome these limitations.

Chapter 8, Searching Data, presents the mechanisms that are useful for searching data effectively.

Chapter 9, Performing Table and Database Operations, covers ways to perform some operations that influence and can be applied on entire tables or databases as a whole. Finally, it deals with table maintenance operations for table repair and optimization.

Chapter 10, Benefiting from the Relational System, is where we start covering the advanced features of phpMyAdmin. The chapter explains how to define inter-table relations. It also explains how to install the linked-tables infrastructure —a prerequisite for the advanced features.

Chapter 11, Entering SQL Commands, teaches us how to enter our own SQL commands. The chapter also covers the Query window—the window used to edit an SQL query. Finally, it also shows us how to obtain the history of typed commands.

Chapter 12, Generating Multi-table Queries, covers the multi-table query generator, which allows us to produce these queries without actually typing them.

Chapter 13, Synchronizing Data and Supporting Replication, teaches us how to synchronize databases on the same server, or from one server to another one. It then covers how to manage MySQL replication.

Chapter 14, Using Bookmarks, covers one of the features of the linked-tables infrastructure. It explains how to record bookmarks and how to manipulate them. Finally, it covers how to pass parameters to bookmarks.

Chapter 15, Documenting the System, gives an overview of how to produce documentation that explains the structure of a database, by using the tools offered by phpMyAdmin.

Chapter 16, Transforming Data Using MIME, explains how to apply transformations to data in order to customize its format at view time.

Chapter 17, Supporting MySQL 5.0 and 5.1, covers phpMyAdmin's support for the MySQL features that are new in these versions.

Chapter 18, Tracking Changes, teaches us how to record structure and data changes done from the phpMyAdmin interface.

Chapter 19, Administrating the MySQL Server with phpMyAdmin, is about the administration of a MySQL server, focusing on user accounts and privileges. The chapter discusses how a system administrator can use phpMyAdmin's server management features for day-to-day user account maintenance, server verification, and server protection.

Appendix A, The History of phpMyAdmin, provides a history of the project, from its roots back in 1998 through the project re-launch in 2001, and its subsequent evolution.

Appendix B, Troubleshooting and Support, explains how to troubleshoot phpMyAdmin by examining some of its error messages, and proposing appropriate solutions. It also explains how to interact with the development team for support, bug reports, and contributions.

What you need for this book

You need to have access to a server or workstation that has the following installed:

- A web server with PHP 5.2 or later
- MySQL 5.0 or later

Who this book is for

If you are a developer, system administrator, or web designer who wants to manage MySQL databases and tables efficiently, then this book is for you. This book assumes that you are already well-acquainted with MySQL basics. This book is a must-read for every serious phpMyAdmin user who would like to use this outstanding application to its full power.

Conventions

In this book, you will find a number of styles of text that distinguish between different kinds of information. Here are some examples of these styles, and an explanation of their meaning.

Code words in text are shown as follows: "The `cookie` authentication mode is superior to `http` in terms of the functionalities offered".

A block of code is set as follows:

```
cd phpMyAdmin
mkdir config
chmod 777 config
```

When we wish to draw your attention to a particular part of a code block, the relevant lines or items are set in bold:

```
$cfg['Servers'][$i]['pmadb']            = 'marc_book';
$cfg['Servers'][$i]['bookmarktable']    = 'pma_bookmark';
$cfg['Servers'][$i]['relation']         = 'pma_relation';
```

Any command-line input or output is written as follows:

```
tar -xzvf phpMyAdmin-3.3.2-all-languages.tar.gz
```

New terms and **important words** are shown in bold. Words that you see on the screen, in menus or dialog boxes for example, appear in the text like this: "If **Show hidden messages** appears and we click on this link, messages that might have been shown earlier are revealed".

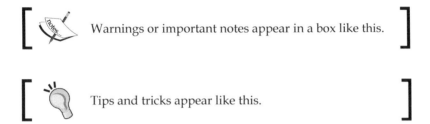

Warnings or important notes appear in a box like this.

Tips and tricks appear like this.

Reader feedback

Feedback from our readers is always welcome. Let us know what you think about this book—what you liked or may have disliked. Reader feedback is important for us to develop titles that you really get the most out of.

To send us general feedback, simply send an e-mail to feedback@packtpub.com, and mention the book title via the subject of your message.

If there is a book that you need and would like to see us publish, please send us a note in the **SUGGEST A TITLE** form on www.packtpub.com or e-mail suggest@packtpub.com.

If there is a topic that you have expertise in and you are interested in either writing or contributing to a book, see our author guide on www.packtpub.com/authors.

Customer support

Now that you are the proud owner of a Packt book, we have a number of things to help you to get the most from your purchase.

Downloading the example code for this book

You can download the example code files for all Packt books you have purchased from your account at http://www.PacktPub.com. If you purchased this book elsewhere, you can visit http://www.PacktPub.com/support and register to have the files e-mailed directly to you.

Errata

Although we have taken every care to ensure the accuracy of our content, mistakes do happen. If you find a mistake in one of our books—maybe a mistake in the text or the code—we would be grateful if you would report this to us. By doing so, you can save other readers from frustration and help us improve subsequent versions of this book. If you find any errata, please report them by visiting http://www.packtpub.com/support, selecting your book, clicking on the **errata submission form** link, and entering the details of your errata. Once your errata are verified, your submission will be accepted and the errata will be uploaded on our website, or added to any list of existing errata, under the Errata section of that title. Any existing errata can be viewed by selecting your title from http://www.packtpub.com/support.

Piracy

Piracy of copyright material on the Internet is an ongoing problem across all media. At Packt, we take the protection of our copyright and licenses very seriously. If you come across any illegal copies of our works, in any form, on the Internet, please provide us with the location address or website name immediately so that we can pursue a remedy.

Please contact us at copyright@packtpub.com with a link to the suspected pirated material.

We appreciate your help in protecting our authors, and our ability to bring you valuable content.

Questions

You can contact us at questions@packtpub.com if you are having a problem with any aspect of the book, and we will do our best to address it.

1
Getting Started with phpMyAdmin

I wish you a warm welcome to this book! The goal of this first chapter is to:

- Know the position of this software product in the web spectrum
- Be aware of all its features
- Become proficient at installing and configuring it

Introducing phpMyAdmin

This section describes the place of phpMyAdmin in the context of PHP/MySQL web applications.

Web applications

The Web has evolved! In the last few years the Web has changed dramatically. In its infancy, the Web was a medium used mainly to convey **static** information ("Look, my home-page is on the Web!"). Now, large parts of the Web carry information that is **dynamically generated** by application programs on which enterprises, and even individuals, rely for their intranets and public websites.

Because of the clear benefits of databases—better accessibility and structuring of information—web applications are mostly database driven. While the frontend is usually a well-known (and quickly deployed) web browser, there is a database system at the backend. Application programs provide the interface between the browser and the database.

Those who are not operating a database-driven website are not using the medium to its fullest capability. Also, they could be lagging behind competitors who have made the switch. So, it is not a question of whether we *should* implement a database-driven site, but rather about *when* and *how* to implement it.

Why web applications? Because they improve the user experience and involve users in the process by opening up possibilities such as:

- Gathering feedback about the site
- Letting users communicate with us and with each other through forums
- Ordering goods from our e-commerce site
- Enabling easily-editable web-based information (content management)
- Designing and maintaining databases from the Web

Nowadays, **WWW** might stand for **World Wide Wave** — a big wave that profoundly modifies the way developers think about user interface, data presentation, and most of all, the way data reaches users and comes back to the data center.

PHP and MySQL: The leading open source duo

When we look at the web applications platforms currently offered by host providers, we will see that most prevalent is the PHP/MySQL combination.

Well-supported by their respective homesites — `http://www.php.net` and `http://www.mysql.com` — this duo has enabled developers to build a lot of ready-made open source web applications and, most importantly, enabled in-house developers to quickly put solid web solutions in place.

MySQL, which is mostly compliant with the SQL:2003 standard, is a database system well known for its speed, robustness, and a small connection overhead. This is important in a web context where pages must be served as quickly as possible.

PHP, usually installed as a module on the web server, is a popular scripting language in which applications are written to communicate with MySQL (or other database systems) on the backend and browsers on the frontend. Ironically, the acronym's significance has evolved along with the evolution of the Web, from Personal HomePage to Professional HomePage to its current recursive definition: PHP: Hypertext Processor. An explanation of the successive name changes can be seen in PHP's source code at `http://svn.php.net/viewvc/archived/php3/trunk/CHANGES?r1=5246&r2=5459`. Available on millions of web domains, PHP drives its own wave of quickly-developing applications.

What is phpMyAdmin?

phpMyAdmin (see the official home page at `http://www.phpmyadmin.net`) is a web application written in PHP; it contains (like most web applications) XHTML, CSS, and JavaScript client code. This application provides a complete web interface for administering MySQL databases, and is widely recognized as the leading application in this field. Being open source since its birth, it has enjoyed support from numerous developers and translators worldwide (being translated into 58 languages at the time of writing this book). The project is currently hosted at Sourceforge.net and developed using their facilities by the phpMyAdmin team.

Host providers everywhere are showing their trust in phpMyAdmin by installing it on their servers. The popular cPanel (a website control application) interfaces with phpMyAdmin. In addition, we can install our own copy of phpMyAdmin inside our webspace, as long as our provider respects the minimum requirements (see the *System requirements* section later in this chapter).

The goal of phpMyAdmin is to offer the complete web-based management of MySQL servers and data, and to keep up with the evolution of MySQL and web standards. While the product is always evolving, it supports all standard operations, along with extra features.

The development team constantly fine-tunes the product based on the reported bugs and requested features, releasing new versions regularly.

phpMyAdmin offers features that cover basic MySQL database and table operations. It also has an internal relational system that maintains metadata to support advanced features. Finally, system administrators can manage users and privileges from phpMyAdmin. It is important to note that phpMyAdmin's choice of available operations depends on the rights the user has on a specific MySQL server.

Project documentation

Further information about phpMyAdmin is available on the homesite's documentation page, located at `http://www.phpmyadmin.net/home_page/docs.php`. Moreover, the development team, helped by the community, maintains a wiki at `http://wiki.phpmyadmin.net`.

Installing phpMyAdmin

It's time to install the product and configure it minimally for first-time use.

Our reason for installing phpMyAdmin could be one of the following:

- Our host provider did not install a central copy
- Our provider installed it, but the version installed is not current
- We are working directly on our enterprise's web server

Required information

Some host providers offer an integrated web panel where we can manage accounts, including MySQL accounts, and also a file manager that can be used to upload web content. Depending on this, the mechanism that we use to transfer phpMyAdmin source files to our webspace may vary. We will need some specific information (listed below) before starting the installation:

- The web server's name or address: Here, we will assume it to be `www.mydomain.com`.
- Our web server's account information (username, password): This information will be used for either FTP or SFTP transfer, SSH login, or web control panel login.
- The MySQL server's name or IP address: If this information is not available, a good alternative choice is `localhost`, which means that the MySQL server is located on the same machine as the web server. We will assume this to be localhost.
- Our MySQL server's account information (username, password).

System requirements

The up-to-date requirements for a specific phpMyAdmin version are always stated in the accompanying `Documentation.html` file. For phpMyAdmin 3.3, the minimum PHP version required is PHP 5.2 with **session** support and the **Standard PHP Library (SPL)**. Moreover, the web server must have access to a MySQL server (version 5.0 or later)—either locally or on a remote machine. It is strongly recommended that the PHP `mcrypt` extension be present for improved performance in cookie authentication mode (more on this in *Chapter 2, Configuring Authentication and Security*). In fact, on a 64-bit server, this extension is required.

On the browser side, cookie support must be activated, whatever authentication mode we use.

Downloading the files

There are various files available in the **Download** section of `http://www.phpmyadmin.net`. There might be more than one version offered here, and it is always a good idea to download the latest stable version. We only need to download one file, which works regardless of the platform (browser, web server, MySQL, or PHP version). For version 3.3, there are two groups of files—`english` and `all-languages`. If we need only the English interface, we can download a file whose name contains "english"—for example, `phpMyAdmin-3.3.2-english.zip`. On the other hand, if we have the need for at least one other language, choosing `all-languages` would be appropriate.

If we are using a server supporting only PHP4—for which the PHP team has discontinued support since December 31, 2007—the latest stable version of phpMyAdmin is not a good choice for download. I recommend using version 2.11.x, which is the latest branch that supports PHP4.

The files offered have various extensions: `.zip`, `.tar.bz2`, `.tar.gz`, `.7z`. Download a file having an extension for which you have the corresponding extractor. In the Windows world, `.zip` is the most universal file format, although the files are bigger than `.gz` or `.bz2` files (which are common in the Linux/Unix world). The `.7z` extension denotes a 7-Zip file, which is a format that achieves a higher compression ratio than the other formats offered—an extractor is available at `http://www.7-zip.org`. In the following examples, we will assume that the chosen file was `phpMyAdmin-3.3.2-all-languages.zip`.

After clicking on the appropriate file, the nearest mirror site will be chosen by Sourceforge.net. The file will start to download, and we can save it on our computer.

Installing on different platforms

The next step depends on the platform you are using. The following sections detail the procedures for some common platforms. You may proceed directly to the relevant section.

Installing on a remote server using a Windows machine

Using the File explorer, we double-click the phpMyAdmin-3.3.2-all-languages. zip file that we just downloaded on the Windows machine. A file extractor will start, showing us all of the scripts and directories inside a main phpMyAdmin-3.3.2- all-languages directory.

Use whatever mechanism your file extractor offers to save all the files, including subdirectories, to some location on your workstation. Here, we have chosen C:\. Therefore, a C:\phpMyAdmin-3.3.2-all-languages directory has been created for extraction.

Now, it's time to transfer the entire directory structure C:\phpMyAdmin-3.3.2-all- languages to the web server in our webspace. We use our favorite SFTP or FTP software, or the web control panel, for the transfer.

The exact directory under which we transfer phpMyAdmin may vary. It could be our public_html directory or another directory to which we usually transfer web documents. For further instructions about the exact directory to be used, or the best way to transfer the directory structure, we can consult our host provider's help desk.

After the transfer is complete, these files can be removed from our Windows machine as they are no longer needed.

Installing on a local Linux server

Let's say we chose phpMyAdmin-3.3.2-all-languages.tar.gz and downloaded it directly to some directory on the Linux server. We move it to our web server's document root directory (for example, /var/www/html) or to one of its subdirectories (for example, /var/www/html/utilities). We then extract it by issuing the following shell command or by using any graphical file extractor that our window manager offers:

```
tar -xzvf phpMyAdmin-3.3.2-all-languages.tar.gz
```

We must ensure that the permissions and ownership of the directory and files are appropriate for our web server. The web server user or group must be able to read them.

Installing on local Windows servers (Apache, IIS)

The procedure here is similar to that described in the *Installation on a remote server using a Windows machine* section, except that the target directory will be under our DocumentRoot (for Apache) or our wwwroot (for IIS). Of course, we do not need to transfer anything after modifications are made to config.inc.php (described in the next section), as the directory is already on the webspace.

Apache is usually run as a service. Hence, we have to ensure that the user under whom the service is running has normal read privileges to access our newly-created directory. The same principle applies to IIS, which uses the IUSR_machinename user. This user must have read access to the directory. You can adjust permissions in the Security/permissions tab of the directory's properties.

Configuring phpMyAdmin

Here, we will learn how to prepare and use the configuration file containing the parameters to connect to MySQL, and which can be customized as per our requirements.

Before configuring, we can rename the directory phpMyAdmin-3.3.2-all-languages to something like phpMyAdmin or just something easier to remember. This way, we and our users can visit an easily-remembered URL to start phpMyAdmin. On most servers, the directory part of URLs is case-sensitive, so we should communicate the exact URL to our users. We can also use a symbolic link if our server supports this feature.

The config.inc.php file

This file contains valid PHP code that defines the majority of the parameters (expressed by PHP variables) that we can change in order to tune phpMyAdmin to our own needs. There are also normal PHP comments in it, and we can comment our changes.

Be careful not to add any blank lines at the beginning or end of the file; doing so would hamper the execution of phpMyAdmin.

Note that phpMyAdmin looks for this file in the first level directory — the same one where index.php is located.

In versions before 2.8.0, a generic `config.inc.php` file was included in the downloaded kit. Since 2.8.0, this file is no longer present in the directory structure. Since version 2.9.0, a `config.sample.inc.php` file is included, and this can be copied and renamed to `config.inc.php` to act as a starting point. However, it is recommended that you use the web-based setup script (explained in this chapter) instead, for a more comfortable configuration interface.

There is another file—`layout.inc.php`—that contains some configuration information. Because phpMyAdmin offers theme management, this file contains the theme-specific colors and settings. There is one `layout.inc.php` file per theme, located in `themes/themename`, for example, `themes/original`. We will cover modifying some of those parameters in *Chapter 4, Taking First Steps*, under the *Customizing the browse mode* section.

Avoiding false error messages about permissions on config.inc.php

In its normal behavior, phpMyAdmin verifies that the permissions on this file do not allow everyone to modify it. This means that the file should not be writable to the world. Also, it displays a warning if the permissions are not correct. However, in some situations (for example, an NTFS file system mounted on a non-Windows server), the permission detection fails. In these cases, you should set the following parameter to `false`:

```
$cfg['CheckConfigurationPermissions'] = false;
```

The following sections explain various methods for adding or changing a parameter in the `config.inc.php` file.

Configuration principles

phpMyAdmin's behavior, given that no configuration file is present, has changed in version 3.1.0. In versions 3.0 and earlier, the application used its default settings as defined in `libraries/config.default.php` and tried to connect to a MySQL server on `localhost`—the same machine where the web server is running—with user as `root` and no password. This is the default set-up produced by most MySQL installation procedures, even though it is not really secure. Therefore, if our freshly-installed MySQL server were still to have the default root account, we would have logged on automatically and would have seen a warning given by phpMyAdmin about such lack of security.

If the notion of a MySQL `root` user eludes you, now might be the time to browse `http://dev.mysql.com/doc/refman/5.1/ en/privilege-system.html`, in order to learn the basics about MySQL's privilege system.

Since version 3.1.0, the development team has wanted to promote a more flexible login panel. This is why, with the lack of a configuration file, phpMyAdmin displays the cookie-based login panel by default (more details on this in *Chapter 2, Configuring Authentication and Security*, which explains that with the default configuration, it's not possible to log in with an empty password):

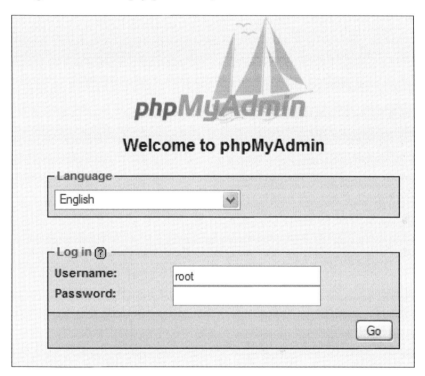

We can verify this fact by visiting `http://www.mydomain.com/phpMyAdmin` and substituting the appropriate values for the domain part and the directory part. If we are able to log in, it means that there is a MySQL server running on the same host as the web server (`localhost`) and we've just made a connection to it. However, not having created a configuration file means that we would not be able to manage other hosts via our installation of phpMyAdmin. Moreover, many advanced phpMyAdmin features (for example, query bookmarks, full relational support, column transformation, and so on) would not be activated.

The cookie-based authentication method uses Blowfish encryption for storing credentials in browser cookies. If no configuration file exists, a Blowfish secret key is generated and stored in session data, which can open the door to security issues. This is why the following warning message is displayed: **The configuration file now needs a secret passphrase (blowfish_secret)**.

At this point, we have some choices:

- Use phpMyAdmin without a configuration file
- Use the web-based setup script to generate a `config.inc.php` file
- Create a `config.inc.php` file manually

These options are presented in the following sections. We should note that even if we use the web-based setup script, we should familiarize ourselves with the `config.inc.php` file format, because the setup script does not cover all of the possible configuration options.

Web-based setup script

The web-based setup mechanism is strongly recommended in order to avoid syntax errors that could result from the manual creation of the configuration file. Also, because this file must respect PHP's syntax, it's common for new users to experience problems in this phase of the installation.

 A warning is in order here: The current version has only a limited number of translation languages for the setup interface.

To access the setup script, we must visit `http://www.mydomain.com/phpmyadmin/setup`. Here is what appears upon initial execution:

In most cases, the icons beside each parameter point to the respective phpMyAdmin official wiki and to their documentation, providing you with more information about this parameter and its possible values.

If **Show hidden messages** appears and we click on this link, messages that might have been displayed earlier are revealed:

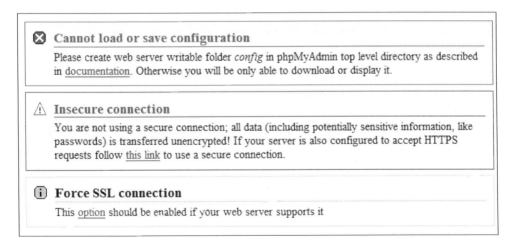

There are three warnings here. As taking care of the first message will require more manipulations, we will handle it in a moment. Let's cover the second message—**Insecure connection**. This message appears if we are accessing the web server over HTTP—an insecure protocol. As we are possibly going to input confidential information, such as the username and password, in the setup phase, it's recommended that you communicate over HTTPS, at least for this phase. HTTPS uses **Secure Socket Layer (SSL)** to encrypt the communication and make eavesdropping on the line impossible. If our web server supports HTTPS, we can simply follow the proposed link. This will restart the setup process, this time over HTTPS. We have made this assumption in our example.

The third warning encourages you to use the ForceSSL option, which will automatically switch to HTTPS when using phpMyAdmin (not related to the setup phase).

The first warning tells us that phpMyAdmin did not find a writable directory with the name config. This is normal as it was not present in the downloaded kit. Also, as the directory is not yet there, we observe that the **Save**, **Load**, and **Delete** buttons in the interface are gray. In this config directory, we can:

- Save the working version of the configuration file during the setup process
- Load a previously-prepared config.inc.php file

It's not absolutely necessary that we create this configuration directory, as we can download the config.inc.php file produced by the setup procedure to our client machine. We can then upload it to phpMyAdmin in the first-level directory via the same mechanism (say FTP) that we used to upload phpMyAdmin. In any case, we'll create this directory.

The principle here is that the web server must be able to write to this directory. There is more than one way to achieve this. Here is one that would work on a Linux server—adding read, write, and execute permissions for everyone on this directory:

```
cd phpMyAdmin
mkdir config
chmod 777 config
```

Having done that, we refresh the page in our browser and we see:

In the configuration dialog, a drop-down menu permits the user to choose the proper end-of-line format. We should choose the format that corresponds to the platform (**UNIX/Linux** or **Windows**) on which we will open later, with a text editor, the `config.inc.php` file.

A single copy of phpMyAdmin can be used to manage many MySQL servers, but for now we will define parameters describing our first MySQL server. We click **New server**, and the server configuration panel is shown.

A complete explanation of these parameters can be found in the following sections of this chapter, and also in *Chapter 10, Benefiting from the Relational System*. For now, we notice that the setup process has detected that PHP also supports the `mysqli` extension. Therefore, this is the one that is chosen by default. This extension is the programming library used by PHP to communicate with MySQL.

It's recommended you abide by the philosophy proposed by the interface, and keep **cookie** as the **Authentication type**. We assume that our MySQL server is located on `localhost`. Hence, we keep this value, and all of the proposed values intact, except for the following:

- **Verbose name of this server**: We enter **my server**
- **User for config auth**: We remove **root** and leave it empty

You can see that any parameter that is changed from its default value appears in a different color. Moreover, a small arrow becomes available, the purpose of which is to restore a field to its default value. Hence, you can feel free to experiment with changing parameters, knowing that you can easily revert to the proposed value. At this point, the panel should look like this:

We then click on **Save** and are brought back to the **Overview** panel. This save operation did not yet save anything to disk; changes were saved in memory. We are warned that a Blowfish secret key was generated. However, we don't have to remember it, as it's not keyed in during login process, but is used internally. For the curious, you can switch to the **Features** panel and click on the **Security** tab to see which secret key was generated. Back to the **Overview** panel. Now our setup process knows about one MySQL server, and there are links that enable us to **Edit** or **Delete** these server settings:

Servers				
#	Name	Authentication type	DSN	
1	my server	cookie	mysqli://localhost	Edit | Delete

We can have a look at the generated configuration lines by using the **Display** button; and then we can analyze these parameters using the explanations given in the *Description of some configuration parameters* section later in this chapter.

At this point, this configuration is still just in memory, so we need to save it. This is done via the **Save** button on the **Overview** panel. It saves `config.inc.php` in the special `config` directory that we created previously. This is a directory strictly used for configuration purposes. If, for any reason, it was not possible to create this `config` directory, you just have to **Download** the file and upload it to the web server directory where phpMyAdmin is installed.

The last step is to copy `config.inc.php` from the `config` directory to the top-level directory—the one that contains `index.php`. By copying this file, it becomes owned by the user instead of by the web server, ensuring that further modifications are possible. This copy can be done via FTP or through commands such as:

```
cd config
cp config.inc.php ..
```

As a security measure and until the configuration steps are completed, it's recommended that you change the permission on the `config` directory—for example, with the `chmod ugo-rwx config` command. This is to block any unauthorized reading and writing in this directory.

Other configuration parameters can be set with these web-based setup pages. To do so, we would have to:

1. Enable read and write access to the `config` directory

2. Copy the `config.inc.php` to this directory

3. Ensure that read and write access are provided to this file for the web server

4. Start the web-based setup tool

After the configuration steps are done, it's recommended that you completely remove the `config` directory, as this directory is only used by the web-based setup script. Since version 3.2.0, phpMyAdmin displays the following warning on the home page (see *Chapter 3, Over Viewing the Interface*) if it detects that this directory still exists:

Directory config, which is used by the setup script, still exists in your phpMyAdmin directory. You should remove it once phpMyAdmin has been configured.

You are invited to peruse the remaining menus to get a sense of the available configuration possibilities, either now or later when we cover a related subject.

In order to keep this book's text lighter, we will only refer to the parameters' textual values in the following chapters.

Manually creating config.inc.php

We can create this text file from scratch by using our favorite text editor, or by using `config.sample.inc.php` as a starting point. The exact procedure depends upon which client operating system we are using. We can refer to the next section for further information.

The default values for all possible configuration parameters that can be located inside `config.inc.php` are defined in `libraries/config.default.php`. We can take a look at this file to see the syntax used, as well as further comments about configuration. See the important note about this file in the *Upgrading phpMyAdmin* section later in this chapter.

Tips for editing config.inc.php on a Windows client

This file contains special characters (Unix-style end of lines). Hence, we must open it with a text editor that understands this format. If we use the wrong text editor, this file will be displayed with very long lines. The best choice is a standard PHP editor such as NetBeans or Zend Studio for Eclipse. Another choice would be WordPad, metapad, or UltraEdit.

Every time the `config.inc.php` file is modified, it will have to be transferred to our webspace again. This transfer is done via an FTP or an SFTP client. You have the option to use a standalone FTP/SFTP client such as FileZilla, or save it directly via FTP/SFTP, if your PHP editor supports this feature.

Description of some configuration parameters

In this chapter and the next one, we will concentrate on the parameters that deal with connection and authentication. Other parameters will be discussed in the chapters where the corresponding features are explained.

PmaAbsoluteUri

The first parameter we will look at is: `$cfg['PmaAbsoluteUri'] = '';`.

PMA is a familiar abbreviation for **phpMyAdmin**. For configuration parameters, the chosen convention is to capitalize the first letter, producing `Pma` in this case. At some places in its code, phpMyAdmin sends an HTTP `Location` header and must know the absolute URI of its installation point. Using an absolute URI in this case is required by RFC 2616, section 14.30.

In most cases, we can leave this one empty, as phpMyAdmin tries to auto-detect the correct value. If we browse a table later, and then edit a row and click on **Save**, we will receive an error message from our browser saying, for example, **This document does not exist**. This means that the absolute URI that phpMyAdmin built in order to reach the intended page was wrong, indicating that we must manually put the correct value in this parameter.

For example, we would change it to:

```
$cfg['PmaAbsoluteUri'] = 'http://www.mydomain.com/phpMyAdmin/';
```

Server-specific sections

The next section of the file contains server-specific configurations, each starting with:

```
$i++;
$cfg['Servers'][$i]['host']              = '';
```

If we examine only the normal server parameters (other parameters will be covered starting in *Chapter 10, Benefiting from the Relational System*), we see a section that looks like the following for each server:

```
$i++;
$cfg['Servers'][$i]['host']              = '';
$cfg['Servers'][$i]['port']              = '';
$cfg['Servers'][$i]['socket']            = '';
$cfg['Servers'][$i]['connect_type']      = 'tcp';
$cfg['Servers'][$i]['extension']         = 'mysqli';
$cfg['Servers'][$i]['compress']          = FALSE;
$cfg['Servers'][$i]['controluser']       = '';
$cfg['Servers'][$i]['controlpass']       = '';
$cfg['Servers'][$i]['auth_type']         = 'cookie';
$cfg['Servers'][$i]['user']              = '';
$cfg['Servers'][$i]['password']          = '';
$cfg['Servers'][$i]['only_db']           = '';
$cfg['Servers'][$i]['hide_db']           = '';
$cfg['Servers'][$i]['verbose']           = '';
```

In this section, we have to enter in `$cfg['Servers'][$i]['host']`, either the hostname or IP address of the MySQL server—for example, `mysql.mydomain.com` or `localhost`. If this server is running on a non-standard port or socket, we need to enter the correct values in `$cfg['Servers'][$i]['port']` or `$cfg['Servers'][$i]['socket']`. See the section on `connect_type` for more details about sockets.

The displayed server name inside phpMyAdmin's interface will be the one entered in `'host'` (unless we enter a non-blank value in the following parameter). For example:

```
$cfg['Servers'][$i]['verbose'] = 'Test server';
```

This feature can thus be used to display a **different server hostname as seen** by the users on the login panel and on the main page, although the real server name can be seen as part of the user definition (for example, `root@localhost`) on the main page.

extension

The traditional mechanism PHP uses to communicate with a MySQL server, as available in PHP before version 5, is the `mysql` extension. This extension is still available in PHP 5. However, a new extension called `mysqli` has been developed and should be preferred for PHP 5, because of its improved performance and its support of the full functionality of the MySQL family 4.1.x. This extension is designed to work with MySQL version 4.1.3 and higher. As phpMyAdmin supports both extensions, we can choose either one for a particular server. We indicate the extension we want to use in `$cfg['Servers'][$i]['extension']`.

connect_type, socket, and port

Both the `mysql` and `mysqli` extensions automatically use a socket to connect to MySQL if the server is on `localhost`. Consider this configuration:

```
$cfg['Servers'][$i]['host']          = 'localhost';
$cfg['Servers'][$i]['port']          = '';
$cfg['Servers'][$i]['socket']        = '';
$cfg['Servers'][$i]['connect_type']  = 'tcp';
$cfg['Servers'][$i]['extension']     = 'mysql';
```

The default value for `connect_type` is `tcp`. However, the extension will use a socket because it concludes that this is more efficient as the `host` is `localhost`. So in this case, we can use `tcp` or socket as the `connect_type`. To force a real TCP connection, we can specify `127.0.0.1` instead of `localhost` in the `host` parameter. Because the `socket` parameter is empty, the extension will try the default socket. If this default socket, as defined in `php.ini`, does not correspond to the real socket assigned to the MySQL server, we have to put the socket name (for example, `/tmp/mysql.sock`) in `$cfg['Servers'][$i]['socket']`.

If the hostname is not `localhost`, a TCP connection will occur — here, on the special port 3307. However, leaving the port value empty would use the default 3306 port:

```
$cfg['Servers'][$i]['host']          = 'mysql.mydomain.com';
$cfg['Servers'][$i]['port']          = '3307';
$cfg['Servers'][$i]['socket']        = '';
$cfg['Servers'][$i]['connect_type']  = 'tcp';
$cfg['Servers'][$i]['extension']     = 'mysql';
```

compress configuration

Beginning with PHP 4.3.0 and MySQL 3.23.49, the protocol used to communicate between PHP and MySQL allows a compressed mode. Using this mode provides better efficiency. To take advantage of this mode, simply specify:

```
$cfg['Servers'][$i]['compress']        = TRUE;
```

PersistentConnections

Another important parameter (which is not server-specific but applies to all server definitions) is `$cfg['PersistentConnections']`. For every server we connect to using the `mysql` extension, this parameter, when set to TRUE, instructs PHP to keep the connection to the MySQL server open. This speeds up the interaction between PHP and MySQL. However, it is set to FALSE by default in `config.inc.php` because persistent connections are often a cause of resource depletion on servers. So you will find MySQL refusing new connections. For this reason, the option is not even available for the `mysqli` extension. Hence, setting it to TRUE here would have no effect if you are connecting with this extension.

Upgrading phpMyAdmin

Normally, upgrading is just a matter of installing the newer version into a separate directory and copying the previous version's `config.inc.php` to the new directory. If the previous version is phpMyAdmin 2.6.0 or earlier, we cannot copy its `config.inc.php` to the new version because the file format has changed a lot.

An upgrade path or the first-installation path, which should *not* be taken, is to copy `libraries/config.default.php` to `config.inc.php`. This is because the default configuration file is version-specific and is not guaranteed to work for future versions.

New parameters appear from version to version. These are documented in `Documentation.html` and defined in `libraries/config.default.php`. If a configuration parameter is not present in `config.inc.php`, its value from `libraries/config.default.php` will be used. Therefore, we do not have to include it in `config.inc.php` if the default value suits us.

Special care must be taken to propagate the changes we might have made to the `layout.inc.php` files, depending on the themes used. We may even have to copy our custom themes subdirectories if we added our own themes to the structure.

Summary

This chapter covered how the web has evolved as a means of delivering applications, and why we should use PHP/MySQL to develop these applications. The chapter also gave an overview of why phpMyAdmin is recognized as a leading application to interface MySQL from the Web, and provided a brief list of its features. It then discussed common reasons for installing phpMyAdmin, steps for downloading it from the main site, basic configuration, uploading phpMyAdmin to our web server, and also described how to upgrade it.

Now that the basic installation has been done, the next chapter will deal with the configuration subject in depth, by exploring the authentication and security aspects.

2
Configuring Authentication and Security

There are many ways of configuring authentication in phpMyAdmin depending on our goals, the presence of other applications, and the level of security we need. This chapter explores the available possibilities.

Logging in to MySQL through phpMyAdmin

When we type in a username and password, although it seems that we are logging in to phpMyAdmin, we are not! The authentication system is a function of the MySQL server. We are merely using phpMyAdmin (which is running on the web server) as an interface that sends our username and password information to the MySQL server. Strictly speaking, we do not log in **to** phpMyAdmin, but **through** phpMyAdmin.

> This is why, in user support forums about phpMyAdmin, people asking for help about authentication are often referred back to their MySQL server's administrator, because a lost MySQL username or password is not a phpMyAdmin problem.

This section explains the various authentication modes offered by phpMyAdmin.

Logging in to an account without a password

MySQL's default installation leaves a server open to intrusion because it creates a MySQL account named `root` without a password—unless a password has been set by the MySQL distributor. The recommended remedy for this weakness in security is to set a password for the root account. In the eventuality that we cannot set one or do not want to set one, we will have to make a configuration change to phpMyAdmin. Indeed, a server-specific configuration parameter, `$cfg['Servers']` `[$i]['AllowNoPassword']`, has been introduced in phpMyAdmin 3.2.0. Its default value is `false`, which means that no account is permitted to log in without a password. Generally, this directive should remain `false` to avoid this kind of access via phpMyAdmin, as hackers are actively probing the web for insecure MySQL servers. Go through the *Securing phpMyAdmin* section for other ideas about protecting your server.

 If the `AllowNoPassword` parameter is set to `false` and a login attempt is made without a password, an **Access denied** message is displayed.

Authenticating a single user with config

We might need to automatically connect to a MySQL server via phpMyAdmin, using a fixed username and password, without even been asked for it. This is the precise goal of the `config` authentication type.

For our first example, we will use this `config` authentication, which is easy to understand. However, in the *Authenticating multiple users* section, we will see more powerful and versatile ways of authenticating.

 Using the `config` authentication type leaves our phpMyAdmin open to intrusion, unless we protect it as explained in the *Securing phpMyAdmin* section of this chapter.

Here we ask for `config` authentication, and enter our username and password for this MySQL server:

```
$cfg['Servers'][$i]['auth_type'] = 'config';
$cfg['Servers'][$i]['user']      = 'marc';
$cfg['Servers'][$i]['password']  = 'bingo';
```

We can then save the changes we made in `config.inc.php`.

Testing the MySQL connection

Now it's time to start phpMyAdmin and try connecting with the values we configured. This will test the following:

- The values we entered in the `config` file or on the web-based setup
- The setup of the PHP component inside the web server, if we did a manual configuration
- Communication between web and MySQL servers

We start our browser and point it to the directory where we installed phpMyAdmin, as in `http://www.mydomain.com/phpMyAdmin/`. If this does not work, we try `http://www.mydomain.com/phpMyAdmin/index.php`. (This would mean that our web server is not configured to interpret `index.php` as the default starting document.)

If you still get an error, refer to *Appendix B* for troubleshooting and support. We should now see phpMyAdmin's home page. *Chapter 3, Over Viewing the Interface* gives an overview of the panels seen now.

Authenticating multiple users

We might want to allow a single copy of phpMyAdmin to be used by a group of persons, each having their own MySQL username and password, and seeing only the databases they have rights to. Or we might prefer to avoid having our username and password in clear text in `config.inc.php`.

Authentication types offered

Instead of relying on a username and password stored in `config.inc.php`, phpMyAdmin will communicate with the browser and get authentication data from it. This enables **true login** for all users defined in a specific MySQL server, without having to define them in the configuration file. There are three modes offered that allow a controlled login to MySQL via phpMyAdmin: `http`, `cookie`, and `signon`. We will have to choose the one that suits our specific situation and environment (more on this in a moment). The `http` and `cookie` modes may require that we first define a control user.

The control user

Defining the control user has two purposes:

- On a MySQL server running with `--skip-show-database`, the control user permits the use of multi-user authentication. This aspect is described in the current section, even though servers running with this option are not commonly seen.

- On all versions of MySQL server, this user is necessary to be able to use the advanced relational features of phpMyAdmin, which are described starting in *Chapter 10, Benefiting from the Relational System*.

For authentication purposes, the control user is a special user (the usual name we choose for it is pma) who has the rights to read some fields in the special **mysql** database (which contains all of the user definitions). phpMyAdmin sends queries with this special control user only for the specific needs of authentication, and not for normal operation. The commands to create the control user are available in phpMyAdmin's `Documentation.html` and may vary from one version to another. This documentation contains the most current commands.

When our control user is created in the MySQL server, we fill in the parameters as shown in the following example:

```
$cfg['Servers'][$i]['controluser'] = 'pma';
$cfg['Servers'][$i]['controlpass'] = 'bingo';
```

 I use the `bingo` password when I teach pMyAdmin; it's recommended to avoid using the same password for your own installation. MySQL itself does not seem to enforce limits on the password size, but standard password guidelines apply. Please refer to `http://en.wikipedia.org/wiki/Password_strength` for suggestions.

Logging out

A mechanism is available to tell phpMyAdmin which URL it should display after a user has logged out. This feature **eases integration with other applications** and works for all authentication types that permit logging out. Here is an example:

```
$cfg['Servers'][$i]['LogoutURL'] = 'http://www.mydomain.com';
```

This directive must contain an absolute URL, including the protocol.

Authenticating with HTTP

This mode—http—is the traditional mode offered in HTTP, in which the browser asks for the username and password, sends them to phpMyAdmin, and keeps sending them until all of the browser's windows are closed.

To enable this mode, we simply use the following line:

```
$cfg['Servers'][$i]['auth_type'] = 'http';
```

This mode has some limitations:

- PHP, depending on the version, might not support HTTP authentication. It works when PHP is running as a module under Apache; for other cases, we should consult the PHP documentation for our version.

- If we want to protect phpMyAdmin's directory with a .htaccess file (see the *Securing phpMyAdmin* section of this chapter), this will interfere with the HTTP authentication type; we cannot use both.

- Browsers usually store the authentication information to save retyping credentials but bear in mind that these credentials are saved in an unencrypted format.

- There is no support for proper logout in the HTTP protocol; hence, we might have to close all browser windows to be able to log in again with the same username.

Even considering these limitations, this mode may be a valuable choice as it's a bit faster than cookie processing.

Authenticating users with cookie values

The cookie authentication mode is superior to http in terms of the functionalities offered. It offers true login and logout, and can be used with PHP running on any kind of web server. It presents a login panel (see the following figure) from within phpMyAdmin. This can be customized, as we have the application source code. However, as you may have guessed, for cookie authentication, the browser must accept cookies coming from the web server—true for all authentication modes.

This mode stores the username typed in the login screen into a permanent cookie in our browser, while the password is stored as a temporary cookie. In a multi-server configuration, the username and password corresponding to each server are stored separately. To protect the username and password secrecy against attack methods that target cookie content, they are encrypted using the Blowfish cipher. So, to use this mode, we have to define (once) in config.inc.php, a secret password that will be used to securely encrypt all passwords stored as cookies from this phpMyAdmin installation.

This password is set via the `blowfish_secret` directive:

```
$cfg['blowfish_secret'] = 'jgjgRUD875G%/*';
```

In the previous example, an arbitrary string of characters was used; this password can be very complex as nobody will ever need to type it on a login panel. If we fail to configure this directive, a random secret password is generated by phpMyAdmin but it will last only for the current working session. Therefore, some features such as recalling the previous username on the login panel won't be available.

Then, for each server-specific section, use the following:

```
$cfg['Servers'][$i]['auth_type'] = 'cookie';
```

The next time we start phpMyAdmin, we will see the login panel as shown in the following screenshot:

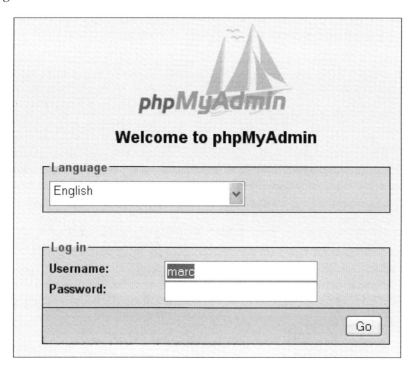

By default, phpMyAdmin displays (in the **Log in** panel) the last username for which a successful login was achieved for this particular server, as retrieved from the permanent cookie. If this behavior is not acceptable (someone else who logs in from the same workstation should not see the previous username), we can set the following parameter to FALSE:

```
$cfg['LoginCookieRecall'] = FALSE;
```

There is a security feature to add a specific time limit for the validity of a password. This feature helps to protect the working session. After a successful login, our password is stored (encrypted) in a cookie, along with a timer. Every action in phpMyAdmin resets the timer. If we stay inactive for a certain number of seconds, as defined in `$cfg['LoginCookieValidity']`, we are disconnected and have to log in again. Increasing this parameter does not work in all cases, because PHP's own `session.gc_maxlifetime` directive can get in the way. Please refer to http://php. net/manual/en/session.configuration.php for an explanation of this directive. Therefore, if phpMyAdmin detects that the value of `session.gc_maxlifetime` is less than the configured `$cfg['LoginCookieValidity']`, a warning is displayed on the main page. The default is 1440 seconds; this matches the `php.ini`'s default value for the `session.gc_maxlifetime` parameter.

The Blowfish algorithm used to protect the username and password requires many computations. To achieve the best possible speed, the PHP's `mcrypt` extension and its accompanying library must be installed on our web server. Otherwise, phpMyAdmin relies on an internally-coded algorithm, which works but causes delays of several seconds on almost every operation done from phpMyAdmin! This is because the username and password information must be decoded on every mouse click to be able to connect to MySQL.

To help users realize that this extension is really important, a message is displayed on the main page when phpMyAdmin detects its absence. The `$cfg['McryptDisableWarning']` directive controls this message. By default, a value of `false` implies that the message is shown.

Authenticating through the signon mode

The `signon` mode enables us to use the credentials from another application to authenticate to phpMyAdmin. Some applications have their own authentication mechanism, so it's convenient to be able to use this fact to avoid another cumbersome login panel. In order for this to work, this other application has to store the proper credentials into PHP's session data to be retrieved later by phpMyAdmin.

Storing credentials in PHP's session is not guaranteed to be safe, according to the PHP manual: http://php.net/manual/en/ session.security.php.

To enable this mode, we start with this directive:

```
$cfg['Servers'][$i]['auth_type'] = 'signon';
```

Let's suppose that the authenticating application has used a session named `FirstApp` to store the credentials. We tell this to phpMyAdmin:

```
$cfg['Servers'][$i]['SignonSession'] = 'FirstApp';
```

We must take care of users that try to access phpMyAdmin before accessing the other application; in this case, phpMyAdmin will redirect users to the authenticating application. This is done with:

```
$cfg['Servers'][$i]['SignonURL'] = 'http://www.mydomain.com/FirstApp';
```

How does the authenticating application store credentials in a format that phpMyAdmin can understand? An example is included as `scripts/signon.php`. In this script, there is a simple HTML form to input the credentials and logic that initializes the session—we would use `FirstApp` as a session name, and create the user, password, host, and port information within this session:

```
$_SESSION['PMA_single_signon_user'] = $_POST['user'];

$_SESSION['PMA_single_signon_password'] = $_POST['password'];

$_SESSION['PMA_single_signon_host'] = $_POST['host'];

$_SESSION['PMA_single_signon_port'] = $_POST['port'];
```

> Note that `FirstApp` does not need to ask the MySQL's credentials to the user. These could be hardcoded inside the application, as they are secret or there is a known correspondence between the credentials of this application and that of MySQL's.

The authenticating application then uses a way of its choice—a link or a button—to let its users start phpMyAdmin.

Configuring for multiple server support

The `config.inc.php` file contains at least one server-specific section; however, we can add more, enabling a single copy of phpMyAdmin to manage many servers. Let us see how to configure more servers.

Defining servers in the configuration file

In the server-specific sections of the `config.inc.php` file, we see lines referring to `$cfg['Servers'][$i]` for each server. Here, the variable `$i` is used so that you can easily cut and paste whole sections of the configuration file in order to configure more servers. While copying such sections, we should take care that the `$i++;` instruction, which precedes each section and is crucial to delimit the server sections, is also copied.

Then, at the end of the sections, the following line controls what happens at start-up:

```
$cfg['ServerDefault'] = 1;
```

The default value, 1, means that phpMyAdmin will connect by itself to the first server defined, or present this server choice by default when using HTTP or cookie authentications. We can specify any number, for the corresponding server-specific section. We can also enter the value 0, signifying no default server; in this case a list of available servers will be presented at login time.

This configuration can also be done via web-based setup. Given here is an example of a multi-server definition, with the default server being set to **let the user choose**.

With no default server defined, phpMyAdmin will present a server choice:

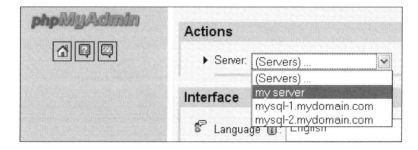

Authenticating through an arbitrary server

Another mechanism can be used if we want to be able to connect to an undefined MySQL server. First, we have to set the following parameter:

```
$cfg['AllowArbitraryServer'] = TRUE;
```

We also have to put back the default value of 1 into $cfg['ServerDefault'] and use the cookie authentication type. We will then be able to choose the server and enter a username and a password.

 Allowing an arbitrary server means that any MySQL server accessible from our web server could be connected to via phpMyAdmin. Therefore, this feature should be used in conjunction with a reinforced security mechanism (see the *Securing phpMyAdmin* section).

As seen here, we still can choose one of the defined servers in **Server Choice**. In addition, we can also enter an arbitrary server name, a username, and a password:

As the tool tip indicates, you can also enter a port number (of course, separated from the hostname/IP address by a space), if this MySQL server is listening on a non-standard port.

Securing phpMyAdmin

Security can be examined at various levels:

- How we can protect the phpMyAdmin installation directory
- Which workstations can access phpMyAdmin
- The databases that a legitimate user can see
- How in-transit data protection and access protection can be enforced via a physical USB key on the workstation
- How we can use a logging system to record login attempts

Protecting phpMyAdmin at the directory level

Suppose an unauthorized person is trying to execute our copy of phpMyAdmin. If we use the simple `config` authentication type, anyone knowing the URL of our phpMyAdmin will have the same effective rights to our data as we do. In this case, we should use the directory protection mechanism offered by our web server (for example, `.htaccess`, a filename with a leading dot) to add a level of protection.

If we decide to use `http` or `cookie` authentication types, our data would be safe enough. However, we should take normal precautions with our password (including its periodic change).

The directory where phpMyAdmin is installed contains sensitive data. Not only the configuration file, but also all scripts stored there, must be protected from alteration. We should ensure that apart from us, only the web server's effective user has read access to the files contained in this directory, and that only we can write to them.

 phpMyAdmin's scripts never have to modify anything inside of this directory, except when we use the **Save export file to server** feature (explained in *Chapter 6, Exporting Data and Structure (Backup)*).

Another recommendation is to rename the default `phpMyAdmin` directory to something less obvious; this discourages the probing of our server. This is called security by obscurity and can be very effective—but please avoid choosing other obvious names, such as `admin`.

Another possible attack is from other developers who have an account on the same web server as we do. In this kind of attack, someone can try to open our `config.inc.php` file. As this file is readable by the web server, someone could try to `include` our file from their PHP scripts. This is why it's recommended to use PHP's `open_basedir` feature, possibly applying it to all directories from which such attacks could originate.

Displaying error messages

Version 3.0 has introduced a new PHP error trapping behavior in phpMyAdmin, based on PHP's custom error handler mechanism. One of the benefits of this error handler is the avoidance of path disclosure, which is considered a security weakness. The default settings related to this are:

```
$cfg['Error_Handler'] = array();
$cfg['Error_Handler']['display'] = false;
```

You should leave the default value for display as false, unless you are developing a new phpMyAdmin feature and want to see all PHP errors and warnings.

Protecting with IP-based access control

An additional level of protection can be added, this time verifying the **Internet Protocol (IP)** address of the machine from which the request to use phpMyAdmin is received. To achieve this level of protection, we construct rules allowing or denying access, and specify the order in which these rules will be applied.

Defining rules

The format of a rule is:

```
<'allow' | 'deny'> <username> [from] <source>
```

The `from` keyword is optional. Here are some examples:

Rule	Description
allow Bob from 1.2.3.4	User `Bob` is allowed access from IP address `1.2.3.4`.
allow Bob from 1.2.3/24	User `Bob` is allowed from any address matching the network `1.2.3` (this is CIDR IP matching).
deny Alice from 4.5/16	User `Alice` is denied access when located on network `4.5`.

Rule	Description
allow Melanie from all	User `Melanie` can login from anywhere.
allow Julie from localhost	Equivalent to 127.0.0.1
deny % from all	`all` can be used as an equivalent to 0.0.0.0/0, meaning any host. Here, the `%` sign means any user.

Usually we will have several rules. Let's say we wish to have the two rules that follow:

```
allow Marc from 45.34.23.12
allow Melanie from all
```

We have to put them in `config.inc.php` (in the related server-specific section) as follows:

```
$cfg['Servers'][$i]['AllowDeny']['rules'] =
    array('allow Marc from 45.34.23.12', 'allow Melanie from all');
```

When defining a single rule or multiple rules, a PHP array is used. We must follow its syntax, enclosing each complete rule within single quotes and separating each rule from the next with a comma. Thus, if we have only one rule, we must still use an array to specify it like this:

```
$cfg['Servers'][$i]['AllowDeny']['rules'] =
    array('allow Marc from 45.34.23.12');
```

The next parameter explains the order in which rules are interpreted.

Order of interpretation for rules

By default, this parameter is empty:

```
$cfg['Servers'][$i]['AllowDeny']['order'] = '';
```

This means that no IP-based verification is made.

Suppose we want to allow access by default, denying access only to some username/IP pairs. We should use:

```
$cfg['Servers'][$i]['AllowDeny']['order'] = 'deny,allow';
```

In this case, all `deny` rules will be applied first, followed by `allow` rules. If a case is not mentioned in the rules, access is granted. Being more restrictive, we'd want to deny by default. We can use:

```
$cfg['Servers'][$i]['AllowDeny']['order'] = 'allow,deny';
```

In this case, all `allow` rules are applied first, followed by `deny` rules. If a case is not mentioned in the rules, access is denied. The third (and most restrictive) way of specifying the order of rules is:

```
$cfg['Servers'][$i]['AllowDeny']['order'] = 'explicit';
```

Now, `deny` rules are applied before `allow` rules. But for them to be accepted, a username/IP address must be listed in the `allow` rules, and not in the `deny` rules.

Blocking root access

As the `root` user is present in almost all MySQL installations, it's often the target of attacks. A parameter permits us to easily block all phpMyAdmin logins of the MySQL's `root` account, by using the following:

```
$cfg['Servers'][$i]['AllowRoot'] = FALSE;
```

Some system administrators prefer to disable the `root` account at the MySQL server level, creating another less obvious account that possesses the same privileges. This has the advantage of blocking root access from all sources, and not just from phpMyAdmin.

Protecting in-transit data

HTTP is not inherently immune to network sniffing (grabbing sensitive data off the wire). So, if we want to protect not only our username and password but all of the data that travels between our web server and the browser, we have to use HTTPS.

To do so, assuming that our web server supports HTTPS, we just have to start phpMyAdmin by putting `https` instead of `http` in the URL: `https://www.mydomain.com/phpMyAdmin/`.

If we are using `PmaAbsoluteUri` auto-detection:

```
$cfg['PmaAbsoluteUri'] = '';
```

phpMyAdmin will see that we are using HTTPS in the URL and react accordingly.

If not, we must put the `https` part in this parameter as follows:

```
$cfg['PmaAbsoluteUri'] = 'https://www.mydomain.com/phpMyAdmin';
```

We can automatically switch users to an HTTPS connection with this setting:

```
$cfg['ForceSSL'] = TRUE;
```

Authenticating using Swekey hardware

Support for the Swekey hardware authentication USB key has been merged into cookie-based authentication in phpMyAdmin. Reference for this USB key is available at `http://phpmyadmin.net/auth_key`. A Swekey can be used with all compatible web applications to add a level of security, based on the possession of this physical device. In the case of phpMyAdmin, it does not replace the normal MySQL authentication.

Configuring Swekey authentication

The `contrib/swekey.sample.conf` sample file should be used as a starting point to configure this feature. This file contains sample configuration commands and comments from the vendor. The principle is simple—each Swekey device contains a unique ID, and this ID must be associated with a MySQL username in the Swekey configuration file. These lines are part of the sample file:

```
000000000000000000000000000763A:root
0000000000000000000000000089E4:steve
000000000000000000000000000231E:scott
```

This means that the person responsible for the phpMyAdmin configuration tracks which Swekey is given to each user and puts this information in the file. The vendor does not need to be informed about this association. They only keep track of which Swekeys are sold and which are deactivated. Hence, a Swekey can be passed from one user to another, provided that the configuration is updated accordingly.

Other security-related directives are in the sample file, and it's recommended to refrain from changing them—`SERVER_CHECK`, `SERVER_RNDTOKEN`, and `SERVER_STATUS` in particular. This is because these directives access servers via `https`, which is a guarantee of a secure channel between our web server and the vendor's.

Once modified, this file should be copied over to a directory outside of the web server's document root (suggested place is `/etc/swekey-pma.conf`). Then, a configuration parameter in `config.inc.php` must be set as well:

```
$cfg['Servers'][$i]['auth_swekey_config'] = '/etc/swekey-pma.conf';
```

Using phpMyAdmin in a Swekey context

Let's see what happens now when phpMyAdmin is started and no Swekey is connected to your workstation:

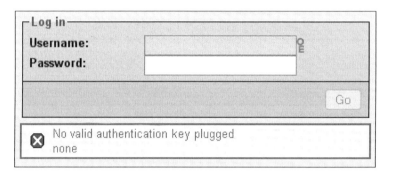

We notice three changes:

- The username field cannot be typed in
- A small key icon is displayed
- An error message appears

It's normal that the username field is deactivated, as usernames are now taken from the Swekey configuration file. The icon can be clicked to reach the vendor's website. There is a testing mechanism on this site, to verify if a Swekey is connected. Drivers can also be downloaded in case the automatic installation did not work.

Now if you connect your Swekey, assuming that user `marc` has been defined and associated to this device, a reassuring panel is displayed:

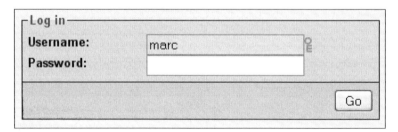

Security note

It would not make sense to rely on the protection offered by this device, if our users have access to a webspace on which they can install their own copy of phpMyAdmin. Obviously, phpMyAdmin has to be configured accordingly to make use of the Swekey. Hence, a user-installed copy of phpMyAdmin would circumvent the protection. This means that a host provider should permit access to his MySQL server only from a web server on which he or she installed a controlled copy of phpMyAdmin, and on which other users cannot install their own copy.

Access logging

When PHP is running as an Apache module, extra PHP functions are made available to the application. One of these is `apache_note()`, which is referenced at `http://php.net/apache_note`. Although the name of this function might not be evident, it can be used to set name-value pairs inside of the Apache system. This information is accessible to other Apache modules; we can take advantage of this to ask Apache to include some information of our choice in its access log.

Subsequently, log files analyzing tools can be used to gather information about our legitimate users or possible break-in attempts.

Available information

If phpMyAdmin detects the presence of the `apache_note()` function, it automatically creates the following notes during the login process:

- userID: This contains the username for which a login attempt was made
- userStatus: This contains a message explaining the outcome of the login attempt

The possible status messages are:

Status message	Description
"ok"	The user is logged in
"mysql-denied"	The MySQL server refused this login attempt
"allow-denied"	phpMyAdmin's allow/deny rules denied this login attempt
"root-denied"	phpMyAdmin's `$cfg['Servers'][$i]['AllowRoot']` directive (set to false) blocked a root login attempt

Status message	Description
"empty-denied"	phpMyAdmin's `$cfg['Servers'][$i]['AllowNoPassword']` directive is set to false and a login attempt without a password was made

Configuring Apache

Up to now, the notes are only present inside the Apache system. Normally we want to see them, therefore we will modify Apache's logging configuration to achieve this goal. The exact recipe for this depends on the configuration file name chosen by the distributor of Apache, but we'll use the most common one: `httpd.conf`.

This file usually contains a `LogFormat` directive that controls which information goes into one of Apache's log file. phpMyAdmin's documentation suggests this modified directive:

```
LogFormat "%h %l %u %t \"%r\" %>s %b \
\"%{Referer}i\" \"%{User-Agent}i\" %{userID}n %{userStatus}n" \  pma_
combined
```

We recognize the `userID` and `userStatus` notes coming from phpMyAdmin, coated with Apache's special characters. Hence we can apply this newly-configured `pma_combined` format to Apache's access log with:

```
CustomLog "logs/access_log" pma_combined
```

After restarting Apache, all login attempts will be logged and can be analyzed for statistical or security purposes.

Summary

This chapter gave us an overview of how to use a single copy of phpMyAdmin to manage multiple servers, and also the use of authentication types to fulfill the needs of a users' group while protecting authentication credentials. The chapter also covered the ways of securing our phpMyAdmin installation.

In the next chapter, we'll take a look at all of the panels and windows that comprise the user interface of phpMyAdmin.

3
Over Viewing the Interface

Before delving into task-oriented chapters, such as searching and the like, it's appropriate to have a look at the general organization of phpMyAdmin's interface. We'll also look at the configuration parameters and settings that influence the interface as a whole.

Over viewing panels and windows

The phpMyAdmin interface is composed of various panels and windows, each one having a specific function. We will first see a quick overview of each panel and then take a detailed look at them later in this chapter.

Login panels

The login panel that appears depends on the authentication type chosen. For the `http` type, it will take the form of our browser's HTTP authentication pop-up screen. For the `cookie` type, the phpMyAdmin-specific login panel will be displayed. (This is covered in *Chapter 2*, *Configuring Authentication and Security*.) For external authentication (`signon`), the login panel is handled by the external application itself. By default, a **Server** choice dialog and a **Language** selector are present on this panel.

However, if we are using the `config` authentication type, no login panel is displayed, and the first displayed interface contains the navigation and the main panels.

Navigation and main panels

The navigation and main panels go together and are displayed during most of our working session with phpMyAdmin. The **navigation panel** is our guide through the databases and tables. The **main panel** is the working area where the data is managed and results appear. Its exact layout depends on the choices made in the navigation panel and the sequence of operations performed. For the majority of languages (which are written left-to-right), the navigation panel is located on the left side and the main panel is on the right. However, for right-to-left languages such as Hebrew, these panels are reversed.

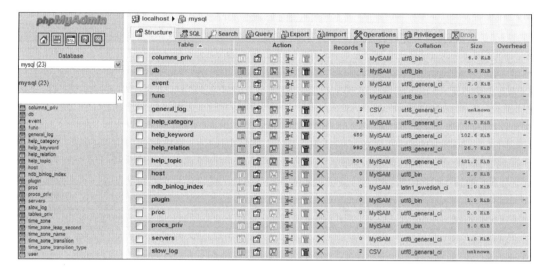

Home page

The main panel can take the form of the home page. The home page will then contain various links related to MySQL operations or phpMyAdmin information, a **Language** selector, and possibly the themes selector.

Views

In the main panel, we can see the **Database** view (where we can take various actions for a specific database), or the **Table** view (where we can access many functions to manage a table). There is also a **Server** view, which is useful for both system administrators and non-administrator users. All these views have a top menu, which takes the form of tabs that lead to different subpages used to present information regrouped by common functions (table structure, privileges, and so on).

Please do not confuse the term view—used here in the interface sense—with the MySQL 5.0's notion of SQL views (covered in *Chapter 17, Supporting MySQL 5.0 and 5.1*).

Query window

This is a distinct window that is usually opened from the navigation panel, and sometimes from the main panel when editing an SQL query. Its main purpose is to facilitate work on queries and display the results in the main panel.

Starting page

When we start phpMyAdmin, we will see the following (depending on the authentication type specified in `config.inc.php` and on whether it has more than one server defined in it):

- One of the login panels
- The navigation and main panels, with the home page displayed in the main panel

Customizing general settings

This section describes settings that have an impact on many panels. These settings modify the appearance of titles in windows, of information icons, and how the list of tables is sorted. The whole visual style of all pages is controlled by the theme system, which is covered here altogether. This section also deals with how to restrict the list of databases seen by users.

Configuring the window title

When the navigation and main panels are displayed, the window's title changes to reflect which MySQL server, database, and table are active. phpMyAdmin also shows some information about the web server's hostname if `$cfg['ShowHttpHostTitle']` is set to TRUE. What is displayed depends on another setting—`$cfg['SetHttpHostTitle']`. If this setting is empty (as it is by default), the true web server's hostname appears in the title. We can put another string, such as "my Web server", and this will be shown instead of the true hostname.

Seeing the web server's hostname can come in handy when we have many phpMyAdmin windows open, thus being connected to more than one web server. Of course, each phpMyAdmin window can itself give access to many MySQL servers.

Configuring icons

When various warnings, errors, or information messages are displayed, they can be accompanied by an icon, if $cfg['ErrorIconic'] is set to TRUE. Another parameter, $cfg['ReplaceHelpImg'], when set to TRUE, displays a small icon containing a question mark at every place where documentation is available for a specific subject. These two parameters are set to TRUE by default.

Natural sort order for database and table names

Usually, computers sort items in lexical order, which gives the following results for a list of tables:

```
table1
table10
table2
table3
```

phpMyAdmin implements "natural sort order" by default, as specified by $cfg['NaturalOrder'] being TRUE. Thus, the database and table lists in the navigation and main panels are sorted as:

```
table1
table2
table3
table10
```

Creating site-specific headers and footers

Some users may want to display a company logo, a link to their company's helpdesk, or other information on the phpMyAdmin interface. In the main phpMyAdmin directory, for this purpose, we can create two scripts—config.header.inc.php and config.footer.inc.php. We can put our own PHP or XHTML code in these scripts, and it will appear either at the beginning (for header) or at the end (for footer) of the cookie login and the main panel pages.

For example, create a config.footer.inc.php script containing these lines:

```
<hr />
<em>All the information on this page is confidential.</em>
```

This would produce the intended message on all pages:

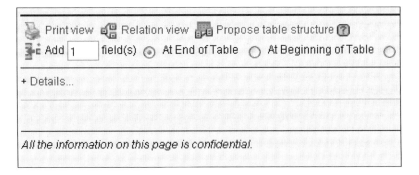

Displaying MySQL documentation links

phpMyAdmin displays links to the MySQL documentation at various places on its interface. These links refer to the exact point in the official MySQL documentation to learn about a specific MySQL command. We can customize the location and manual type referred to, with the following configuration parameters:

```
$cfg['MySQLManualBase'] = 'http://dev.mysql.com/doc/refman';
$cfg['MySQLManualType'] = 'viewable';
```

About the manual base, users who prefer to keep a copy of this documentation on a local server would specify a local link here. For the manual type, the most up-to-date possible values are explained as comments in `config.inc.php`.

Themes

A theme system is available in phpMyAdmin starting with version 2.6.0. The color parameters and the various icons are located in a directory structure under the `themes` subdirectory. For each available theme, there is a subdirectory named after the theme. It contains:

- `layout.inc.php` for the theme parameters
- `css` directory with the various CSS scripts
- `img` directory containing any icons or other imagery (such as logos)
- `screen.png`: A screenshot of this theme

The downloaded kit contains two themes, but there are more available at `http://phpmyadmin.net/home_page/themes.php`. Installing a new theme is just a matter of downloading the corresponding `.zip` file and extracting it under the `themes` subdirectory.

In case someone would like to build a custom theme that contains JavaScript code, please note that some phpMyAdmin 3.3 pages are using the MooTools JavaScript library, and all phpMyAdmin 3.4 pages will be including the jQuery library.

Configuring themes

In `config.inc.php`, the `$cfg['ThemePath']` parameter contains `'themes'` by default, indicating which subdirectory the required structure is located in. This can be changed to point to another directory where our company's specific phpMyAdmin themes are located.

The default chosen theme is specified in `$cfg['ThemeDefault']`, and is set to `'original'`. If no theme selection is available for users, this theme will be used.

The `original` subdirectory should never be deleted; phpMyAdmin relies on it for normal operations.

Selecting themes

On the home page, we can offer a theme selector to users. Setting `$cfg['ThemeManager']` to TRUE (the default) shows the selector:

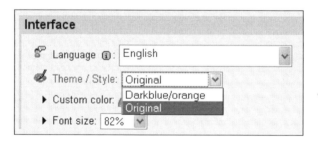

To help choose a suitable theme, the **Theme / Style** link displays a panel containing screenshots of the available themes and a **Get more themes** link. We can then click on **take it** under the theme we want. The chosen theme is remembered in a cookie. By default, the remembered theme applies to all servers that we connect to. To make phpMyAdmin remember one theme per MySQL server, we set `$cfg['ThemePerServer']` to TRUE.

Assigning colors using the color picker

Here is a feature—the custom color picker— that may seem frivolous but has its utility. We'll first discuss the *how* and then the *why*.

Located on the home page, the small rainbow icon gives access to a picker that controls the background color of both panels. The phpMyAdmin team merged the MooRainbow code from Djamil Legato (`http://moorainbow.woolly-sheep.net`) to offer this feature.

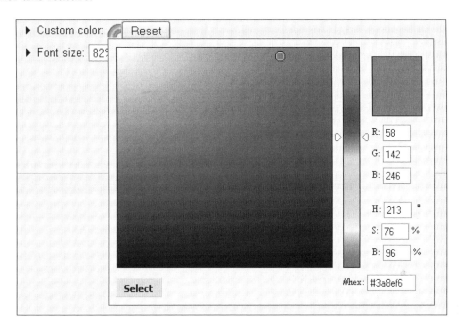

You can operate the picker in many ways—moving the slider, moving the mouse in the big square, or directly entering values into the fields. When you are done, you click on **Select** to clear the picker.

The purpose of this feature is to help users who are working simultaneously on many MySQL servers, and like to have visual clues about each server. Another possible scenario is a busy database administrator who takes calls from customers and opens many phpMyAdmin windows. He then assigns priorities by using the color picker, say red for top priority—you get the idea.

Sliders

You'll see on some pages, a small plus sign followed by a controlling label—either **Options** or **Details**. A click on the label opens a slider to reveal a section of the interface, which is believed to be less often used in day-to-day work. As some people prefer to immediately see the whole interface—at the expense of screen space—there is a configuration parameter that controls how the sliders are initially set:

```
$cfg['InitialSlidersState'] = 'closed';
```

The default value of `closed` means that sliders must be opened by clicking on the label; you might have guessed that the reverse value is `open`. A third value, `disabled`, can be used by slider-allergic users. This JavaScript feature comes from the MooTools library located at `http://mootools.net`.

Limiting URL lengths

Some web servers—for example, Internet Information Server (IIS)—have problems handling long URLs. As phpMyAdmin creates such URLs on the generated pages, we need a way to indicate when a link would be too long and should be replaced by a form with buttons. The `$cfg['LinkLengthLimit']` directive acts as this limit, with a default value of 1000 which seems appropriate for such servers.

Restricting the list of databases

Sometimes it's useful to avoid showing, in the navigation panel, all the databases a user has access to. phpMyAdmin offers two ways of restricting this—`only_db` and `hide_db`.

To specify the list of what can be seen, the `only_db` parameter is used. It may contain a database name or a list of database names. Only these databases will be seen in the navigation panel:

```
$cfg['Servers'][$i]['only_db'] = 'payroll';
$cfg['Servers'][$i]['only_db'] = array('payroll', 'hr');
```

The database names can contain MySQL wildcard characters such as _ and %. These wildcard characters are described at `http://dev.mysql.com/doc/refman/5.1/en/account-names.html`. If an array is used to specify many databases, they will be displayed on the interface in the same order as they are listed in the array.

Another feature of `only_db` is that you can use it not to restrict the list, but instead to put emphasis on certain names that will be displayed on top of the list. Here, the `myspecial` database name will appear first, followed by all other names:

```
$cfg['Servers'][$i]['only_db'] = array('myspecial', '*');
```

We can also indicate which database names must be hidden with the `hide_db` parameter. It contains a regular expression (`http://en.wikipedia.org/wiki/ Regular_expression`) representing what to exclude. If we do not want users to see any database whose name begins with `secret`, we should use:

```
$cfg['Servers'][$i]['hide_db'] = '^secret';
```

These parameters apply to all users for this server-specific configuration.

 These mechanisms do not replace the MySQL privilege system. Users' rights on other databases still apply, but they cannot use phpMyAdmin's navigation panel to reach their other databases or tables.

Character sets, collations, and language

A **character set** describes how symbols for a specific language or dialect are encoded. A **collation** contains rules to compare and sort the characters of a character set. The character set used to store our data may be different from the one used to display it, leading to data discrepancies. Thus, a need to transform the data arises.

Since MySQL 4.1.x, the MySQL server does the character recoding work for us. Also, MySQL enables us to indicate the character set and collation for each database, each table, and even each field. A default character set for a database applies to each of its tables, unless it's overridden at the table level. The same principle applies to every field.

Collations

When strings have to be compared and sorted, precise rules must be followed by the system (MySQL in this case). For example, is "A" equivalent to "a"? Is "André" equivalent to "Andre"? A set of these rules is called a collation.

A proper choice of collation is important for obtaining the intended results when searching data (for example, from phpMyAdmin's **Search** page), and also when sorting data.

For an introduction to collations, see `http://dev.mysql.com/doc/mysql/en/ Charset-general.htm`, and for a more technical explanation of the algorithms involved, refer to `http://www.unicode.org/reports/tr10/`.

Unicode and UTF-8

> *Unicode is an industry standard designed to allow text and symbols [...] to be consistently represented and manipulated by computers.*

For more information, visit `http://en.wikipedia.org/wiki/Unicode` and `http://www.unicode.org`.

Unicode currently supports more than 600 languages, which is its main advantage over other character sets available with ISO or Windows. This is especially important with a multi-language product such as phpMyAdmin.

To represent or encode these Unicode characters, many **Unicode Transformation Formats (UTF)** exist. A popular transformation format is UTF-8, which uses one to four octets per character. For more details, visit `http://en.wikipedia.org/wiki/UTF-8`.

Note that the browser must support UTF-8 (as most current browsers do). The phpMyAdmin distribution kit includes a UTF-8 version of every language file in the `lang` subdirectory.

Selecting languages

A **Language** selector appears on the login panel (if any) and on the home page. The default behavior of phpMyAdmin is to use the language defined in our browser's preferences, if there is a corresponding language file for this version.

The default language used — in case the program cannot detect one — is defined in `config.inc.php`, in the `$cfg['DefaultLang']` parameter with `'en-utf-8'`. This value can be changed. The possible values for language names are defined in the `libraries/select_lang.lib.php` script as an array.

Even if the default language is defined, each user (especially on a multi-user installation) can choose his or her preferred language from the selector. The user's choice will be remembered in a cookie whenever possible.

We can also force a single language by setting the `$cfg['Lang']` parameter with a value, such as `'fr-utf-8'`. Starting with version 2.7.0, another parameter, `$cfg['FilterLanguages']`, is available. Suppose we want to shorten the list of available languages to **English** and **Français** (French), as these are the ones used exclusively by our users. This is accomplished by building a regular expression indicating which languages we want to display based on the ISO 639 codes of these languages. To continue with our example, we would use:

```
$cfg['FilterLanguages']  = '^(fr|en)';
```

In this expression, the caret (^) means **starting with** and the pipe (|) means **or**. The expression indicates that we are restricting the list to languages whose corresponding ISO codes start with fr or en.

By default, this parameter is empty, meaning that no filter is applied to the list of available languages.

The small information icon beside **Language** gives access to phpMyAdmin's translator page, which lists, by language, the official translator and the contact information. This way, we can reach the translator for corrections, or to offer help with untranslated messages.

Effective character sets and collations

On the home page, we can see the **MySQL charset** information and a **MySQL connection collation** selector. Here is the **MySQL charset** information:

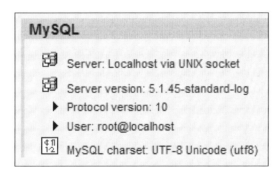

The character set information (as seen here after **MySQL charset**) comes directly from the $charset variable located in the language file that corresponds to the currently-selected language. It's used to generate HTML information, which tells the browser what the page's character set is.

We can also choose which character set and collation will be used for our connection to the MySQL server using the **MySQL connection collation** dialog. This is passed to the MySQL server. MySQL then transforms the characters that will be sent to our browser into this character set. MySQL also interprets what it receives from the browser according to the character set information. Remember that all tables and fields have a character set information describing how their data is encoded.

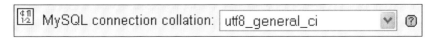

Normally, the default value should work. However, if we are entering some characters using a different character set, we can choose the proper character set in this dialog.

The following parameter defines both the default connection collation and the character set:

```
$cfg['DefaultConnectionCollation'] = 'utf8_unicode_ci';
```

Navigation panel

The navigation panel contains the following elements:

- The logo (see the next section)
- The server list (if `$cfg['LeftDisplayServers']` is set to TRUE)
- The **Home** link or icon (which takes you back to the phpMyAdmin home page)
- A **Log out** link or icon (if logging out is possible)
- A link or icon leading to the **Query window**
- Icons to display phpMyAdmin and MySQL documentation
- A table name filter (under certain conditions; see later in the *Table name filter* section)
- The databases and tables with statistics about the number of tables per database

If `$cfg['MainPageIconic']` is set to TRUE (the default), we see the **icons**. However, if it's set to FALSE, we see the **Home**, **Log out**, and **Query window** links.

The navigation panel can be resized by clicking and moving the vertical separation line in the preferred direction to reveal more data, in case the database or table names are too long for the default navigation panel size.

We can even customize the appearance of this panel. Generally, all parameters are located in `themes/themename/layout.inc.php` unless stated otherwise. `$cfg['LeftWidth']` contains the default width of the navigation panel in pixels. The background color is defined in `$cfg['LeftBgColor']` with a default value of `'#D0DCE0'`. The `$cfg['LeftPointerColor']` parameter, with a default value of `'#CCFFCC'`, defines the pointer color. (The pointer appears when we are using the Full mode, which is discussed shortly.) To activate the navigation pointer for any theme being used, a master setting, `$cfg['LeftPointerEnable']`, exists in `config.inc.php`. Its default value is TRUE.

Configuring the logo

The logo display behavior is controlled by a number of parameters. First, $cfg['LeftDisplayLogo']$ has to be set to TRUE, to enable any displaying of the logo. It is set to true by default. A click on this logo brings the interface to the page listed in the $cfg['LeftLogoLink']$ parameter, which is usually the main phpMyAdmin page (default value main.php), but can be any URL. Finally, the $cfg['LeftLogoLinkWindow']$ parameter indicates in which window the new page appears after clicking on the logo. By default, it's on the main page (value main). However, it could be on a brand new window by using the value new.

The logo image itself comes from the logo_left.png file, which is located in each specific theme's directory structure.

Database and table list

The following examples show that no database has been chosen yet:

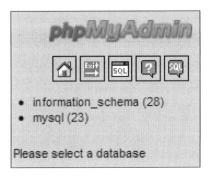

It is also possible to see a **No databases** message instead of the list of databases. This means that our current MySQL rights do not allow us to see any existing databases.

A MySQL server always has at least one database (named **mysql**), but in this case, we do not have the right to see it. Moreover, as of MySQL 5.0.2, a special database called **information_schema** appears at all times in the database list unless it's hidden via the $cfg['Servers']$ [$i]['only_db']$ or the $cfg['Servers']$ [$i]['hide_db']$ mechanisms. It contains a set of views describing the metadata visible for the logged-in user.

We may have the right to create one, as explained in *Chapter 4, Taking First Steps*.

Light mode

The navigation panel can be shown in two ways—the Light mode and the Full mode. The Light mode is used by default, as defined by a TRUE value in $cfg['LeftFrameLight']. This mode shows a drop-down list of the available databases, and only tables of the currently-chosen database are displayed. It's more efficient than Full Mode; the reason is explained in the *Full mode* section appearing later in this chapter. Here we have chosen the **mysql** database:

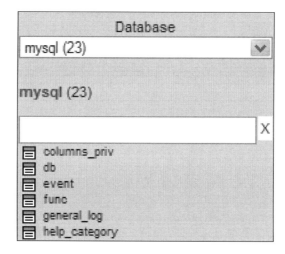

Clicking on a name opens the main panel in the **Database** view, and clicking on a table name opens the main panel in the **Table** view to browse this table. (See the *Main panel* section of this chapter for details.)

Tree display of database names

A user, for example **marc**, might be allowed to work on a single database. Some system administrators offer a more flexible scheme by allowing user **marc** to create many databases, provided all have their names starting with **marc**, such as **marc_airline** and **marc_car**. In this situation, the navigation panel can be set to display a tree of these database names, such as this:

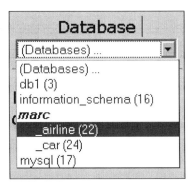

This feature is currently offered only in Light mode, and is controlled by the following parameters:

```
$cfg['LeftFrameDBTree']        = TRUE;
$cfg['LeftFrameDBSeparator'] = '_';
```

The default value of TRUE in `$cfg['LeftFrameDBTree']` ensures that this feature is activated. A popular value for the separator is ' _ '. Should we need more than one set of characters to act as a separator, we just have to use an array such as:

```
$cfg['LeftFrameDBSeparator'] = array('_', '+');
```

Table name filter

In Light mode only, if a database is currently selected, a table name filter is displayed just under the current database name. As we enter a subset of the table names in this filter, the list of tables is reduced to match this subset. The right-hand side **X** control can be used to empty the filter:

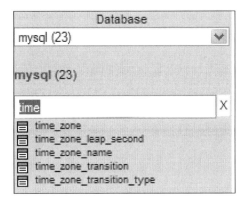

Full mode

The previous examples were shown in Light mode, but setting the $cfg['LeftFrameLight']$ parameter to FALSE produces a complete layout of our databases and tables using collapsible menus (if supported by the browser):

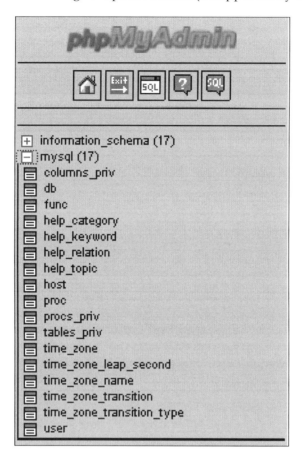

The number of tables in each database is shown in brackets. The Full mode is not selected by default; it can increase network traffic and server load if our current rights give us access to a large number of databases and tables. Links must be generated in the navigation panel to enable table access and quick-browse access to every table. Also, the server has to count the number of rows for all tables.

Table short statistics

Moving the cursor over a table name displays comments about the table (if any), and the number of rows currently within it:

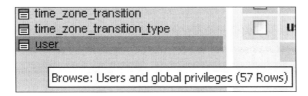

Table quick-access icon

Starting with version 3.0, it was established that the most common action on a table is to browse it. Therefore, a click on the table name itself opens it in browse mode. The small icon beside each table name is a quick way to perform another action on each table, and by default, it brings us to the **Structure** view.

The $cfg['LeftDefaultTabTable']$ parameter controls this action. It has a default value of $'tbl\_structure.php'$, which is the script showing the table's structure. Other possible values for this parameter are listed in Documentation.html. If we prefer to revert to the pre-3.0 behavior, where a click on the table name opened it in the **Structure** page and a click on the quick-access icon led to the **Browse** page, we have to set the following directives:

- $cfg['LeftDefaultTabTable'] = 'sql.php';$
- $cfg['DefaultTabTable'] = 'tbl\_structure.php';$

Nested display of tables within a database

MySQL's data structure is based on two levels—databases and tables. This does not allow subdivisions of tables per project, a feature often requested by MySQL users. They must rely on having multiple databases, but this is not always allowed by their provider. To help them with this regard, phpMyAdmin introduces a **nested-levels** feature, based on the table naming.

Let's say we have access to the **db1** database, and we want to represent two projects, **marketing** and **payroll**. Using a special separator (by default a double underscore) between the project name and the table name, we create the **payroll__employees** and **payroll__jobs tables**, achieving a visually interesting effect:

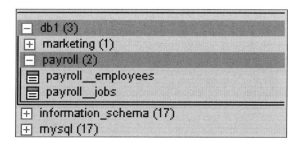

This feature is parameterized with $cfg['LeftFrameTableSeparator'] (set here to '__') to choose the characters that will mark each level change, and $cfg['LeftFrameTableLevel'] (set here to '1') for the number of sublevels.

 The nested-level feature is intended only for improving the navigation panel's look. The proper way to reference the tables in MySQL statements stays the same—for example, db1.payroll__jobs.

A click on the project name (here **payroll**) in the navigation panel opens this project in the main panel, showing only those tables associated with that project:

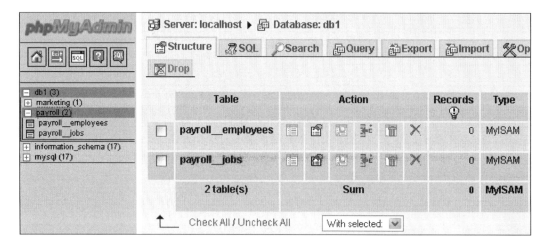

Choosing from the server list

If we have to manage multiple servers from the same phpMyAdmin window and often need to switch between servers, it might prove useful to always have the list of servers in the navigation panel:

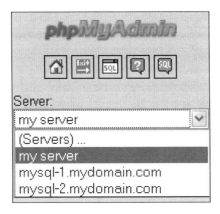

For this, the $cfg['LeftDisplayServers']$ parameter must be set to TRUE. The list of servers can have two forms: a drop-down list or links. Which form appears depends on $cfg['DisplayServersList']$. By default, this parameter is set to FALSE, so we see a drop-down list of servers. Setting $cfg['DisplayServersList']$ to TRUE produces a list of links to all defined servers:

Handling many databases or tables

This section describes some techniques for coping with a server holding a huge number of databases and tables.

Limits on the interface

Before phpMyAdmin 2.11, it was difficult to work with the interface if we had access to hundreds or even thousands of databases, or hundreds of tables in the same database. Loading of the navigation panel was slow, or did not work at all. In 2.11, the interface has been reworked to take care of this.

Two new parameters, shown here with their default values, establish a limit on the number of databases and tables displayed, by adding a page selector and navigation links:

```
$cfg['MaxDbList'] = 100;
$cfg['MaxTableList'] = 250;
```

The effect of `$cfg['MaxDbList']` can be seen on the main panel in **Server** view:

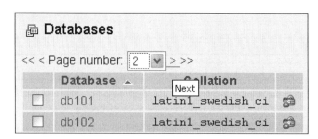

We can also see the effect in the navigation panel:

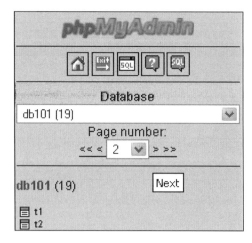

Improving fetch speed

Three configuration parameters have an effect on the speed of database name retrieval and table counting. The first one is

```
$cfg['Servers'][$i]['ShowDatabasesCommand'] = 'SHOW DATABASES';
```

Every time phpMyAdmin needs to obtain the list of databases from the server, it uses the command listed in this parameter. The default command SHOW DATABASES is fine in ordinary situations. However, on servers with many databases, speed improvements can be observed by trying other commands, such as one of these:

- SHOW DATABASES LIKE '#user#_%'
- SELECT DISTINCT TABLE_SCHEMA FROM information_schema.SCHEMA_PRIVILEGES
- SELECT SCHEMA_NAME FROM information_schema.SCHEMATA

In the first example, #user# is replaced by the current username. In extreme situations (thousands of databases), a user who installs his own copy of phpMyAdmin should put False in this parameter. This would block the fetching of any database names, and would require the population of the $cfg['Servers'][$i]['only_db'] parameter with this user's database list.

Another parameter that can help is $cfg['Servers'][$i]['CountTables'], which has a default value of True. Setting it to False would instruct phpMyAdmin to avoid counting the tables when producing the list of databases and tables in the navigation panel (in Full mode).

Finally, some users have speed issues, at least under MySQL 5.1, with information retrieval from **INFORMATION_SCHEMA**. The phpMyAdmin team would like to use this SQL-standard way of requesting information from the server, but the reality of its MySQL implementation leaves room for improvement. Therefore the $cfg['Servers'][$i]['DisableIS'] directive, with its default value of TRUE, disables the use of **INFORMATION_SCHEMA** for a major portion of the phpMyAdmin code. For your server, it may be worth setting this to FALSE to see if response time improves.

Main panel

The main panel is the principal working area, and all the possible views for it are explained in the following sections. Its appearance can be customized. The background color is defined in $cfg['RightBgColor']$, and the default color is #F5F5F5. We can also select a background image by setting the URI of the image we want (for example, http://www.domain.com/images/clouds.jpg) in $cfg['RightBgImage']$.

Home page

The home page may contain a varying number of links depending on the login mode and the user's rights. A normal user may see it as:

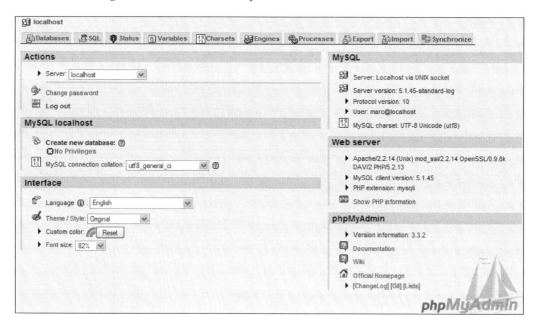

The **Home** link from the navigation panel is used to display this page. It shows the phpMyAdmin and MySQL versions, the MySQL server name, and the logged-in user. In order to reveal less information about our web server and MySQL server, we could set $cfg['ShowServerInfo']$ to FALSE. Another setting, $cfg['ShowPhpInfo']$, can be set to TRUE if we want to see the **Show PHP Information** link on the home page; by default its value is FALSE. The reason for the **No privileges** message and how to fix this condition is covered in *Chapter 4, Taking First Steps*. We see some links that relate to MySQL or phpMyAdmin itself. The **Log out** link might not be there if the user did not log in, as indicated by the configuration file's $cfg['Servers'][$i]['auth_type']$ parameter being set to config.

In this example, a normal user is allowed to change his or her password from the interface by using the **Change password** link, which displays the following dialog:

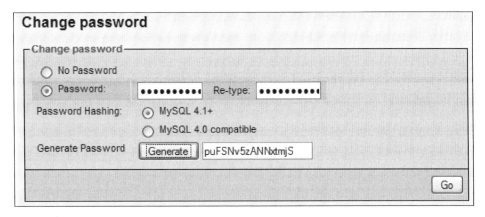

We can either choose our new password by typing it twice, or use the **Generate** button (only available in JavaScript-enabled browsers). In this case, the new password is shown in a clear field for us to take good note of it, and is automatically filled into the dialog for changing the password effectively. It is highly recommended to generate passwords in this way, as they are most likely more secure than a human-chosen password. To disallow the **Change password** link from the home page, we set $cfg['ShowChgPassword']$ to FALSE. Privileged users have more options on the home page. They can always create databases and have more links to manage the server as a whole—for example, the **Privileges** link (more on this in *Chapter 19, Administrating the MySQL Server with phpMyAdmin*).

Database view

phpMyAdmin goes into this view (shown in the screenshot that follows) every time we click on a database name in the navigation panel.

This is where we can see an overview of the database—the existing tables, a link to create a table, the tabs to the Database view subpages, and some special operations that we might do on this database in order to generate documentation and statistics. There is a checkbox beside each table to perform global operations on that table (covered in *Chapter 9, Performing Table and Database Operations*). The table is chosen by using the checkbox or by clicking anywhere on the row's background. We can also see each table's size, if $cfg['ShowStats']$ is set to TRUE. This parameter also controls the display of table-specific statistics in the **Table** view.

The initial screen that appears here is the database **Structure** subpage. We note here that almost every column header, such as **Table**, **Records**, and **Size**, is a link that can be used to sort the corresponding column (*Chapter 4, Taking First Steps*, covers sorting). Although sorting by descending table name might not be that useful, sorting by descending size is definitely something we should do from time to time.

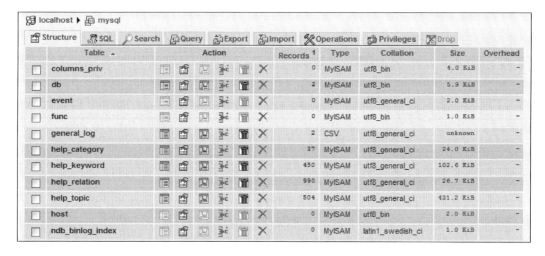

We might want a different initial subpage to appear when entering the **Database** view. This is controlled by the $cfg['DefaultTabDatabase'] parameter and the available choices are given in the configuration file as comments.

The number of records is obtained by using a quick method—the SHOW TABLE STATUS statement—and not by using SELECT COUNT(*) FROM TABLENAME. This quick method is usually accurate, except for InnoDB tables, which returns an approximate number of records. To help get the correct number of records even for InnoDB the $cfg['MaxExactCount'] parameter is available. If the approximate number of records is lower than this parameter's value (by default, 20000), the slower SELECT COUNT(*) method will be used.

Do not put a value too high for the MaxExactCount parameter. You would get correct results, but only after waiting for a few minutes, if there are hundreds of thousands of records in your InnoDB table. To examine **the number of records as** displayed for InnoDB, please refer to *Chapter 10, Benefiting from the Relational System*, where we actually have an InnoDB table to play with.

A user might be surprised when seeing the term **KiB** in the **Size** and **Overhead** columns. phpMyAdmin has adopted the **International Electrotechnical Commission (IEC)** binary prefixes (see `http://en.wikipedia.org/wiki/Binary_prefix`). The displayed values are defined in each language file. Here is the definition for English:

```
$byteUnits = array('B', 'KiB', 'MiB', 'GiB', 'TiB', 'PiB', 'EiB');
```

Table view

This is a commonly-used view, giving access to all table-specific subpages. By default, the initial screen is the table's **Browse** screen, which shows the first page of this table's data. Note that the header for this screen always shows the current database and table names. We also see the comments set for the table:

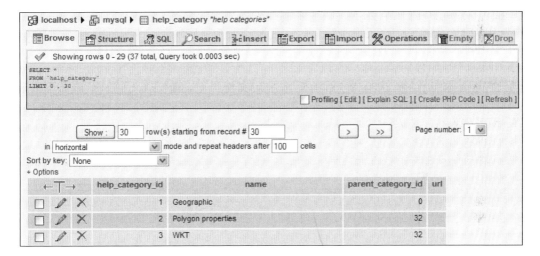

The `$cfg['DefaultTabTable']` parameter defines the initial subpage on the **Table** view. Some users prefer to avoid seeing the first page's data because in production they routinely run saved queries or enter the **Search** subpage (explained in *Chapter 8, Searching Data*).

Server view

The **Server** view is entered each time we go back to the home page. A privileged user will of course see more choices in the **Server** view. The **Server** view panel was created to group together related server management subpages and enable easy navigation between them.

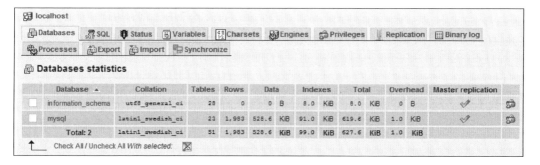

The default **Server** page is controlled by the $cfg['DefaultTabServer'] parameter. This parameter defines the initial starting page as well. For multi-user installations, it's recommended to keep the default value (main.php), which displays the traditional home page. We could choose to display server statistics instead by changing this parameter to server_status.php, or to see the user's list with server_privileges.php. Other possible choices are explained in the configuration file, and the server administration pages are explained in *Chapter 19, Administrating the MySQL Server with phpMyAdmin.*

Icons for the home page and menu tabs

A configuration parameter, $cfg['MainPageIconic'], controls the appearance of icons at various places on the main panel:

- On the home page
- At the top of the page when listing the **Server**, **Database**, and **Table** information
- On the menu tabs in **Database**, **Table**, and **Server** views

This parameter is set to TRUE by default, producing, for example:

We can also display menu items without tabs by setting the $cfg['LightTabs'] parameter to True, producing:

Opening a new phpMyAdmin window

Sometimes we want to compare data from two tables at once, or we have some other need necessitating multiple phpMyAdmin windows. At the bottom of almost every page, a small icon is available for opening another window in phpMyAdmin with the current panel's content. Moreover, this icon can be used to create a browser bookmark that points to the current phpMyAdmin page (but we will need to be logged in to access the data).

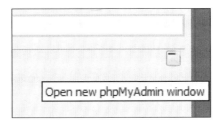

Query window

It's often convenient to have a distinct window in which we can type and refine queries, and which is synchronized with the main panel. This window is called the **Query window**. We can open this window by using the small SQL icon, or the **Query window** link from the navigation panel's icons or links zone.

This link or icon is displayed if $cfg['QueryFrame'] is set to TRUE. A value of TRUE for $cfg['QueryFrameJS'] tells phpMyAdmin to open a distinct window and update it by using JavaScript commands; of course, this only works for a JavaScript-enabled browser. If this is set to FALSE, clicking on **Query** window will only open the main panel, and will display the normal SQL subpage.

 The full usability of the **Query window** is only achieved with the distinct window mode.

The **Query** window itself has subpages, and it appears here over the main panel:

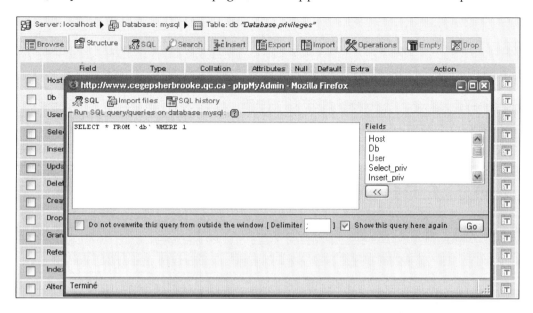

We can choose the dimensions (in pixels) of this window with $cfg['QueryWindowWidth']$ and $cfg['QueryWindowHeight']$. *Chapter 11, Entering SQL Commands*, explains the **Query** window in more detail, including the available SQL query history feature.

Summary

This chapter covered:

- The language selection system
- The purpose of the navigation and main panels
- The contents of the navigation panel, including Light mode and Full mode
- The contents of the main panel, with its various views depending on the **context**
- The **Query** window and the customization of MySQL documentation links

The next chapter will guide you with simple steps to accomplish—with a freshly-installed phpMyAdmin—initial table creation, data insertion, and retrieval.

4
Taking First Steps

Having seen the overall layout of phpMyAdmin's panel, we are ready to create a database, create our first table, insert some data into it, and browse it. These first steps are intentionally simple, but they will give you the foundation on which more complex operations will be achieved later. At the end of the chapter, we will have at our disposition the two basic tables on which the remaining exercises are based.

Creating a database

Before creating a table, we must ensure that we have a database for which the MySQL server's administrator has given us the CREATE privilege. Various possibilities exist:

- The administrator has already created a database for us, and we see its name in the navigation panel; we don't have the right to create an additional database

- We have the right to create databases from phpMyAdmin

- We are on a shared host, and the host provider has installed a general Web interface (for example, cPanel) to create MySQL databases and accounts; in this case, we should visit this web interface now and ensure that we have created at least one database and one MySQL account.

Note that a configuration parameter, $cfg['ShowCreateDb'], controls the display of the **Create new database** dialog. By default, it's set to true, which shows the dialog.

No privileges?

If you do not have the required privileges to create a database, the home page displays a **No privileges** message under the **Create new database** label. This means that you must work with the databases that have been already created for you, or ask the MySQL server's administrator to give you the necessary CREATE privilege.

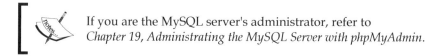

If you are the MySQL server's administrator, refer to *Chapter 19, Administrating the MySQL Server with phpMyAdmin.*

First database creation is authorized

If phpMyAdmin detects that we have the right to create a database, the home page appears as shown in the following figure:

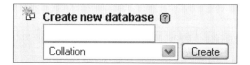

In the input field, a suggested database name appears if the $cfg['SuggestDBName'] parameter is set to TRUE—which is the default setting. The suggested database name is built according to the privileges we possess.

If we are restricted to the use of a prefix, the prefix might be suggested in the input field. (A popular choice for this prefix is the username, which may or may not be followed by an underscore character.) Note that, in this case, the prefix is followed by an ellipsis mark, added by phpMyAdmin. We should remove this ellipsis mark and complete the input field with an appropriate name.

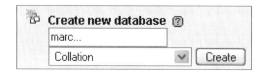

The **Collation** choice can be left unchanged for now. With this dialog, we could pick a default character set and collation for this database. This setting can be changed later (see *Chapter 9, Performing Table and Database Operations*, for more information on this).

We will assume here that we have the right to create a database named **marc_book**. We enter **marc_book** in the input field and click on **Create**. Once the database has been created, we will see the following screen:

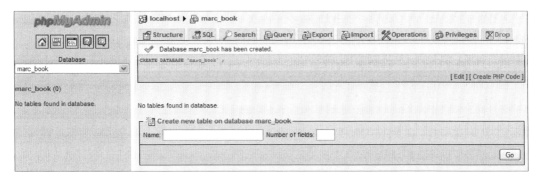

Notice the following:

- The title of the main panel has changed to reflect the fact that we are now located in this database.

- A confirmation message regarding the creation is displayed.

- The navigation panel has been updated; we see **marc_book (0)**. Here, the name indicates that the **marc_book** database has been created, and the number **0** indicates that it contains no tables.

- By default, the SQL query sent to the server by phpMyAdmin to create the database is displayed in color.

> phpMyAdmin displays the query it generated, because `$cfg['ShowSQL']` is set to TRUE. Looking at the generated queries can be a good way of learning SQL.

As the generated queries can be large and take much of the on-screen room, the `$cfg['MaxCharactersInDisplayedSQL']` acts as a limit. Its default value of `1000` should be a good balance between seeing too few and seeing too many of the queries, especially when performing large imports.

It's important to examine the phpMyAdmin feedback to ascertain the validity of the operations that we make through the interface. In this way, we can detect errors such as typos in the names, or the creation of a table in the wrong database. phpMyAdmin retrieves error messages from the MySQL server and displays them in the interface.

Creating our first table

Now that we have a new database, it's time to create a table in it. The example table we will create is named **book**.

Choosing the fields

Before creating a table, we should plan the information we want to store. This is usually done during database design. In our case, a simple analysis leads us to the following book-related data we want to keep:

- International Standard Book Number (ISBN)
- Title
- Number of pages
- Author identification

For now, it's not important to have the complete list of fields (or columns) for our **book** table. We will modify it by prototyping the application now and refining it later. At the end of the chapter, we will add a second table, **author**, containing information about each author.

Creating a table

We have chosen our table name and we know the number of fields. We enter this information in the **Create new table** dialog and click on **Go** to start creating the table. At this point it does not matter if the number of fields is exactly known, as a subsequent panel will allow the addition of fields when creating the table:

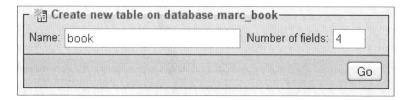

We then see a panel specifying field information. As we asked for **4** fields, we get four rows. Each row refers to information specific to one field. The following image represents the left side for this panel:

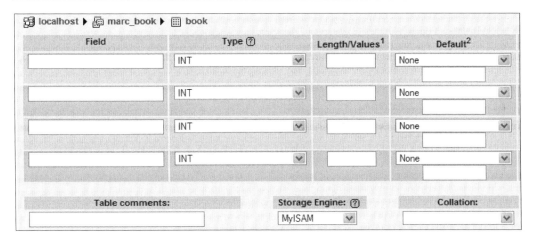

And the next one represents the right side:

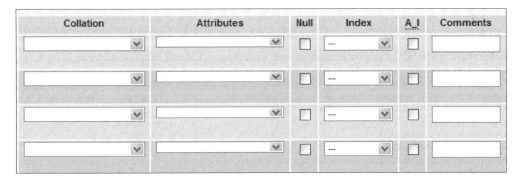

Had we asked to create a table with less than four fields, the display would be oriented vertically — we'll see an example of that at the end of the chapter.

The MySQL documentation explains the valid characters for the table and field names (if we search for **Legal names**). This may vary depending on the MySQL version. Usually, any character that is allowed in a filename (except the dot and the slash) is acceptable in a table name, and the length of the name must not exceed 64 characters. The 64-character limit exists for field names as well, but we can use any character.

We enter our field names in the **Field** column. Each field has a type, and the most commonly-used types are located at the beginning of the drop-down list.

The **VARCHAR** (variable character) type is widely used when the field content is alphanumeric, because the contents will occupy only the space needed for it. This type requires a maximum length, which we specify. If we forget to do so, a small pop-up message reminds us later when we save the page. For the page count and the author identification, we have chosen **INT** type (integer), as depicted in the following screenshot:

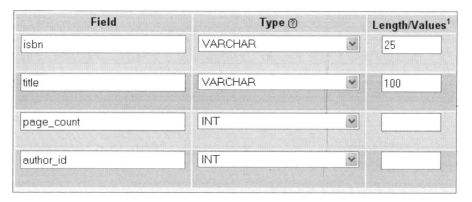

There are other attributes for fields, but we will leave them empty in this example. You might notice the **Add 1 Field(s)** dialog at the bottom of the screen. We can use it to add some fields to this table creation panel by entering the appropriate value and hitting **Go**. The number of rows will change according to the new number of fields, leaving the information already entered in the first four fields intact. Before saving the page, let's define some keys.

Choosing keys

A table should normally have a primary key (a field with unique content that represents each row). Having a primary key is recommended for row identification, better performance, and possible cross-table relations. A good value here is the ISBN; so, in the **Index** dialog we select **PRIMARY** for the **isbn** field. Other possibilities for index type include **INDEX**, **UNIQUE**, and **FULLTEXT** (more on this in *Chapter 5, Changing Data and Structure*).

 Index management (also referred to as Key management) can be done at initial table creation, or later in the **Structure** subpage of Table view.

To improve the speed of the queries that we will make by author ID, we should add an index on this field. The rightmost part of our screen now looks like this:

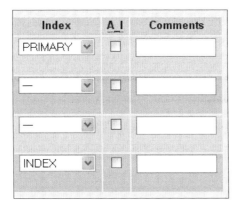

At this point, we could pick a different **Storage Engine** from the corresponding drop-down menu. However, for the time being, we will just accept the default storage engine.

Now we are ready to create the table by clicking on **Save**. If all goes well, the next screen confirms that the table has been created; we are now in the **Structure** subpage of the Table view:

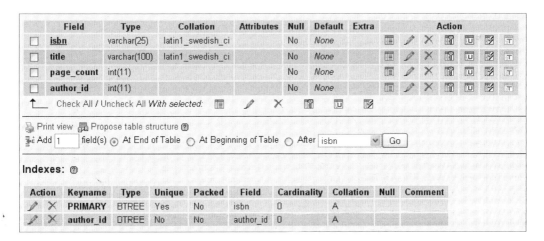

Of the various tabs leading to other subpages, some are not active, because it would not make sense to browse or search a table if there are no rows in it. However, it would be acceptable to export a table, as we can export a table's structure even if it contains no data.

Inserting data manually

Now that we have a table, let's put some data in it manually. Before we do that, here are some useful references on data manipulation within this book:

- *Chapter 5, Changing Data and Structure* explains how to change data and structure

- *Chapter 7, Importing Data and Structure* explains how to import data from existing files

- *Chapter 9, Performing Table and Database Operations* explains how to copy data from other tables

- *Chapter 10, Benefiting from the Relational System* explains the relational system (in our case, we will want to link to the **author** table)

For now, click on the **Insert** link, which will lead us to the data-entry (or edit) panel. This screen has room to enter information for two rows, that is two books in our example. This is because the default value of $cfg['InsertRows']$ is 2. In the lower part of the screen, the dialog **Restart insertion with 2 rows** can be used if the default number of rows does not suit our needs. But beware, any data already on the screen would be lost. By default, the **Ignore** checkbox is ticked, which means that the second group of fields will be ignored. But as soon as we enter some information in one field of this group and exit the field, the **Ignore** box is automatically unchecked if JavaScript is enabled in the browser.

We can enter the following sample information for two books:

- ISBN: 1-234567-89-0, title: A hundred years of cinema (volume 1), 600 pages, author ID: 1

- ISBN: 1-234567-22-0, title: Future souvenirs, 200 pages, author ID: 2

We start by entering data for the first and the second rows. The **Value** column width obeys the maximum length for the character fields. For this example, we leave the lower drop-down selector with its default value of **Insert as new row**. We then click on **Go** to insert the data. There is a **Go** button after each set of columns that represent a row, and another one on the lower part of the screen. All of these have the same effect of saving the entered data, but are provided for convenience.

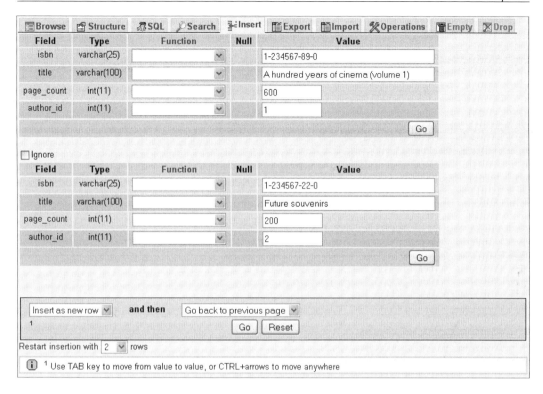

If our intention had been to enter data for more books after these two, we would have selected **Insert another new row** from the first drop-down menu before clicking on **Go**. This would then insert the data we have provided and reload the screen so that it's ready for us to insert more.

Data entry panel tuning for CHAR and VARCHAR

By default, phpMyAdmin displays an input field on a single line for the field types CHAR and VARCHAR. This is controlled by setting $cfg['CharEditing'] to 'input'. Sometimes, we may want to insert line breaks (new lines) within the field. This can be done by changing $cfg['CharEditing'] to 'textarea'. This is a global setting, and will apply to all the fields of all the tables, for all users of this copy of phpMyAdmin. In this mode, the insertion of line breaks may be done manually with the *Enter* key, or by copying and pasting lines of text from another on-screen source.

We can tune the number of columns and rows of this text area with:

```
$cfg['CharTextareaCols']   = 40;
$cfg['CharTextareaRows']   = 2;
```

Here, 2 for $cfg['CharTextareaRows']$ means that we should be able to see at least two lines before the browser starts to display a vertical scroll bar. These settings apply to all **CHAR** and **VARCHAR** fields. Applying those settings would generate a different **Insert** screen, as follows:

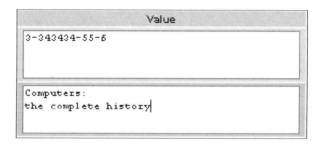

 With this entry mode, the maximum length of each field no longer applies visually. It would be enforced by MySQL at insert time.

Browse mode

There are many ways to enter Browse mode. In fact, it's used each time the query results are displayed. We can enter this mode by clicking on the table name in the navigation panel, or by clicking on **Browse** when we are in the Table view for a specific table:

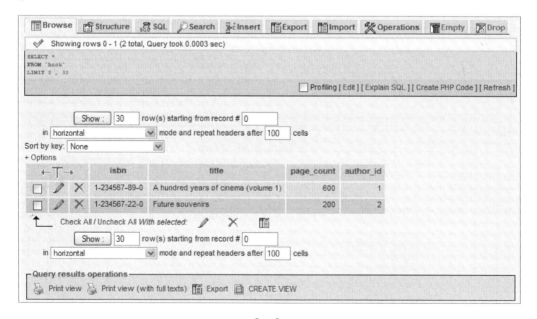

SQL query links

In the **Browse** results, the first part displayed is the query itself, along with a few links. The displayed links may vary depending on our actions and some configuration parameters.

The **Profiling** checkbox is covered in *Chapter 17, Supporting MySQL 5.0 and 5.1*.

The **Edit** link appears if `$cfg['SQLQuery']['Edit']` is set to TRUE. Its purpose is to open the **Query window** so that you can edit this query (see *Chapter 11, Entering SQL Commands*, for more details).

Explain SQL is displayed if `$cfg['SQLQuery']['Explain']` is set to TRUE. We will see in *Chapter 5, Changing Data and Structure* what this link can be used for.

The **Create PHP Code** link can be clicked to reformat the query to the syntax expected in a PHP script. It can then be copied and pasted directly at the place where we need the query in the PHP script we are working on. Note that after a click, this link changes to **Without PHP Code**, which would bring back the normal query display. This link is available if `$cfg['SQLQuery']['ShowAsPHP']` is set to TRUE.

Refresh is used to execute the same query again. The results might change, as a MySQL server is a multi-user server, and other users or processes might be modifying the same tables. This link is shown if `$cfg['SQLQuery']['Refresh']` is set to TRUE.

All four of these parameters have a default value of TRUE in `config.inc.php`.

Navigation bar

The Navigation bar is displayed at the top of the results and also at the bottom. Column headers can be repeated at certain intervals among results depending on the value entered in **repeat headers after...**.

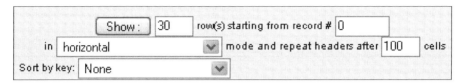

The Navigation bar enables us to navigate from page to page, displaying an arbitrary number of records (or rows), starting at some point in the results. As we entered browse mode by clicking on **Browse**, the underlying query that generated the results includes the whole table. However, this is not always the case.

Notice that we are positioned at record number **0**, and are seeing records in **horizontal** mode.

The default display mode is `'horizontal'`, as defined in `$cfg['DefaultDisplay']`. We can also set this to `'vertical'` if we usually prefer this mode. Even if our preferred mode is set in this configuration parameter, we can always use the **Show** dialog to change it on the fly.

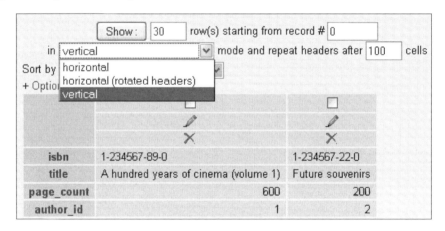

Another possibility for $cfg['DefaultDisplay']$ is the 'horizontalflipped' value (which can also be selected on screen via the **horizontal (rotated headers)** choice), which rotates the column headers by 90 degrees. If we try this choice, another parameter, $cfg['HeaderFlipType']$, plays a role. Its default value, css, displays true rotated headers. Not every browser supports this (at least Firefox and Chrome do not); however, Internet Explorer 8 and Opera do support this feature, and produce:

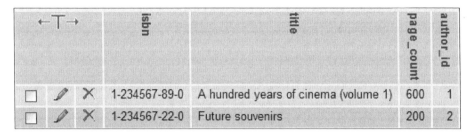

On other browsers, it seems the best we can achieve is by setting $cfg['HeaderFlipType']$ to fake.

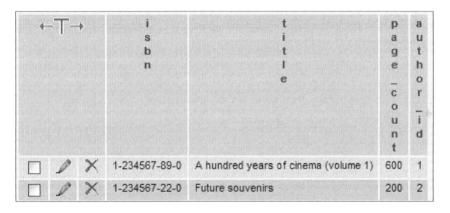

We are currently using a table containing a small number of rows. With larger tables, we could see a more complete set of navigation buttons. To simulate this, let's use the **Show** dialog to change the default number of rows from **30** to **1**; we then click on **Show**. We can see that the navigation bar adapts itself:

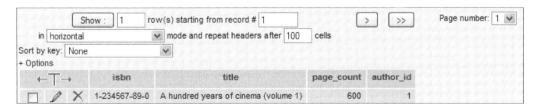

This time, there are buttons labeled <<, <, >, and >> for easy access to the first page, previous page, next page, and the last page of the results respectively. The buttons appear only when necessary; for example, the **first page** button is not displayed if we already are on the first page. These symbols are displayed in this manner as the default setting of $cfg['NavigationBarIconic'] is TRUE. A FALSE here would produce buttons like **Next** and **End**, whereas a value of 'both' would display **> Next** and **>> End**.

There is also a **Page number** drop-down menu, to go directly to one of the pages located near the current page. As there can be hundreds or thousands of pages, this menu is kept small and contains the commonly requested pages: A few page numbers before and after the current page, a few pages at the beginning and at the end, and a sample of page numbers based on a computed interval.

By design, phpMyAdmin always tries to give quick results, and one way to achieve this result is to add a LIMIT clause in SELECT. If a LIMIT clause is already there in the original query, phpMyAdmin will respect it. The default limit is 30 rows, set in $cfg['MaxRows']. If there are many users on the server, limiting the number of rows returned helps to keep the server load to a minimum.

Another button is available on the navigation bar, but must be activated by setting $cfg['ShowAll'] to TRUE. It would be very tempting for users to use this button often. Hence, on a multi-user installation of phpMyAdmin, it's recommended that the button be left to its default value of disabled (FALSE). When enabled, the navigation bar is augmented with a **Show all** button. Clicking on this button retrieves all of the rows of the current results set, which might hit the execution time limit in PHP or a memory limit on the server; most browsers would also crash when asked to display thousands of rows. The exact number of rows that can be safely displayed cannot be predicted as it depends on the actual data present in columns and on the browser's capabilities.

 If we enter a big number in the **Show...rows** dialog, the same results will be achieved (and we may face the same problems).

Query results operations

A section labeled **Query results operations** is located under the results. This contains links to print the results (with or without the FULL TEXT columns), to export these results (see the *Exporting partial query results* section in *Chapter 6, Exporting Data and Structure (Backup)*), or to create a view from this query (more on this in Chapter 17, *Supporting MySQL 5.0 and 5.1*).

Sorting results

In SQL, we can never be sure of the order in which the data is retrieved, unless we explicitly sort the data. Some implementations of the retrieving engine may show results in the same order as the one in which data was entered, or according to a primary key. However, a sure way to get results in the order we want is by sorting them explicitly.

When browsing results are displayed, any column header can be clicked to sort on this column, even if it's not part of an index. Let's click on the **author_id** column header:

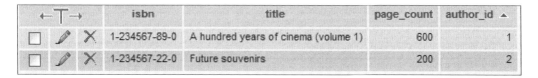

We can confirm that the sorting has occurred, by watching the SQL query at the top of the screen; it now contains an **ORDER BY** clause.

We now see a small red triangle pointing upwards beside the **author_id** header. This means that the current sort order is "ascending". Moving the mouse cursor over the **author_id** header makes the red triangle change direction, to indicate what will happen if we click on the header again—a sort by descending **author_id**.

Another way to sort is by key. The **Sort** dialog shows all of the keys already defined. Here we see a key named **PRIMARY**—the name given to our primary key on the **isbn** field when we checked **Primary** for this field at creation time:

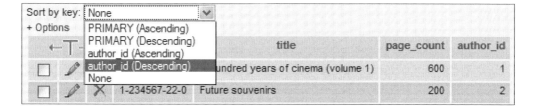

This might be the only way to sort on multiple fields at once (for multi-field indexes).

The default initial sort order is defined in $cfg['Order']$, with ASC for ascending, DESC for descending. The sort order can also be SMART, which means that fields of type DATE, TIME, DATETIME, and TIMESTAMP would be sorted in descending order, whereas other field types will be sorted in ascending order.

Headwords

Because we can change the number of records displayed on a page, it's quite possible that we do not see all of the data. In this case, it would help to see headwords— indications about the first and last row of displayed data. This way, you can click on **Next** or **Previous** without scrolling to the bottom of the window.

However, which column should phpMyAdmin base this headwords generation on? A simple assumption has been made: If you click on a column's header to indicate your intention of sorting on this column, phpMyAdmin uses this column's data as a headword. For our current book table, we do not have enough data to clearly notice the benefits of this technique. However, we can nonetheless see that after a sort the top part of the screen now contains this message:

```
Showing rows 0 - 1 (2 total, Query took 0.0006 sec)
   [author_id: 1 - 2]
```

Here, the message between square brackets means that **author_id** number **1** is on the first displayed row and number **2** is on the last one.

Color-marking rows

When moving the mouse between rows, the row background color can change to the color defined in `$cfg['BrowsePointerColor']`. This parameter can be found in `themes/themename/layout.inc.php`. To enable this, the browse pointer for all themes— `$cfg['BrowsePointerEnable']` — must be set to TRUE (the default) in `config.inc.php`.

It may be interesting to visually mark some rows when we have many columns in the table and must constantly scroll left and right to read data. Another option is to highlight the importance of some rows for personal comparison of data, or when showing data to people. Highlighting is done by clicking on the row. Clicking again removes the highlighting from the row. The chosen color is defined by `$cfg['BrowseMarkerColor']` (see `themes/themename/layout.inc.php`). This feature must be enabled by setting `$cfg['BrowseMarkerEnable']` to TRUE, this time in `config.inc.php`. This sets the feature for all themes. We can mark more than one row. Marking the row also activates the checkbox for this row.

←T→			isbn	title	page_count	author_id
☑	🖉	✕	1-234567-89-0	A hundred years of cinema (volume 1)	600	1
☐	🖉	✕	1-234567-22-0	Future souvenirs	200	2

Limiting the length of each column

In the previous examples, we always saw the full contents of each column, as each column had a number of characters that was within the limit defined by $cfg['LimitChars']. This is a limit enforced on all non-numeric fields. If this limit was lower (say 10), the display would be as follows:

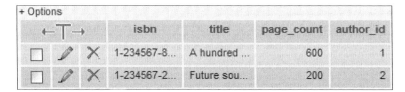

This would help us see more columns at the same time (at the expense of seeing less of each column).

Display options

In order to see the full texts, we will now make use of the **Options** slider, which reveals some display options. The option that concerns us at the moment is the **Partial Texts/Full Texts** pair; we can choose **Full Texts** to see all of the text that was truncated. Even if we elect not to change the $cfg['LimitChars'] parameter, there will be a time when asking for full texts will be useful (when we work with the TEXT field type—more on this in *Chapter 5, Changing Data and Structure*).

A quicker way of seeing the full texts is to click on the big **T**, which is located just on top of the **Edit** and **Delete** icons. Another click on this **T** toggles the display from full to partial.

Browsing distinct values

There is a quick way to display all distinct values and the number of occurrences for each value for each field. This feature is available on the **Structure** page. For example, we want to know how many different authors we have in our book table and how many books each one wrote. On the line describing the field we want to browse (here **author_id**), we click on the **Browse distinct values** icon or link:

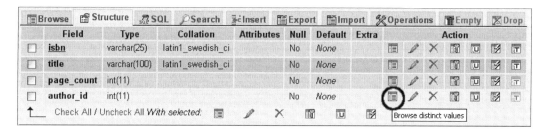

We have a limited test set, but can nonetheless see the results:

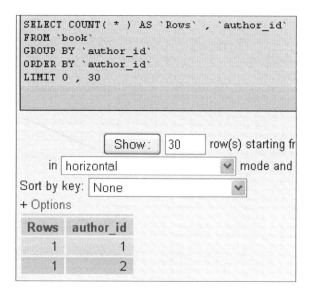

Customizing the browse mode

The following are additional parameters that control the appearance of results. These parameters—except $cfg['RepeatCells']—are located in themes/themename/layout.inc.php.

Additional parameter	Effect on appearance of result
$cfg['Border']	The HTML tables used to present results have no border by default because this parameter is set to 0; we can set this to a higher number (for example, 1 or 2) to add borders to the tables.
$cfg['ThBgcolor']	The tables mentioned have headers with #D3DCE3 as the default background color.
$cfg['BgcolorOne'], $cfg['BgcolorTwo']	When displaying rows of results, two background colors are used alternately; by default, those are #CCCCCC and #DDDDDD.
$cfg['RepeatCells']	When many rows of data are displayed, we may lose track of the meaning of each column. By default, at each 100th cell, the column headers are displayed.

Creating an additional table

In our (simple) design, we know that we need another table—the **author** table. The **author** table will contain:

- Author identification
- Full name
- Phone number

To create this table, we must go back to the Database view. We click on **marc_book** in the navigation panel, and request the creation of another table with three fields, as indicated in the following screenshot:

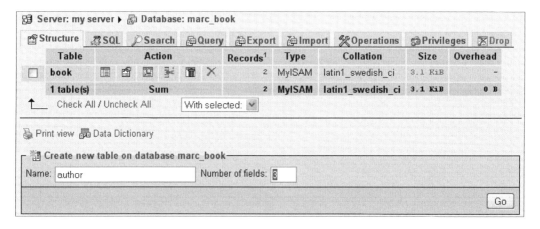

Using the same techniques used when creating the first table, we enter the data shown in the following screenshot:

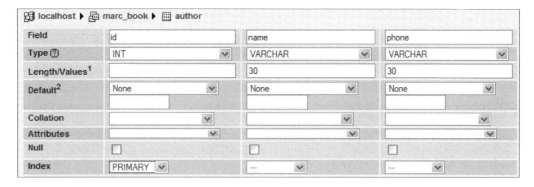

As we have three fields or less, the display is now in vertical mode (see the *Vertical mode* section in *Chapter 5, Changing Data and Structure* for more details).

The field name **id**, which is our primary key in this new table, relates to the author_id field from the book table. After saving the table structure, we enter some data for authors 1 and 2. Use your imagination for this!

Summary

This chapter explained how to create a database and tables, and how to enter data manually into the tables. It also covered how to confirm the presence of data by using the browse mode, which includes the SQL query links, navigation bar, sorting options, and row marking.

The next chapter explains how to edit data rows and covers the various aspects of deletion of rows, tables, and databases.

5

Changing Data and Structure

Data is not static, it changes often. This chapter focuses on editing and deleting data and its supporting structures—tables and databases.

Changing data

In this section we cover the various ways of editing and deleting data.

Entering edit mode

When we browse a table or view the results from a search on any single-table query, small icons appear on the left or right of each table row, as shown in the following screenshot:

The row can be edited with the pencil-shaped icon and deleted with the X-shaped icon. The exact form and location of these controls are governed by:

```
$cfg['PropertiesIconic']    = TRUE;
$cfg['ModifyDeleteAtLeft']  = TRUE;
$cfg['ModifyDeleteAtRight'] = FALSE;
```

We can decide whether to display them on the left side, the right side, or on both sides. The $cfg['PropertiesIconic']$ parameter can have the values TRUE, FALSE, or both. TRUE displays icons as seen in the previous screenshot, FALSE displays **Edit** and **Delete** (or their translated equivalent) as links, and both displays the icon as well as the text.

The small checkbox beside each row is explained in the *Multi-row edit* and the *Deleting many rows* sections later in this chapter.

Clicking on the **Edit** icon or link displays the following panel, which is similar to the data entry panel (except for the lower part):

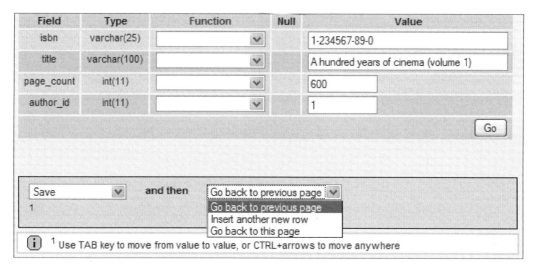

In this panel, we can change data by typing directly (or by cutting and pasting via the normal operating system mechanisms). We can also revert to the original contents using the **Reset** button.

By default, the lower drop-down menus are set to **Save** (so that we make changes to this row) and **Go back to previous page** (so that we can continue editing another row on the previous results page). We might want to stay on the current page after clicking on **Go**—in order to save and then continue editing— in which case we can choose **Go back to this page**. If we want to insert yet another new row after saving the current row, we just have to choose **Insert another new row** before saving. The **Insert as new row** choice—below the **Save** choice—is explained in the *Duplicating rows of data* section later in this chapter.

Moving to the next field with the tab key

People who prefer to use the keyboard can use the *Tab* key to go to the next field. Normally, the cursor goes from left to right and from top to bottom, so it would travel into the fields in the **Function** column (more on this in a moment). However, to ease data navigation in phpMyAdmin, the normal order of navigation has been altered. The *Tab* key first goes through each field in the **Value** column, and then through each one in the **Function** column.

Moving with arrows

Another way of moving between fields is with the *Ctrl + arrow* keys. This method might be easier than using the *Tab* key when there are many fields on the screen. For this to work, the $cfg['CtrlArrowsMoving']$ parameter must be set to true, which is the default value.

 On a Mac OS X 10.5 with spaces enabled, *Ctrl* + arrow keys are the default shortcut to switch between virtual desktops, so this technique cannot be used for moving between fields.

Handling NULL values

If the table's structure permits a NULL value inside a field, a small checkbox appears in the field's **Null** column. Selecting this puts a NULL value in the field. Whenever data is typed into the **Value** column for this field, the **Null** checkbox is cleared automatically. (This is only possible in JavaScript-enabled browsers.)

Here, we have modified the structure of the **phone** field in the author table to permit a NULL value (refer to the *Editing field attributes* section later in this Chapter). The **Null** checkbox is not selected here:

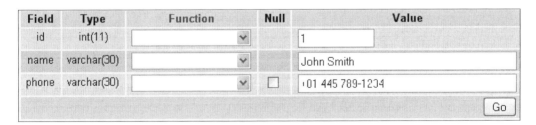

Field	Type	Function	Null	Value
id	int(11)			1
name	varchar(30)			John Smith
phone	varchar(30)		☐	ı01 445 789-1234
				Go

The data is erased after selecting the **Null** box, as shown in the following screenshot:

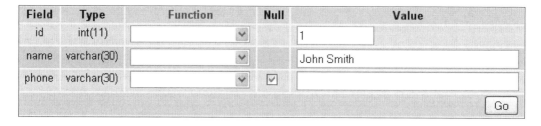

Field	Type	Function	Null	Value
id	int(11)	☐		1
name	varchar(30)	☐		John Smith
phone	varchar(30)	☐	☑	
				Go

The **Edit** panel will appear this way if this row is ever displayed on the screen again.

Applying a function to a value

The MySQL language offers some functions that we may apply to data before saving our work. Some of these functions appear in a drop-down menu beside each field, if `$cfg['ShowFunctionFields']` is set to TRUE.

The function list is defined in the `$cfg['Functions']` array. As usual, the default values for these arrays are located in `libraries/config.default.php`. We may change them by copying the required section into `config.inc.php`; if we do so, as these values can change from version to version, we should take care of merging our changes with the values of the new version. The most commonly-used functions for a certain data type are displayed first in the list. Some restrictions are defined in the `$cfg['RestrictColumnTypes']` and `$cfg['RestrictFunctions']` arrays, to control which functions are displayed first.

Here are the definitions that restrict the function names that are displayed for the VARCHAR type:

```
$cfg['RestrictColumnTypes'] = array(
        'VARCHAR' => 'FUNC_CHAR', [...]

$cfg['RestrictFunctions'] = array(
        'FUNC_CHAR' => array(
            'ASCII',
            'CHAR',
            'SOUNDEX',
            'LCASE',
            'UCASE',
            'PASSWORD',
            'OLD_PASSWORD',
            'MD5',
            'SHA1',
            'ENCRYPT',
```

```
            'COMPRESS',
            'UNCOMPRESS',
            'LAST_INSERT_ID',
            'USER',
            'CONCAT'
       ),   [...]
```

As depicted in the following screenshot, we apply the **UPPER** function to the title when saving this row:

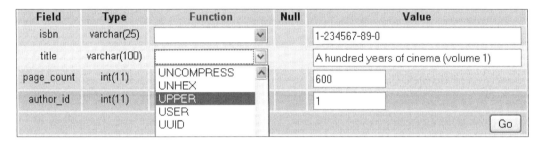

To gain some screen space (to be able to see more of the data), this feature may be disabled by setting `$cfg['ShowFunctionFields']` to `FALSE`. Moreover, the **Function** column header is clickable, so we can disable this feature on the fly.

When this feature is disabled — either by clicking on the header or via the configuration parameter — a **Show: Function** link appears in order to display this **Function** column with a single click:

Show : Function			
Field	**Type**	**Null**	**Value**
isbn	varchar(25)		1-234567-89-0
title	varchar(100)		A hundred years of cinema (volume 1)
page_count	int(11)		600
author_id	int(11)		1
			Go

Duplicating rows of data

During the course of data maintenance (for permanent duplication or for test purposes), we often have to generate a copy of a row. If this is done in the same table, we must respect the rules of key uniqueness.

Here is an example of row duplication. Our author has written Volume 2 of his book about cinema. Hence, the fields that need a slight change are the ISBN, title, and page count. We bring the existing row on screen, change these three fields, and choose **Insert as new row**, as shown in the following screenshot:

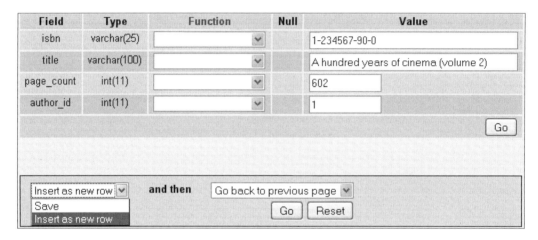

When we click on **Go**, another row is created with the modified information, leaving the original row unchanged:

Multi-row editing

The multi-row edit feature enables us to use checkboxes on the rows that we want to edit, and use the **Edit** link (or the pencil-shaped icon) in the **With selected** menu. The **Check All / Uncheck All** links can also be used to quickly select or deselect all of the boxes. We can also click anywhere on the row's data to activate the corresponding checkbox. To select a range of checkboxes, we can click the first checkbox in the range, and then *Shift* + click the last checkbox in the range:

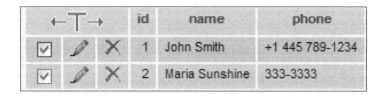

This brings up an Edit panel containing all of the chosen rows. The editing process may continue while the data from these rows is seen, compared, and changed.

When we select the checkboxes for some rows, we can also perform two other actions on the rows: delete (see the *Deleting many rows* section in this chapter) and export (see *Chapter 6, Exporting Structure and Data (backup)*).

Editing the next row

Sequential editing is possible on tables that have a primary key on an integer field. Our `author` table meets this criteria. Let's see what happens when we start editing the row that has the **id** value **1**:

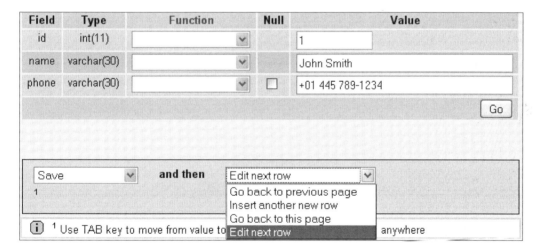

The editing panel appears, and we can edit author number **1**. However, in the drop-down menu, the **Edit next row** choice is available. If chosen, the next author —the first one whose primary key value is greater than the current primary key value—will be available for edit.

Deleting data

phpMyAdmin's interface enables us to delete the following:

- Single rows of data
- Multiple rows in a table
- All of the rows in a table
- All of the rows in multiple tables

Deleting a single row

We can use the small X-shaped icon beside each row to delete the row. If the value of $cfg['Confirm']$ is set to TRUE, every MySQL DELETE statement has to be confirmed before execution. This is the default, because it might not be prudent to allow a row to be deleted with just one click!

The form of the confirmation varies, depending on the browser's ability to execute JavaScript. A JavaScript-based confirmation pop up would look like the following screenshot:

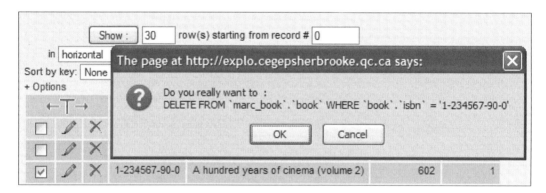

If JavaScript has been disabled in our browser, a distinct panel appears:

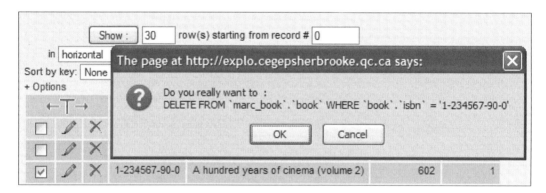

The actual DELETE statement will use whatever information is needed to ensure the deletion of only the intended row. In our case, a primary key had been defined and was used in the WHERE clause. In the absence of a primary key, a longer WHERE clause will be generated based on the value of each field. The generated WHERE clause might even prevent the correct execution of the DELETE operation, especially if there are TEXT or BLOB fields. This is because the HTTP transaction, used to send the query to the web server, may be limited in length by the browser or the server. This is another reason why defining a primary key is strongly recommended.

Deleting many rows

Let's say we examine a page of rows and decide that some rows have to be destroyed. Instead of deleting them one-by-one with the **Delete** link or icon—and because sometimes the decision to delete must be made while examining a group of rows—there are checkboxes beside the rows in Table view mode:

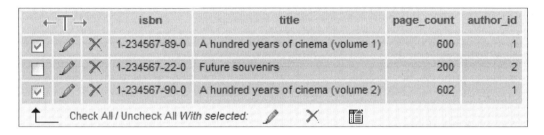

These are used with the **With selected** X-shaped icon. A confirmation screen appears, listing all the rows that are about to be deleted. It is also possible to click anywhere on the row's data to activate the corresponding checkbox.

Deleting all of the rows in a table

To completely erase all of the rows in a table (leaving its structure intact), we go to the Database view and click on the database name in the navigation panel. We then click on the trash can icon located on the same line as the table we want to empty:

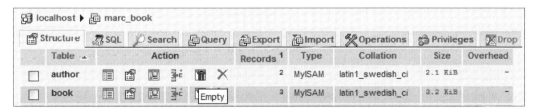

We get a message confirming the TRUNCATE statement (the MySQL statement used to quickly empty a table). For our exercise, we won't delete this precious data!

Emptying a table can also be done in Table view, via the **Empty** link located on the top menu:

 Deleting data, either row-by-row or by emptying a table, is a permanent action. No recovery is then possible, except by using a backup.

Deleting all rows in many tables

The first screenshot in the previous section shows a checkbox to the left of each table name. We can use these to select multiple tables. Then, in the **With selected** menu, we can choose the **Empty** operation, as shown in the following screenshot:

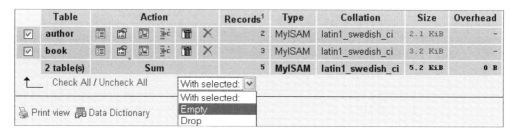

	Table	Action						Records[1]	Type	Collation	Size	Overhead
☑	author							2	MyISAM	latin1_swedish_ci	2.1 KiB	-
☑	book							3	MyISAM	latin1_swedish_ci	3.2 KiB	-
	2 table(s)	Sum						5	**MyISAM**	**latin1_swedish_ci**	**5.2 KiB**	**0 B**

Check All / Uncheck All   With selected: ▾

With selected:
Empty
Drop

Print view   Data Dictionary

Of course, this decision must not be taken lightly!

Deleting tables

Deleting a table erases all of the data and also the table's structure. We can delete tables by using the **Drop** link in **Table** view:

In the Database view, we can delete a specific table by using the X-shaped icon for that table. The same mechanism also exists for deleting more than one table (with the drop-down menu and the **Drop** action).

 The **Empty** and **Drop** actions are marked in red, to better indicate the inherent danger of carrying out these actions on data.

Deleting databases

We can delete an entire database (including all of its tables) using the **Drop** link in the Database view:

By default, $cfg['AllowUserDropDatabase']$ is set to FALSE. So this link is hidden from unprivileged users unless this setting is manually changed to TRUE.

To help us think twice, a special message—**You are about to DESTROY a complete database!**—appears before a database is deleted.

 The database mysql, containing all user and privilege definitions, is highly important. Therefore, the **Drop** button is deactivated for this database, even for administrators.

Changing a table's structure

When developing an application, requirements about the data structure often change because of new or modified needs. Developers must accommodate these changes through judicious table structure editing. This section explores the subject of changing the structure of tables. Specifically, it shows how to add a column to an existing table and how to edit the attributes of a column. We then build on these notions to introduce more specialized column types, and to explain their handling through phpMyAdmin. Finally, we cover the topic of index management.

Adding a field

Suppose that we need a new field to store a book's language and, by default, the books on which we keep data are written in English. We can call the field **language**, which will contain code composed of two characters (**en** by default).

In the **Structure** subpage of the Table view for the **book** table, we can find the **Add field** dialog. Here, we specify how many new fields we want, and where they will go.

The positions of the new fields in the table matter only from a developer's point of view. We usually group the fields logically, so that we can find them more easily in the list of fields. The exact position of the fields will not play a role in the intended results (the output from queries), as these results can be adjusted regardless of the table structure. Usually, the most important fields (including the keys) are located at the beginning of the table. However, it's a matter of personal preference.

We want to put the new field **At End of Table**. So we select the corresponding radio button and click on **Go**:

Other possible choices would be **At Beginning of Table** and **After** (where we would have to choose, from the drop-down menu, the field after which the new field must go).

We see the familiar panel for the new fields, repeated for the number of fields asked for. We fill it in. However, as we want to enter a default value this time, we perform the following two actions:

- Change the **Default** drop-down menu from **None** to **As defined:**
- Enter a default value, **en**

We then click on **Save**:

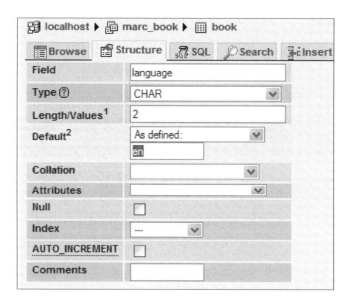

Vertical mode

The previous panel appeared in vertical mode because the default for $cfg['DefaultPropDisplay'] is 3. This means that for three columns or less, the vertical mode is used, and for more than three, horizontal mode would automatically be selected. Here, we can use a number of our choice.

If we set $cfg['DefaultPropDisplay'] to 'vertical', the panel to add new fields (along with the panel to edit a field's structure) will always be presented in vertical order. The advantages of working in vertical mode become obvious, especially when there are more choices for each field, as explained in *Chapter 16*, *Transforming Data Using MIME*.

Horizontal mode

The $cfg['DefaultPropDisplay'] parameter can also take a value of 'horizontal'. Let's see how the panel appears in this mode when we ask for three new fields:

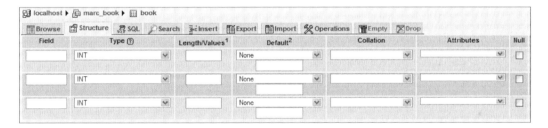

Editing field attributes

On the **Structure** subpage, we can make further changes to our table. For this example, we set $cfg['PropertiesIconic'] to 'both', to see the icons along with their text explanation:

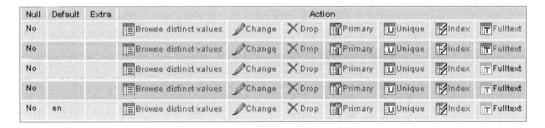

This panel does not allow every possible change to fields. It specifically allows:

- Changing one field's structure, using the **Change** link on a specific field
- Removing a field, using the **Drop** operation
- Adding a field to an existing **Primary** key
- Setting a field as a non-unique **Index** or a **Unique** index
- Setting a **Fulltext** index (offered only if the field type allows it)

These are quick links that may be useful in some situations, but they do not replace the full index management panel. Both of these are explained in this chapter.

We can use the checkboxes to choose fields. Then, with the appropriate **With selected** icons, we can edit the fields or perform a multiple field deletion with **Drop**. The **Check All / Uncheck All** option permits us to easily select or deselect all checkboxes.

TEXT fields

We will now explore how to use the **TEXT** field type, and the relevant configuration values to adjust for the best possible phpMyAdmin behavior. First, we add to the **book** table a **TEXT** field called **description**.

There are three parameters that control the layout of the text area that will be displayed in **Insert** or **Edit** mode for **TEXT** fields. First, the number of columns and rows for each field is defined by:

```
$cfg['TextareaCols']  = 40;
$cfg['TextareaRows']  = 15;
```

This gives (by default) the following space within which to work on a **TEXT** field:

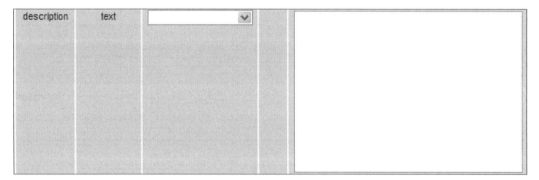

The settings impose only a visual limit on the text area, and a vertical scroll bar is created by the browser if necessary.

Although **MEDIUMTEXT**, **TEXT**, and **LONGTEXT** columns can accommodate more than 32 KB of data, some browsers cannot always edit them with the text area—the mechanism offered by HTML. In fact, experimentation has convinced the phpMyAdmin development team to have the product display a warning message if the contents are larger than 32 KB. The message warns users that the contents may not be editable.

The last parameter has an impact for **LONGTEXT** fields only. The default value of TRUE for $cfg['LongtextDoubleTextarea'] doubles the available editing space.

BLOB (Binary Large Object) fields

BLOB fields are generally used to hold binary data (such as images and sounds), even though the MySQL documentation implies that **TEXT** fields could be used for this purpose. The MySQL 5.1 manual says:

> *In some cases, it may be desirable to store binary data such as media files in BLOB or TEXT columns.*

However, there is another phrase:

> *BLOB columns are treated as binary strings (byte strings).*

This phrase seems to indicate that binary data should really be stored in **BLOB** fields. Thus, phpMyAdmin's intention is to work with **BLOB** fields to hold all binary data.

We will see in *Chapter 16, Transforming Data Using MIME* that there are special mechanisms available to go further with **BLOB** fields, including being able to view some images directly from within phpMyAdmin. Furthermore, *Chapter 17, Supporting MySQL 5.0 and 5.1* covers BLOB streaming support.

First, we add a **BLOB** field named **cover_photo** to our **book** table. If we now browse the table, we can see the field length information, **[BLOB – 0 B]**, for each **BLOB** field:

isbn	title	page_count	author_id	language	description	cover_photo
1-234567-89-0	A hundred years of cinema (volume 1)	600	1	en		[BLOB - 0 B]
1-234567-22-0	Future souvenirs	200	2	en		[BLOB - 0 B]
1-234567-90-0	A hundred years of cinema (volume 2)	602	1	en		[BLOB - 0 B]

This is because the **Show BLOB** display option (do you remember the **Options** slider?) has no check mark by default. So it blocks the display of **BLOB** contents in Browse mode. This behavior is intentional. Usually, we cannot do anything with binary data that is represented in plain text.

Uploading binary content

If we edit one row, we see the **Binary – do not edit** warning and a **Browse...** button. The exact caption on this button depends on the browser used. Even though editing is not allowed, we can easily upload a text or binary file's contents into this **BLOB** column.

Let's choose an image file using the **Browse** button—for example, the logo_left.png file in a test copy of the phpMyAdmin/themes/original/img directory located on our client workstation. If we are seeing **UNHEX** in the function field, we should remove this choice as this is a shortcoming of some phpMyAdmin versions. We then click on **Go**.

We need to keep in mind some limits for the upload size. Firstly, the **BLOB** field size is limited to 64 KB, but in *Chapter 16, Transforming Data Using MIME*, we will change the type of this field to accommodate bigger images. Hence, phpMyAdmin reminds us of this limit with the **Max: 64 KiB** warning. Also, there could be limits inherent to PHP itself (see *Chapter 7, Importing Data and Structure*, for more details). We have now uploaded an image inside this field for a specific row:

isbn	title	page_count	author_id	language	description	cover_photo
1-234567-89-0	A hundred years of cinema (volume 1)	600	1	en		[BLOB - 6.7 KiB]

If we put a check mark for the **Show BLOB Contents** display option, we now see the following in the **BLOB** field:

cover_photo
◆PNG\r\n\Z\n\0\0\0\rIHDR\0\0\0◆\0\0\0\b\0\0\0◆C7w\0\0\0bKGD\0◆\0◆\0◆◆◆◆◆...

To really see the image from within phpMyAdmin, refer to *Chapter 16, Transforming Data Using MIME.*

The $cfg['ProtectBinary']$ parameter controls what can be done when editing binary fields (**BLOB**s and any other field with the `binary` attribute). The default value **blob** blocks **BLOB** fields from being edited, but allows us to edit other fields marked as `binary` by MySQL. A value of **all** would block even `binary` fields from being edited. A value of FALSE would protect nothing, thus allowing us to edit all fields. If we try the last choice, we see the following in the **Edit** panel for this row:

The content of this BLOB field has been converted to hexadecimal form and the **UNHEX** function is selected by default. We probably don't want to edit this image data in hexadecimal form, but this is the best way of safely representing binary data on screen. The reason for this hexadecimal representation is that the **Show binary contents as HEX** display option (in **Browse** mode) is currently selected. But we did not select this option; it was checked because the $cfg['DisplayBinaryAsHex'] directive is TRUE by default.

Should we, instead, decide to not select this option, we would see the following pure binary data for this image:

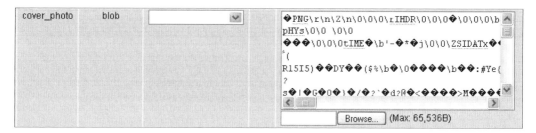

There are chances that this is not our favorite image editor! In fact, data may be corrupted even if we save this row without touching the **BLOB** field. But the need to set $cfg['ProtectBinary'] to FALSE exists, as some users put text in their **BLOB** fields, and they need to be able to modify this text.

MySQL **BLOB** data types are actually similar to their corresponding **TEXT** data types. However, we should keep in mind that a **BLOB** has no character set, whereas a **TEXT** column has a character set that impacts sorting and comparison. This is why phpMyAdmin can be configured to allow the editing of **BLOB** fields.

ENUM and SET fields

Both the ENUM and SET field types are intended to represent a list of possible values. The difference is that the user can choose only one value from a defined list of values with **ENUM**, and more than one value with **SET**. With **SET**, all of the multiple values go into one cell; but multiple values do not imply the creation of more than one row of data.

We add a field named **genre** to the **book** table and define it as an **ENUM**. For now, we choose to put short codes in the value list and make one of them, **F**, into the default value, as shown in the following screenshot:

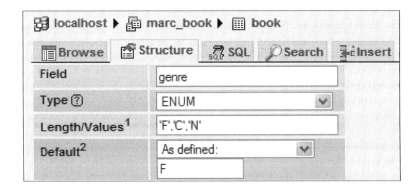

In the value list, we have to enclose each value within single quotes, unlike in the default value field. In our design, we know that these values stand for **Fantasy**, **Child**, and **Novel**. However, for now, we want to see the interface's behavior with short code. In the **Insert** panel, we now see a radio-box interface:

If we decide to have more self-descriptive code, we can go back to **Structure** mode and change the values definition for the **genre** field. We also have to change the default value to one of the possible values, to avoid getting an error message when trying to save this field structure's modification:

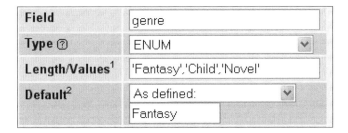

With the modified value list, the **Insert** panel now looks as follows:

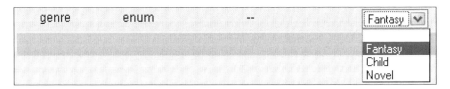

Note that the radio buttons have been replaced by a drop-down list because the possible values are longer.

If we want more than one possible value selected, we have to change the field type to **SET**. The same value list may be used. However, using our browser's multiple value selector (*Ctrl* + click on a Windows or Linux desktop, *Command* + click on a Mac), we can select more than one value, as shown in the following screenshot:

 In a normalized data structure, we would store only the **genre** code in the **book** table and would rely on another table to store the description for each code. We would not use **SET** or **ENUM** in this case.

DATE, DATETIME, and TIMESTAMP fields

We could use a normal character field to store date or time information. But **DATE**, **DATETIME**, and **TIMESTAMP** are more efficient for this purpose. MySQL checks the contents to ensure valid date and time information, and offers special functions to work with these fields.

Calendar pop up

As an added benefit, phpMyAdmin offers a calendar pop up for easy data entry.

We will start by adding a **DATE** field—**date_published**—to our **book** table. If we go into **Insert** mode, we should now see the new field where we can type a date. A **Calendar** icon is also available:

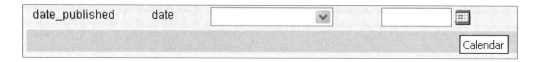

Clicking on this icon brings up a pop-up window, synchronized to this **DATE** field. If there is already a value in the field, the pop up is displayed accordingly. In our case, there is no value in the field, so the calendar shows the current date:

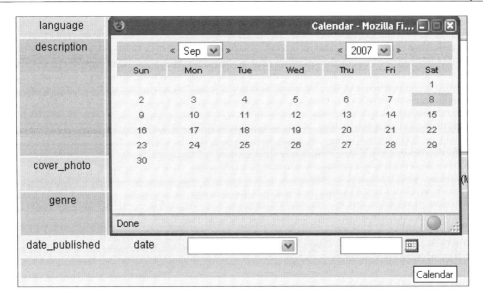

Small symbols on each side of the month and year headers permit easy scrolling through months and years. A simple click on the date we want transports it to our **date_published** field.

For a **DATETIME** or **TIMESTAMP** field, the pop up offers the ability to edit the time part.

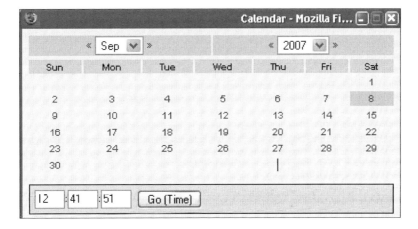

TIMESTAMP options

Starting with MySQL 4.1.2, there are more options that can affect a **TIMESTAMP** column. Let's add to our **book** table, a column named **stamp** of type **TIMESTAMP**. In the **Default** drop-down menu, we could choose **CURRENT_TIMESTAMP**; but we won't for this exercise. However in the **Attributes** column, we choose **on update CURRENT_TIMESTAMP**:

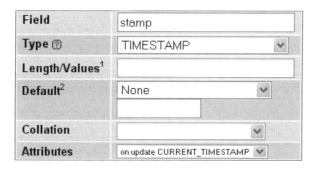

Bit fields

MySQL 5.0.3 introduced true bit-field values. These take the same amount of space in the database as the number of bits in their definition. Let's say we have three pieces of information about each book, and each piece can only be true (1) or false (0):

- Book is hardcover
- Book contains a CD-ROM
- Book is available only in electronic format

We'll use a single **BIT** field to store these three pieces of information. Therefore, we add a field having a length of **3** (which means three bits) to the book table:

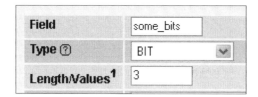

To construct and subsequently interpret the values we store in this field, we have to think in binary, respecting the position of each bit within the field. To indicate that a book is hardcover, does not contain a CD-ROM, and is available only in electronic format, we would use a value of 101.

phpMyAdmin handles `BIT` fields in a binary way. For example, if we edit one row and set a value of `101` in the `some_bits` column, the following query is sent at the time of saving:

```
UPDATE `marc_book`.`book` SET `some_bits` = b '101'
WHERE `book`.`isbn` = '1-234567-89-0' LIMIT 1;
```

The highlighted part of this query shows that the column really receives a binary value. At browse time, the exact field value (which in decimal equals 5—a meaningless value for our purposes) is redisplayed in its binary form, **101**, which helps us to to interpret each discrete bit value.

Managing indexes

Properly maintained indexes are crucial for data retrieval speed. phpMyAdmin has a number of index management options, which will be covered in this section.

Single-field indexes

We have already seen how the **Structure** panel offers a quick way to create an index on a single field, thanks to some quick links such as **Primary**, **Index**, and **Unique**. Under the field list, there is a section of the interface available for managing indexes:

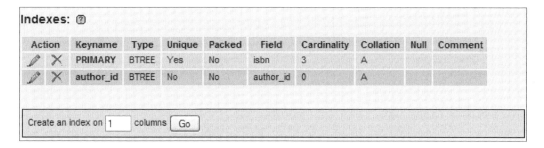

This section has links to edit or delete every index. Here, the **Field** part lists only one field per index, and we can see that the whole field participates in the index. This is because there is no size information after each field name, contrary to what can be seen in our next example.

We will now add an index on the title. However, we want to restrict the length of this index to reduce the space used by the on-disk index structure. The **Create an index on 1 columns** option is appropriate. So we click on **Go**. On the next screen, we specify the index details, as shown here:

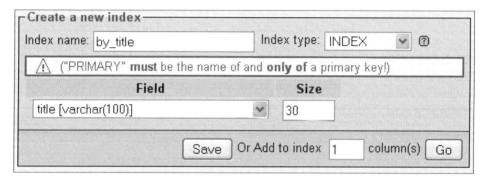

Here is how to fill in this panel:

- **Index name**: A name we invent, that describes the purpose of this index
- **Index type**: We can choose **INDEX**
- **Field**: We select the field that is used as the index, which is the **title** field
- **Size**: We enter **30** instead of **100** (which is the complete length of the field) to save space in the table's physical portion that holds index data

After saving this panel, we can confirm from the following screenshot that the index is created and does not cover the entire length of the title field:

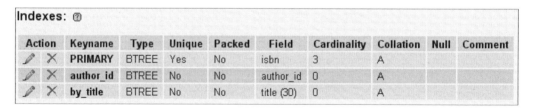

Indexes:

Action	Keyname	Type	Unique	Packed	Field	Cardinality	Collation	Null	Comment
✎ ✗	PRIMARY	BTREE	Yes	No	isbn	3	A		
✎ ✗	author_id	BTREE	No	No	author_id	0	A		
✎ ✗	by_title	BTREE	No	No	title (30)	0	A		

Multi-field indexes and index editing

In the next example, we assume that in a future application we will need to find the books written by a specific author in a specific language. It makes sense to expand our **author_id** index, adding the **language** field to it.

We click on the **Edit** link (the small pencil icon) on the line containing the **author_id** index; this shows the current state of this index. The interface has room to add another field to this index. We could use the **Add to index 1 column(s)** feature should we need to add more than one field. In the field selector, we select **language**. This time we do not have to enter a size, as the whole field will be used in the index. For better documentation, we change the **Index name** (**author_language** is appropriate):

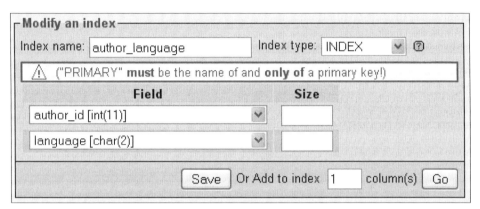

We save this index modification. In the list of indexes, we can confirm our index modification:

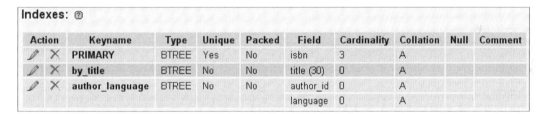

Action	Keyname	Type	Unique	Packed	Field	Cardinality	Collation	Null	Comment
✎ ✕	**PRIMARY**	BTREE	Yes	No	isbn	3	A		
✎ ✕	**by_title**	BTREE	No	No	title (30)	0	A		
✎ ✕	**author_language**	BTREE	No	No	author_id	0	A		
					language	0	A		

FULLTEXT indexes

This special type of index allows for full text searches. It's supported only on `MyISAM` tables for **VARCHAR** and **TEXT** fields. We can use the **Fulltext** quick link in the fields list, or go to the index management panel and choose **Fulltext** from the drop-down menu:

We add a **FULLTEXT** index on the **description** field, so that we are able to locate a book from words present in its description.

Optimizing indexes with EXPLAIN

In this section, we want to get some information about the index that MySQL uses for a specific query, and the performance impact of not having defined an index.

Let's assume we want to use the following query:

```
SELECT   *
FROM `book`
WHERE author_id = 2 AND language = 'es'
```

We want to know which books written by the author whose id is 2, are in the es language—our code for Spanish.

To enter this query, we use the **SQL** link from the database or the table menu, or the SQL query window (see *Chapter 11, Entering SQL Commands*). We enter this query in the query box and click on **Go**. Whether the query finds any results is not important right now.

> ✅ MySQL returned an empty result set (i.e. zero rows). (Query took 0.0006 sec)
>
> ```
> SELECT *
> FROM `book`
> WHERE `author_id` =2
> AND `language` = 'es'
> LIMIT 0 , 30
> ```
>
> ☐ Profiling [Edit] [Explain SQL] [Create PHP Code] [Refresh]

 You could obtain the same query by following the explanations in *Chapter 8, Searching Data* to produce a search for **author_id 2** and language **es**.

Let's look at the links: **[Edit]**, **[Explain SQL]**, **[Create PHP Code]**, and **[Refresh]**.

We will now use the **[Explain SQL]** link to get information about which index (if any) has been used for this query:

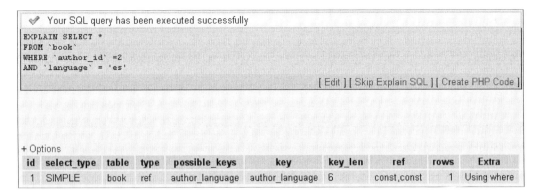

We can see that the **EXPLAIN** command has been passed to MySQL, telling us that the **key** used is **author_language**. Thus, we know that this index will be used for this type of query. If this index had not existed, the result would have been quite different:

Here, **key** (**NULL**) and the **type** (**ALL**) mean that no index would be used, and all rows would need to be examined in order to find the desired data. Depending on the total number of rows, this could have a serious impact on the performance. We can ascertain the exact impact by examining the query timing that phpMyAdmin displays on each result page (**Query took x sec**), and comparing it with or without the index. However, the difference in time can be minimal if we only have limited test data, compared to a real table in production. For more details about the EXPLAIN output format, please refer to http://dev.mysql.com/doc/refman/5.1/en/ explain-output.html.

Detecting index problems

To help users maintain an optimal index strategy, phpMyAdmin tries to detect some common index problems. For example, let's access the `book` table and add an index on the **isbn** column. When we display this table's structure, we get a warning:

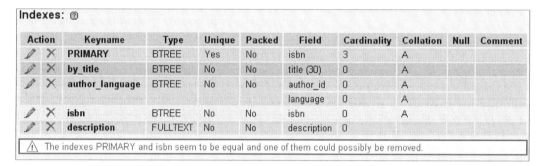

The intention here is to warn us about an inefficient index structure when considering the whole table. We don't need to have two indexes on the same column.

Summary

This chapter examined data changing concepts, such as:

- Editing data
- Including the null field and using the *Tab* key
- Applying a function to a value
- Duplicating rows of data
- Deleting data, tables, and databases

We also saw an overview of structure-changing techniques such as:

- How to add fields, including special field types such as **TEXT, BLOB, ENUM,** and **SET**
- How to use a calendar pop up for **DATE, DATETIME,** and **TIMESTAMP** fields
- How to upload binary data into a **BLOB** field
- How to manage indexes (multi-field and full-text), and how to get feedback from MySQL about which indexes are used in a specific query

In the next chapter, we'll learn how to export a table's structure and data for backup purposes, or to use as a gateway to another application.

6
Exporting Structure and Data (Backup)

Keeping good backups is crucial to a project. Backups consist of up-to-date backups and intermediary snapshots taken during development and production phases. The export feature of phpMyAdmin can generate backups, and can also be used to send data to other applications.

> Please note that phpMyAdmin's export feature produces backups on-demand and it's highly recommended to implement an automatic and scripted backup solution that takes backups on a regular schedule. The precise way to implement such a solution depends on the server's OS.

Dumps, backups, and exports

Let's first clarify some vocabulary. In the MySQL documentation, you will encounter the term **dump**, and in other applications, the term **backup** or **export**. All of these terms have the same meaning in the context of phpMyAdmin.

MySQL includes **mysqldump**—a command-line utility that can be used to generate export files. But the shell access needed for command-line utilities is not offered by every host provider. Also, access to the export feature from within the Web interface is more convenient. This is why phpMyAdmin offers the export feature with more export formats than mysqldump. This chapter will focus on phpMyAdmin's export features.

Before starting an export, we must have a clear picture of the intended goal of the export. The following questions may be of help:

- Do we need the complete database or just some tables?

- Do we need just the structure, just the data, or both?

- Which utility will be used to import the data back in?

- Do we want only a subset of the data?

- What is the size of the intended export, and the link speed between us and the server?

Scope of the export

When we click an **Export** link from phpMyAdmin, we can be in one of the following views or contexts: Database view, Table view, or Server view (more on this later in *Chapter 19, Administrating the MySQL Server with phpMyAdmin*). According to the current context, the resulting export's scope will be a complete database, a single table, or even a multi-database export as in the case of Server view. We will first explain database exports and all of the relevant export types. Then we'll go on with table and multi-database exports, underlining the difference for these modes of exporting.

Exporting a database

In the Database view, click on the **Export** link. The default export panel looks like this:

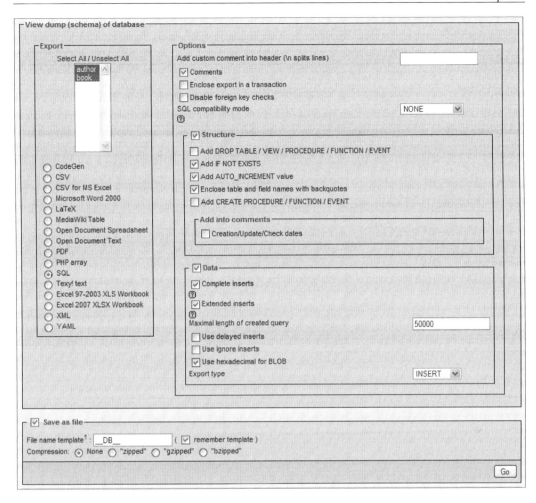

The default values selected here depend on `config.inc.php`, more specifically on the `$cfg['Export']` array of parameters. For example, the `$cfg['Export']` `['format']` parameter is set to `'sql'`, so that the **SQL** export mode is chosen by default.

The export panel has three subpanels. The top panel, **Export**, and the bottom panel, **Save as file**, are always there. However, the third panel varies (using dynamic menu techniques) in order to show the options for the export mode chosen (which is SQL here).

The export subpanel

This subpanel contains a table selector, from where we choose the tables and the format that we want. The SQL format is useful for our needs, as it creates standard SQL commands that would work on any SQL server. Other formats are available, depending on our needs.

We shall now discuss the formats (and the options available once they have been chosen) that can be selected in the **Export** subpanel.

 Even if we can export into many formats, only some of these formats can be imported back using phpMyAdmin.

SQL

We will start by clicking on **Select All**; we want all of the tables. We know that the tables are small, so the on-screen export will not be too large. For the moment, let's deselect the **Extended inserts** checkbox. To produce an export file, we would normally leave the **Save as file** checkbox selected, but to see the results on screen, we deselect it; we then click on **Go**.

The first part of the export comprises comments (starting with the characters --) that detail the utility (and version) that created the file, the date, and other environment information. We then see the CREATE and INSERT queries for each table.

 phpMyAdmin generates ANSI-compatible comments in the export file. These comments start with --. They help with importing the file into other ANSI SQL-compatible systems.

Defining options for SQL export

SQL options are used to define exactly what information the export will contain. We may want to see the structure, the data, or both. Selecting **Structure** generates the section with CREATE queries, and selecting **Data** produces INSERT queries. The following screenshot depicts the general SQL options and the **Structure** options:

The general SQL options are:

- **Add custom comment into header**: We can add our own comments for this export (for example, **Monthly backup**), which will appear in the export headers (after the PHP version number). If the comment has more than one line, we must use the special character \n to separate each line.

- **Comments**: Removing the check mark here causes the export to have no comments at all.

- **Enclose export in a transaction**: Starting with MySQL 4.0.11, we can use the START TRANSACTION statement. This command, combined with SET AUTOCOMMIT=0 at the beginning and COMMIT at the end, asks MySQL to execute the import (when we will re-import this file) in one transaction, ensuring that all the changes are done as a whole.

- **Disable foreign key checks**: In the export file, we can add DROP TABLE statements. However, normally a table cannot be dropped if it's referenced in a foreign key constraint. This option overrides the verification by adding SET FOREIGN_KEY_CHECKS=0 to the export file. This override only lasts for the duration of the export.

- **SQL compatibility mode:** This lets us choose the flavor of SQL that we export. We must have some knowledge about the system into which we intend to import this file. Among the choices are **MySQL 3.23**, **MySQL 4.0**, **Oracle**, and **ANSI**.

The options in the **Structure** section are:

- **Add DROP TABLE / VIEW / PROCEDURE / FUNCTION / EVENT**: Adds a DROP ... IF EXISTS statement before each CREATE statement, for example: DROP TABLE IF EXISTS `author`;. This way, we can ensure that the export file is executed on a database in which the same element already exists, updating its structure but destroying the previous elements' contents.

- **Add IF NOT EXISTS**: Adds the IF NOT EXISTS modifier to CREATE TABLE statements, avoiding an error during import if the table already exists.

- **Add AUTO_INCREMENT value**: Puts auto-increment information from the tables into the export, ensuring that the inserted rows in the tables will receive the next exact auto-increment ID value.

- **Enclose table and field names with backquotes**: In the MySQL world, backquotes are the normal way of protecting table and field names that may contain special characters. In most cases, it's useful to have them. However, backquotes are not recommended if the target server (where the export file will be imported) is running a SQL engine that does not support backquotes.

- **Add CREATE PROCEDURE / FUNCTION / EVENT**: This includes all procedures, functions, and event definitions found in this database, in the export.

- **Add into comments**: This adds information (in the form of SQL comments), which cannot be directly imported, but which nonetheless is valuable and human-readable table information. The amount of information here varies depending on the relational system settings (see *Chapter 10, Benefiting from the Relational System*). In fact, with an activated relational system, we would get the following choices:

Selecting **Relations** and **MIME type** would produce an additional section in the structure export:

```
--
-- COMMENTS FOR TABLE `book`:
--     `isbn`
--          'book number'
--     `page_count`
--          'approximate'
```

```
--      `author_id`
--          'see author table'
--


--
-- MIME TYPES FOR TABLE `book`:
--      `cover_photo`
--          'image_jpeg'
--      `date_released`
--          'text_plain`
--      `description'
--          'text_plain'
--


-- RELATIONS FOR TABLE `book`:
--      `author_id`
--          'author' -> 'id'
--
```

The following screenshot displays options relevant to a **Data** export:

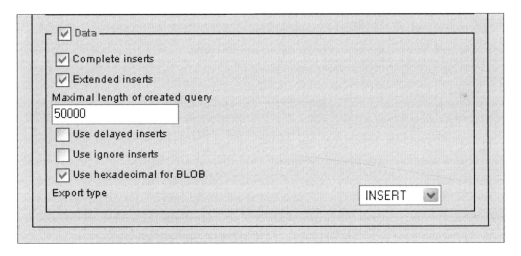

The options available in the **Data** section are:

- **Complete inserts**: Generates the following export for the author table:

```
INSERT INTO `author` (`id`, `name`, `phone`)
VALUES (1, 'John Smith', '+01 445 789-1234');
INSERT INTO `author` (`id`, `name`, `phone`)
VALUES (2, 'Maria Sunshine', '+01 455 444-5683');
```

Notice that every column name is present in every statement. The resulting file is bigger, but will prove more portable on various SQL systems, with the added benefit of being better documented.

- **Extended inserts**: Packs the whole table data into a single INSERT statement:

```
INSERT INTO `author` VALUES (1, 'John Smith','+01 445 789-1234'),
     (2, 'Maria Sunshine', '+01 455 444-5683');
```

This method of inserting data is faster than using multiple INSERT statements, but is less convenient because it makes reading the resultant file harder. **Extended inserts** also produces a smaller file, but each line of this file is not executable in itself because each line does not have an INSERT statement. If you cannot import the complete file in one operation, you cannot split the file with a text editor and import it chunk by chunk.

- **Maximal length of created query**: The single INSERT statement generated for **Extended inserts** might become too big and could cause problems. Hence, we set a limit on the number of characters for the length of this statement.

- **Use delayed inserts**: Adds the DELAYED modifier to INSERT statements. This accelerates the INSERT operation because it's queued to the server, which will execute it when the table is not in use. This is a MySQL non-standard extension, available only for MyISAM, MEMORY, and ARCHIVE tables.

- **Use ignore inserts**: Normally, at import time, we cannot insert duplicate values for unique keys, as this would abort the insert operation. This option adds the IGNORE modifier to INSERT and UPDATE statements, thus skipping the rows that generate duplicate key errors.

- **Use hexadecimal for BLOB**: This option makes phpMyAdmin encode the contents of BLOB fields in 0x format. Such a format is useful because, depending on the software that will be used to manipulate the export file (for example, a text editor or mail program), handling a file containing 8-bit data can be problematic. However, using this option will produce an export of the BLOB that can be twice the size of a file generated without this option.

- **Export type**: The choices are **INSERT**, **UPDATE**, and **REPLACE**. The most well-known of these types is the default **INSERT**—using INSERT statements to import back our data. At import time, however, we could be in a situation where a table already exists and contains valuable data, and we just want to update the fields that are in the current table we are exporting. **UPDATE** generates statements such as UPDATE `author` SET `id` = 1, `name` = 'John Smith', `phone` = '111 1111' WHERE `id` = '1'; updating a row when the same primary or unique key is found. The third possibility, **REPLACE**, produces statements such as REPLACE INTO `author` VALUES (1, 'John Smith', '111-1111');. These act like an INSERT statement for new rows and update existing rows based on primary or unique keys.

The "Save as file" subpanel

In the previous examples, the results of the export operation were displayed on screen and, of course, no compression was made on the data. We can choose to transmit the export file via HTTP by checking the **Save as file** checkbox. This triggers a **Save** dialog in the browser, which ultimately saves the file on our local workstation.

File name template

The name of the proposed file will obey the **File name template**. In this template, we can use the special __**SERVER**__, __**DB**__, and __**TABLE**__ placeholders. These placeholders will be replaced by the current server, database, or table name (for a single-table export). Note that there are two underscore characters before and after the words. We can also use any special character from the PHP `strftime` function; this is useful for generating an export file based on the current date or hour. Finally, we can put any other string of characters (not part of the `strftime` special characters), which will be used literally. The file extension is generated according to the type of export. In this case, it will be `.sql`. Here are some examples for the template:

- __**DB**__ would generate **marc_book.sql**
- __**DB**__-%Y%m%d would give **marc_book-20071206.sql**

The **remember template** option, when activated, stores the entered template settings into cookies (for database, table, or server exports) and brings them back the next time we use the same kind of export.

The default templates are configurable, via the following parameters:

```
$cfg['Export']['file_template_table']       = '__TABLE__';
$cfg['Export']['file_template_database']     = '__DB__';
$cfg['Export']['file_template_server']       = '__SERVER__';
```

Compression

To save transmission time and generate a smaller export file, phpMyAdmin can compress to ZIP, GZIP, or BZIP2 formats. These formats work only if the PHP server has been compiled with the `--with-zlib` (for ZIP and GZIP) or `--with-bz2` (for BZ2) configuration option respectively. The following parameters control which compression choices are presented in the panel:

```
$cfg['ZipDump']            = TRUE;
$cfg['GZipDump']           = TRUE;
$cfg['BZipDump']           = TRUE;
```

A system administrator installing phpMyAdmin for a number of users could choose to set all of these parameters to FALSE, so as to avoid the potential overhead incurred by a lot of users compressing their exports at the same time. This situation usually causes more overhead than if all the users were transmitting their uncompressed files at the same time.

In older phpMyAdmin versions, the compression file was built in the web server memory. Some problems caused by this were:

- File generation depended on the memory limits assigned to running PHP scripts.

- During the time when the file was being generated and compressed, no transmission occurred. Hence, users were inclined to think that the operation was not working and that something had crashed.

- Compression of large databases was impossible to achieve.

The `$cfg['CompressOnFly']` parameter (set to TRUE by default) was added to generate (for `gzip` and `bzip2` formats) a compressed file containing more headers. Now, the transmission starts almost immediately. The file is sent in smaller chunks so that the whole process consumes much lesser memory. The downside of this is a slightly larger resulting file.

Choosing a character set

This section explains a little-known feature—the possibility of choosing the exact character set for our exported file.

This feature is activated by setting `$cfg['AllowAnywhereRecoding']` to TRUE. We can see here the effect on the interface:

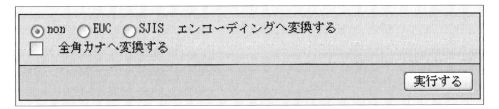

When this parameter is switched on, phpMyAdmin verifies that the conditions for recoding are met. For the actual encoding of data, the PHP component of the web server must support the `iconv` or the `recode` module. If this is not the case and the parameter has been set to TRUE, the following error message will be generated:

Couldn't load the iconv or recode extension needed for charset conversion. Either configure PHP to enable these extensions or disable charset conversion in phpMyAdmin.

If this message is displayed, consult your system's documentation (PHP or the operating system) for the installation procedure.

Another parameter (`$cfg['RecodingEngine']`) specifies the actual recoding engine—the choices being `auto`, `iconv`, and `recode`. If it's set to `auto`, phpMyAdmin will first try the `iconv` module and then the `recode` module.

Kanji support

If phpMyAdmin detects the use of the Japanese language, it checks whether PHP supports the `mb_convert_encoding()` multibyte strings function. If it does, additional radio buttons—**export**, **import**, and **query box**— are displayed on the following pages, so that we can choose between the EUC-JP and SJIS Japanese encodings.

Here is an example taken from the **Export** page:

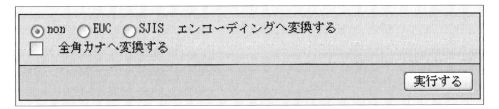

CSV

The comma-separated value (CSV) format is understood by a lot of programs, and you may find it useful for exchanging data. Note that it's a data-only format— there is no SQL structure here:

```
┌─Options ─────────────────────────────────────────────────────────┐
│  Fields terminated by                              │ :          │ │
│  Fields enclosed by                                │ "          │ │
│  Fields escaped by                                 │ \          │ │
│  Lines terminated by                               │ AUTO       │ │
│  Replace NULL by                                   │ NULL       │ │
│  ☐ Remove CRLF characters within fields                          │
│  ☐ Put fields names in the first row                             │
└───────────────────────────────────────────────────────────────────┘
```

The available options are:

- **Fields terminated by**: We put a comma here, which means that a comma will be placed after each field.

- **Fields enclosed by**: We place an enclosing character here (like the quote) to ensure that a field containing the terminating character (comma) is not interpreted as two fields.

- **Fields escaped by**: If the export generator finds the **Fields enclosed by** character inside a field, the **Fields escaped by** character will be placed before it in order to protect it. For example, `"John \"The Great\" Smith"`.

- **Lines terminated by**: This decides the character that ends each line. We should use the correct line delimiter here, according to the operating system on which we will manipulate the resulting export file. The default value of this option comes from the `$cfg['Export']['csv_terminated']` parameter, which contains `'AUTO'` by default. The `'AUTO'` value produces a value of `\r\n` if the browser's OS is Windows and `\n` otherwise. However, this might not be the best choice if the export file is intended for a machine with a different OS.

- **Replace NULL by**: This determines which string occupies the place in the export file of any NULL value found in a field.

- **Remove CRLF characters within fields**: As a column can contain carriage return or line feed characters, this option determines if such characters should be removed from the exported data.

- **Put fields names in the first row**: This gets some information about the meaning of each field. Some programs will use this information to name the column.

Finally, we select the **author** table.

The result is:

```
"id","name","phone"
"1","John Smith","+01 445 789-1234"
"2","Maria Sunshine","+01 455 444-5683"
```

CSV for MS Excel

This export mode produces a CSV file specially formatted for Microsoft Excel. We can select the exact Microsoft Excel edition:

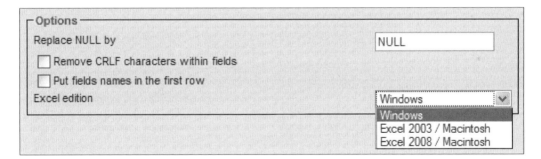

PDF

It's possible to create a PDF report of a table by exporting in PDF. This feature works on only one table at a time, and we must click on the **Save as file** checkbox for normal operation. We can add a title for this report, and it also gets automatically paginated. Non-textual (BLOB) data, as found in the book table, is discarded from this export format.

Here, we test it on the `author` table:

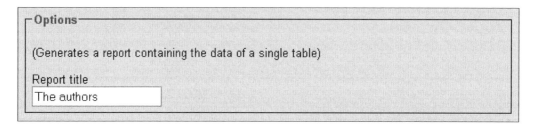

PDF is interesting because of its inherent vectorial nature — the results can be zoomed. Let's have a look at the generated report, as seen in Adobe Reader:

Microsoft Word 2000

This export format directly produces a `.doc` file suitable for all software that understands the Word 2000 format. We find options similar to those in the Microsoft Excel export, and a few more. We can independently export the table's **Structure** and **Data**.

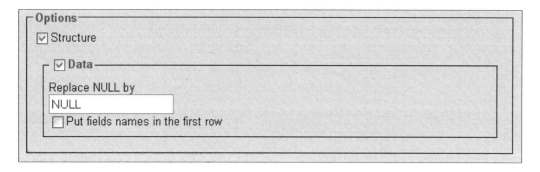

Note that, for this format and the Excel format, we can choose many tables for one export. However, unpleasant results happen if one of these tables has non-textual data. Here are the results for the **author** table:

Database marc_book

Table structure for table author

Field	Type	Null	Default	Comments
id	int(11)	Yes		
name	varchar(30)	Yes		
phone	varchar(30)	Yes	NULL	

Dumping data for table author

id	name	phone
1	John Smith	+01 445-789-1234
2	Maria Sunshine	333-3333

LaTeX

LaTeX is a typesetting language. phpMyAdmin can generate a .tex file that represents the table's structure and/or data in a sideways tabular format.

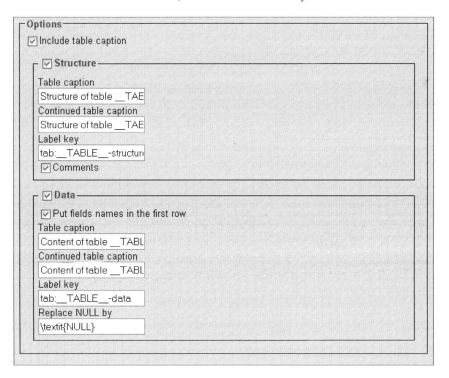

Note that this file is not directly viewable, and must be processed further or converted for the intended final media.

The available options are:

Option	Description
Include table caption	Display captions in the tabular output.
Structure and **Data**	The familiar choice to request structure, data, or both.
Table caption	The caption to appear on the first page.
Continued table caption	The caption to appear on subsequent pages.
Relations, Comments, MIME-type	Other structure information that we want to output. These choices are available if the relational infrastructure is in place (see *Chapter 10*, *Benefiting from the Relational System*, for details).

XML

The XML format is very popular these days for data exchange. Choosing **XML** in the **Export** interface yields no choice for options. What follows is the output of the **author** table:

```
<?xml version="1.0" encoding="utf-8" ?>
<!--
-
- phpMyAdmin XML Dump
- version 3.3.2
- http://www.phpmyadmin.net
-
- Host: localhost
- Generation Time: May 16, 2010 at 09:30 AM
- Server version: 5.1.45
- PHP Version: 5.3.2
-->
<!--
- Database: 'marc_book'
-->
<marc_book>
  <!-- Table author -->
    <author>
```

```
            <id>1</id>
            <name>John Smith</name>
            <phone>+01 445-789-1234</phone>
      </author>
      <author>
            <id>2</id>
            <name>Maria Sunshine</name>
            <phone>333-3333</phone>
      </author>
</marc_book>
```

Open document spreadsheet

The open document spreadsheet format is a subset of the open document (http://en.wikipedia.org/wiki/OpenDocument), which was made popular with the OpenOffice.org office suite. We need to choose only one table to be exported in order to have a coherent spreadsheet. Here is our author table, exported into a file named author.ods, and subsequently looked at from OpenOffice:

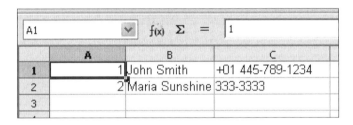

Open document text

Open document text is another subset of the open document standard, this time oriented towards text processing. The available options are as shown in the following screenshot:

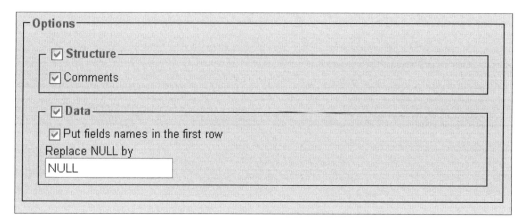

Our `author` table is now exported and appears as follows when viewed in OpenOffice:

Database marc_book

Table structure for table author

Field	Type	Null	Default
id	int(11)	Yes	
name	varchar(30)	Yes	
phone	varchar(30)	Yes	NULL

Dumping data for table author

1	John Smith	+01 445-789-1234
2	Maria Sunshine	333-3333

YAML

YAML stands for **YAML Ain't Markup Language**. YAML is a human-readable data serialization format; its official site is `http://www.yaml.org`. This format has no option that we can choose from within phpMyAdmin. Here is the YAML export for the author table:

```
1:
  id: 1
  name: John Smith
  phone: +01 445-789-1234

2:
  id: 2
  name: Maria Sunshine
  phone: 333-3333
```

CodeGen

The CodeGen option might some day support many formats related to code development. Currently, it can export in NHibernate **Object-relation mapping (ORM)** format. For more details, please refer to `http://en.wikipedia.org/wiki/Nhibernate`.

Texy! text

Texy! is a formatting tool (`http://texy.info/en/`) with its own simplified syntax. Here is an example of export in Texy! format:

```
===Database marc_book

== Table structure for table author
|------
|Field|Type|Null|Default
|------
|//**id**//|int(11)|Yes|NULL
|name|varchar(30)|Yes|NULL
|phone|varchar(30)|Yes|NULL

== Dumping data for table author
|1|John Smith|+01 445 789-1234
|2|Maria Sunshine|333-3333
```

PHP array

In PHP, associative arrays can hold text data; therefore, a PHP array export format is available. It produces a file containing, for example:

```php
<?php
// marc_book.author
$author = array(
  array('id'=>1,'name'=>'John Smith','phone'=>'+1 445 789-1234'),
  array('id'=>2,'name'=>'Maria Sunshine','phone'=>'333-3333')
);
```

Excel 97-2003 and Excel 2007 Workbook

Thanks to the PHPExcel library (`http://www.codeplex.com/PHPExcel`), which is included in phpMyAdmin, it's possible to produce a native Excel 97-2003 or Excel 2007 export file. For this to work, we need a work directory under the main phpMyAdmin directory. This work directory can be created on a Linux system with `mkdir tmp ; chmod o+rwx tmp`. We also need to set the `$cfg['TempDir']` parameter in `config.inc.php` to `'./tmp'`.

> On a shared host, having such an unprotected directory is dangerous as it possibly provides write access to other users of this server.

This export format directly produces a `.xls` or `.xlsx` file suitable for all software that understands these formats. We can specify which string should replace a NULL value. The **Put fields names in the first row** option, when activated, generates the table's column names as the first line of the spreadsheet. Again, the **Save as file** checkbox should be checked. This produces a file where each table's column becomes a spreadsheet column:

MediaWiki table

MediaWiki (`http://www.mediawiki.org/wiki/MediaWiki`) is a popular wiki package which supports the ubiquitous Wikipedia. This wiki software implements a formatting language in which it's possible to describe data in tabular format. Choosing this export format in phpMyAdmin produces a file that can be pasted in a wiki page that we are editing.

Exporting a table

The **Export** link in the Table view brings up the export subpanel for a specific table. It's similar to the database export panel, but there is no table selector. However, there is an additional section for split exports before the **Save as file** subpanel.

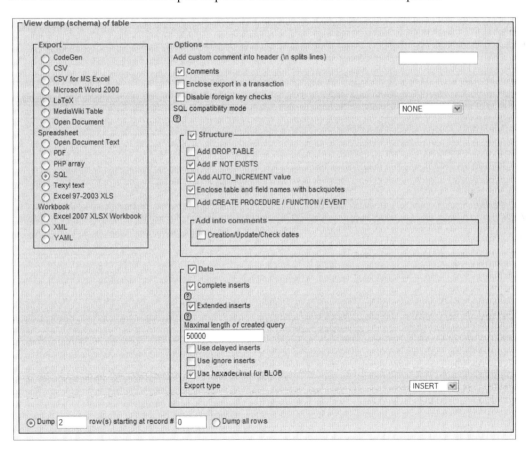

Split-file exports

The **Dump 2 row(s) starting at record # 0** dialog enables us to split the file into chunks. Depending on the exact row size, we can experiment with various values for the number of rows, in order to determine how many rows can be included in a single export file before the memory or execution time limits are reached on the web server. We could then use names like book00.sql and book01.sql for our export files. Should we decide to export all rows, we just select the **Dump all rows** radio box.

Exporting selectively

At various places in phpMyAdmin's interface, we can export the results that we see, or select the rows that we want to export.

Exporting partial query results

When results are displayed from phpMyAdmin (here, the results of a query asking for the books from **author_id 2**), an **Export** link appears at the bottom of the page.

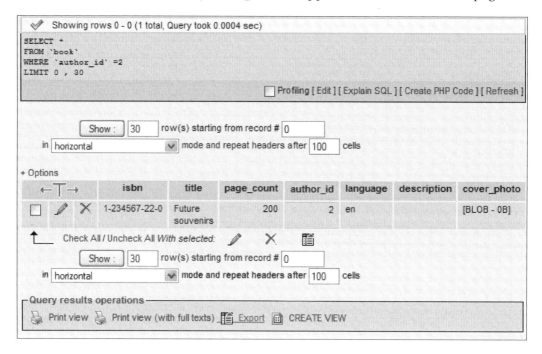

Clicking on this link brings up a special export panel containing the query on the top, along with the other table export options. An export produced via this panel would contain only the data from this result set.

 The results of single-table queries can be exported in all of the available formats, while the results of multi-table queries can be exported only in the CSV, XML, and LaTeX formats.

Exporting and checkboxes

Any time we see the results (when browsing or searching, for example), we can check the checkboxes next to the rows that we want, and use the **With selected: export** icon to generate a partial export file containing just those rows:

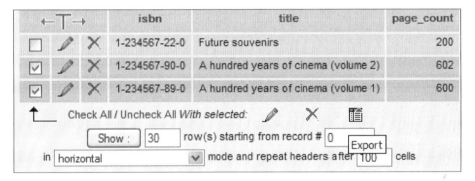

Exporting multiple databases

Any user can export the databases to which he or she has access, in one operation.

On the home page, the **Export** link brings us to the screen shown below. This has the same structure as the other export pages, except for the databases list:

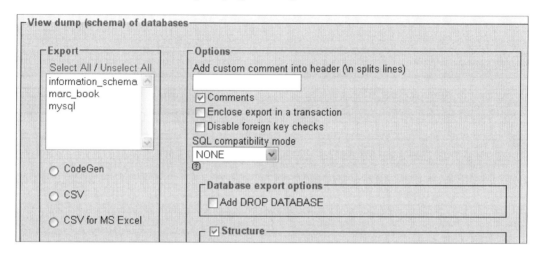

Exporting large databases may or may not work. It depends on their size, the options chosen, and the web server's PHP component settings (especially memory size and execution time).

Saving the export file on the server

Instead of transmitting the export file over the network with HTTP, it's possible to save it directly on the file system of the web server. This could be quicker and less sensitive to execution time limits, because the entire transfer from the server to the client browser is bypassed. Eventually, a file transfer protocol such as FTP or SFTP can be used to retrieve the file, because leaving it on the same machine would not provide good backup protection.

A special directory has to be created on the web server before saving an export file on it. Usually, this is a subdirectory of the main phpMyAdmin directory. We will use save_dir as an example. This directory must have special permissions. First, the web server must have write permissions for this directory. Also, if the web server's PHP component is running in safe mode, the owner of the phpMyAdmin scripts must be the same as the owner of save_dir.

On a Linux system, assuming that the web server is running as group apache, the following commands would do the trick:

```
# mkdir save_dir
# chgrp apache save_dir
# chmod g=rwx save_dir
```

> The correct ownership and permissions mask depend highly upon the chosen web server and the **Server Application Programming Interface (SAPI)** (see http://en.wikipedia.org/wiki/Server_Application_Programming_Interface) used, which influences how directories and files are created and accessed. PHP could be using the scripts' owner as the accessing user, or the web server's user/group itself.

We also have to define the `'./save_dir'` directory name in `$cfg['SaveDir']`. We are using a path relative to the `phpMyAdmin` directory here, but an absolute path would work just as well.

The **Save as file** section will appear with a new **Save on server...** section:

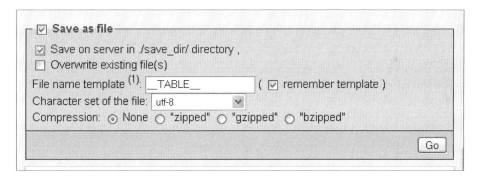

After clicking on **Go**, we will receive either a confirmation message, or an error message (if the web server does not have the required permissions to save the file).

> For saving a file again using the same filename, check the **Overwrite existing file(s)** checkbox.

User-specific save directories

We can use the special string, `%u`, in the `$cfg['SaveDir']` parameter. This string will be replaced by the logged-in username. For example:

```
$cfg['SaveDir'] = './save_dir/%u';
```

This would give us an on screen choice, **Save on server in ./save_dir/marc/ directory**. These directories (one per potential user) must exist and must bear the correct permissions, as already seen in the previous section.

Memory limits

Generating an export file uses a certain amount of memory, depending on the size of the tables and on the chosen options. The `$cfg['MemoryLimit']` parameter can contain a limit (in bytes) on the amount of memory used by PHP scripts in phpMyAdmin—the exporting/importing scripts and other scripts. By default, the parameter is set to `0`, meaning that there is no limit. We could set a limit of 20 megabytes here by using a value of `20M` (the `M` suffix here is very important).

 Note that, if PHP has its safe mode activated, changing `$cfg['MemoryLimit']` has no effect. Instead, the enforced limit comes from the `memory_limit` directive in `php.ini`.

Summary

In this chapter, we examined the various ways of triggering an export—from the Database view, the Table view, or a results page. We also reviewed the various available export formats, their options, the possibility of compressing the export file, and the various places to which the export file could be sent.

In the next chapter, we'll have the opportunity to import our structure and data back again, provided that the chosen format is supported by phpMyAdmin.

7
Importing Structure and Data

In this chapter, we will learn how to import data that we have exported for backup or transfer purposes. Exported data may also come from authors of other applications, and could contain the whole foundation structure of these applications, along with some sample data.

The current phpMyAdmin version (3.3) can import:

- Files containing MySQL statements (usually having a `.sql` suffix, but not necessarily so)
- CSV files (comma-separated values, although the separator is not necessarily a comma); these files can be imported by phpMyAdmin itself or via the MySQL `LOAD DATA INFILE` statement, which enables the MySQL Server to handle the data directly rather than having phpMyAdmin parse it first
- Open Document Spreadsheet files
- Excel files (from versions 97 to 2007)
- XML files (generated by phpMyAdmin)

The binary field upload covered in *Chapter 5, Changing Data and Structure*, can be said to belong to the import family. Future versions might be able to import files in more formats.

 Importing and uploading are synonyms in this context.

In general, an exported file can be imported either to the same database it came from or to any other database; the XML format is an exception to this and a workaround is given in the XML section later in this chapter. Also, a file generated from an older phpMyAdmin version should have no problem being imported by the current version, but the difference between the MySQL version at the time of export and the one at the time of import might play a bigger role regarding compatibility. It's difficult to evaluate how future MySQL releases will change the language's syntax, which could result in import challenges.

The import feature can be accessed from several panels:

- The **Import** menu available from the homepage, the Database view, or the Table view
- The **Import files** menu offered inside the **Query window** (as explained in *Chapter 11, Entering SQL Commands*)

An import file may contain the `DELIMITER` keyword. This enables phpMyAdmin to mimic the `mysql` command-line interpreter. The `DELIMITER` separator is used to delineate the part of the file containing a stored procedure, as these procedures can themselves contain semicolons.

The default values for the `Import` interface are defined in `$cfg['Import']`.

Before examining the actual import dialog, let's discuss some limits issues.

Limits for the transfer

When we import, the source file is usually on our client machine and therefore must travel to the server via HTTP. This transfer takes time and uses resources that may be limited in the web server's PHP configuration.

Instead of using HTTP, we can upload our file to the server by using a protocol such as FTP, as described in the *Reading files from a web server upload directory* section. This method circumvents the web server's PHP upload limits.

Time limits

First, let's consider the time limit. In `config.inc.php`, the `$cfg['ExecTimeLimit']` configuration directive assigns, by default, a maximum execution time of 300 seconds (five minutes) for any phpMyAdmin script, including the scripts that process data after the file has been uploaded. A value of `0` removes the limit, and in theory, gives us infinite time to complete the import operation. If the PHP server is running in safe mode, modifying `$cfg['ExecTimeLimit']` will have no effect. This is because the limits set in `php.ini` or the user-related web server configuration file, (such as `.htaccess` or the virtual host configuration files) take precedence over this parameter.

Of course, the time it effectively takes depends on two key factors:

- Web server load
- MySQL server load

 The time taken by the file, as it travels between the client and the server does not count as execution time because the PHP script only starts to execute after the file has been received on the server. Therefore, the `$cfg['ExecTimeLimit']` parameter has an impact only on the time used to process data (like decompression or sending it to the MySQL server).

Other limits

The system administrator can use the `php.ini` file or the web server's virtual host configuration file to control uploads on the server.

The `upload_max_filesize` parameter specifies the upper limit or maximum file size that can be uploaded via HTTP. This one is obvious, but another less obvious parameter is `post_max_size`. As HTTP uploading is done via the POST method, this parameter may limit our transfers. For more details about the POST method, please refer to `http://en.wikipedia.org/wiki/Http#Request_methods`.

The `memory_limit` parameter is provided to prevent web server child processes from grabbing too much of the server's memory — phpMyAdmin runs inside a child process. Thus, the handling of normal file uploads, especially compressed dumps, can be compromised by giving this parameter a small value. Here, no preferred value can be recommended; the value depends on the size of uploaded data we want to handle and on the size of the physical memory. The memory limit can also be tuned via the `$cfg['MemoryLimit']` parameter in `config.inc.php`, as seen in *Chapter 6, Exporting Structure and Data (Backup)*.

Finally, file uploads must be allowed by setting `file_uploads` to `On`; otherwise, phpMyAdmin won't even show the **Location of the textfile** dialog. It would be useless to display this dialog as the connection would be refused later by the PHP component of the web server.

Handling big export files

If the file is too big, there are ways in which we can resolve the situation. If the original data is still accessible via phpMyAdmin, we could use phpMyAdmin to generate smaller CSV export files, choosing the **Dump n rows starting at record # n** dialog. If this were not possible, we could use a spreadsheet program or a text editor to split the file into smaller sections. Another possibility is to use the upload directory mechanism, which accesses the directory defined in `$cfg['UploadDir']`. This feature is explained later in this chapter.

In recent phpMyAdmin versions, the **Partial import** feature can also solve this file size problem. By selecting the **Allow interrupt...** checkbox, the import process will interrupt itself if it detects that it's close to the time limit. We can also specify a number of queries to skip from the start, in case we successfully import a number of rows and wish to continue from that point.

Uploading into a temporary directory

On a server, a PHP security feature called `open_basedir` (which limits the files that can be opened by PHP to the specified directory tree) can impede the upload mechanism. In this case, or if uploads are problematic for any other reason, the `$cfg['TempDir']` parameter can be set with the value of a temporary directory. This is probably a subdirectory of phpMyAdmin's main directory, into which the web server is allowed to put the uploaded file.

Importing SQL files

Any file containing MySQL statements can be imported via this mechanism. This format is more commonly used for backup/restore purposes. The relevant dialog is available in the Database view or the Table view, via the **Import** subpage, or in the **Query** window.

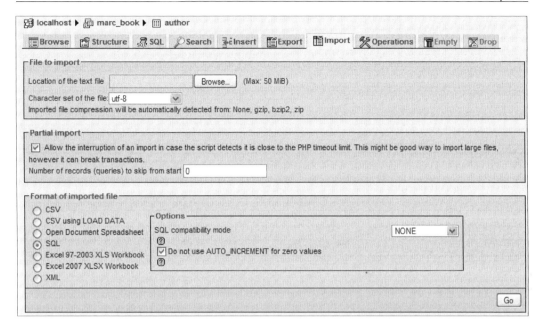

There is no relation between the currently-selected table (here **author**) and the actual contents of the SQL file that will be imported. All of the contents of the SQL file will be imported, and it's those contents that determine which tables or databases are affected. However, if the imported file does not contain any SQL statements to select a database, all statements in the imported file will be executed on the currently-selected database.

Let's try an import exercise. First, we make sure that we have a current SQL export of the **book** table (as explained in *Chapter 6, Exporting Structure and Data (Backup)*). This export file must contain the structure and the data. Then we drop the **book** table—yes, really! We could also simply rename it. (See *Chapter 9, Performing Table and Database Operations*, for the procedure.)

Now it's time to import the file back. We should be on the **Import** subpage, where we can see the **Location of the text file** dialog. We just have to hit the **Browse** button and choose our file.

phpMyAdmin is able to detect which compression method (if any) has been applied to the file. Depending on the phpMyAdmin version, and the extensions that are available in the PHP component of the web server, there is variation in the formats that the program can decompress.

However, to import successfully, phpMyAdmin must be informed of the character set of the file to be imported. The default value is **utf8**. However, if we know that the import file was created with another character set, we should specify it here.

A **SQL compatibility mode** selector is available at import time. This mode should be adjusted to match the actual data that we are about to import, according to the type of the server where the data was previously exported.

Another option, **Do not use AUTO_INCREMENT for zero values**, is selected by default. If we have a value of zero in a primary key and we want it to stay zero instead of being auto-incremented, we should use this option.

To start the import, we click on **Go**. The import procedure continues and we receive a message: **Import has been successfully finished, 2 queries executed**. We can browse our newly-created tables to confirm the success of the import operation.

The file could be imported for testing in a different database or even on another MySQL server.

Importing CSV files

In this section, we will examine how to import CSV files. There are two possible methods—**CSV** and **CSV using LOAD DATA**. The first method is implemented internally by phpMyAdmin and is the recommended one for its simplicity. With the second method, phpMyAdmin receives the file to be loaded and passes it to MySQL. In theory, this method should be faster. However, it has more requirements due to MySQL itself (see the *Requirements* subsection of the *CSV using LOAD DATA* section).

Differences between SQL and CSV formats

There are some differences between the SQL and CSV formats. The CSV file format contains data only, so we must already have an existing table in place. This table does not need to have the same structure as the original table (from which the data comes); the **Column names** dialog enables us to choose which columns are affected in the target table.

Because the table must exist prior to the import, the CSV import dialog is available only from the **Import** subpage in the Table view, and not in the Database view.

Exporting a test file

Before trying an import, let's generate an `author.csv` export file from the `author` table. We use the default values in the **CSV export** options. We can then **Empty** the `author` table—we should avoid dropping this table because we still need the table structure.

CSV

From the **author** table menu, we select **Import** and then **CSV**:

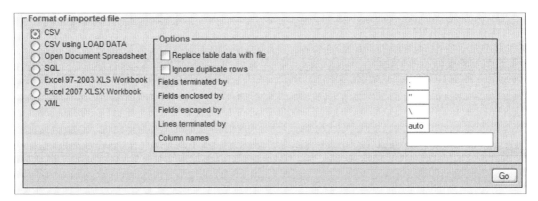

We can influence the behavior of the import in a number of ways. By default, importing does not modify existing data (based on primary or unique keys). However, the **Replace table data with file** option instructs phpMyAdmin to use the REPLACE statement instead of the INSERT statement, so that existing rows are replaced with the imported data.

Using **Ignore duplicate rows**, INSERT IGNORE statements are generated. These cause MySQL to ignore any duplicate key problems during insertion. A duplicate key from the import file does not replace existing data, and the procedure continues for the next line of CSV data.

We can also specify the character that terminates each field, the character that encloses data, and the character that escapes the enclosing character. Usually this is \. For example, for a double quote enclosing character, if the data field contains a double quote, it must be expressed as **"some data \" some other data"**.

For **Lines terminated by**, recent versions of phpMyAdmin offer the **auto** choice, which should be tried first as it detects the end-of-line character automatically. We can also specify manually which characters terminate the lines. The usual choice is **\n** for UNIX-based systems, **\r\n** for DOS or Windows systems, and **\r** for Mac-based system (up to Mac OS 9). If in doubt, we can use a hexadecimal file editor on our client computer (not part of phpMyAdmin) to examine the exact codes.

By default, phpMyAdmin expects a CSV file with the same number of fields and the same field order as the target table. However, this can be changed by entering a comma-separated list of column names in **Column names**, respecting the source file format. For example, let's say our source file contains only the author ID and the author name information:

```
"1","John Smith"
"2","Maria Sunshine"
```

We'd have to put **id, name** in **Column names** in order to match the source file.

When we click on **Go**, the import is executed and we receive a confirmation. We might also see the actual INSERT queries generated if the total size of the file is not too big.

```
Import has been successfully finished, 2 queries executed.
INSERT INTO `author` VALUES ('1', 'John Smith',
  '+01 445 789-1234')# 1 row(s) affected.

INSERT INTO `author` VALUES ('2', 'Maria Sunshine',
  '333-3333')# 1 row(s) affected.
```

CSV using LOAD DATA

With this method, phpMyAdmin relies on the server's LOAD DATA INFILE or LOAD DATA LOCAL INFILE mechanisms to do the actual import, instead of processing the data internally. These statements are the fastest way of importing text in MySQL. They cause MySQL to start a read operation either from a file located on the MySQL server (LOAD DATA INFILE) or from another place (LOAD DATA LOCAL INFILE) which, in this context, is always the web server's file system. If the MySQL server is located on a computer other than the web server, we won't be able to use the LOAD DATA INFILE mechanism.

Requirements

Relying on the MySQL server has some consequences. Using LOAD DATA INFILE requires that the logged-in user possess a global FILE privilege. Also, the file itself must be readable by the MySQL server's process.

Chapter 19, *Administrating the MySQL Server with phpMyAdmin*, explains phpMyAdmin's interface, which can be used by system administrators to manage privileges.

The use of the LOCAL modifier in LOAD DATA LOCAL INFILE must be allowed by the MySQL server and MySQL's client library used by PHP.

Both the LOAD methods are available from the phpMyAdmin LOAD interface, which tries to choose the best possible default option.

Using the LOAD DATA interface

We select **Import** from the **author** table menu. Choosing **CSV using LOAD DATA** brings up the following dialog:

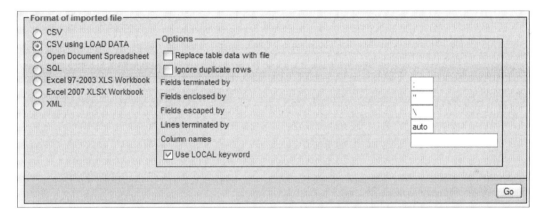

 The available options have already been covered in the *CSV* section.

In the familiar **Location of the text file** question, we choose our author.csv file.

Finally, we can choose the LOAD method, as discussed earlier, by selecting the **Use LOCAL keyword** option. We then click on **Go**.

If all goes well, we can see the confirmation screen as follows:

```
 ✅  Import has been successfully finished, 1 queries executed.

LOAD DATA LOCAL INFILE '/opt/php-upload-tmp/phpPv7pzY' INTO TABLE `author`
FIELDS TERMINATED BY ';' ENCLOSED BY '"' ESCAPED BY '\\' LINES TERMINATED BY
'\r\n'# 2 row(s) affected.

                                          [ Edit ] [ Create PHP Code ]
```

This screen shows the exact **LOAD DATA LOCAL INFILE** statement used. Here is what has happened:

- We chose **author.csv**.
- The contents of this file were transferred over HTTP and received by the web server.
- The PHP component inside the web server saved this file to a work directory (here **/opt/php-upload-tmp/**) and gave it a temporary name.
- phpMyAdmin informed of the location of this working file, built a **LOAD DATA LOCAL INFILE** command, and sent it to MySQL. Note that just one query was executed, which loaded many rows.
- The MySQL server read and loaded the contents of the file into our target table. It then returned the number of affected rows (**2**), which phpMyAdmin displayed in the results page.

Importing other formats

In addition to SQL and CSV formats, phpMyAdmin can import Open Document Spreadsheet, Excel, and XML files. However, these files need to have been exported by phpMyAdmin itself, or closely follow what phpMyAdmin does when exporting.

Open Document Spreadsheet

By default, when we export via phpMyAdmin in this format, the **Put fields names in the first row** option is not selected. This means that the exported file contains only data. At import time, a corresponding option **Column names in first row** is available and should not be selected if the file does not contain the column names in its first row.

However, if the exported file does contain the column names, we can select this option. Therefore, phpMyAdmin will do the following:

- Create a table, using the file name (`author.ods`) as the table name (`author`)
- Use the first row's column contents as column names for this table
- Determine each column's type and appropriate size, based on the data itself
- Insert the data into the table

Other import options exist to indicate what should be done with empty rows and with data containing percentages or currency values.

Excel

For Excel format, the technique about column names being part of the export file—as discussed in the previous section—applies as well.

XML

The amount of structural information that can be created by importing an XML file depends on the options that were chosen at export time. Indeed, if the **Export Structure Schemas** option was selected, the exact CREATE TABLE statement is placed in the exported file. Therefore, the same table structure is available in the restored table.

Likewise, if the **Export contents** option was selected, the whole data is there in the XML file, ready to be imported. There are no options available at import time, as XML is a self-describing format; therefore, phpMyAdmin can correctly interpret what's in the file and react appropriately.

As the original database name is a part of the XML export, the current phpMyAdmin version only supports importing an XML file into the database from which the export originated. To import to a different database, we need to first use a text editor and change the database name inside this line:

```
<pma:database name="marc_book" collation="latin1_swedish_ci"
  charset="latin1">
```

Reading files from a web server upload directory

To get around cases where uploads are completely disabled by a web server's PHP configuration, or where upload limits are too small, phpMyAdmin can read uploaded files from a special directory located on the web server's file system. This mechanism is applicable for SQL and CSV imports.

We first specify the directory name of our choice in the `$cfg['UploadDir']` parameter, for example, `'./upload'`. We can also use the `%u` string, as described in *Chapter 6, Exporting Structure and Data (Backup)*, to represent the user's name.

Now let's go back to the **Import** subpage. We get an error message: **The directory you set for upload work cannot be reached.**

This error message is expected, as the directory does not exist. It is supposed to have been created inside the current `phpMyAdmin` installation directory. The message might also indicate that the directory exists, but can't be read by the web server. (In PHP safe mode, the owner of the directory and the owner of the phpMyAdmin-installed scripts must be the same.)

Using an SFTP or FTP client, we create the necessary directory, and can now upload a file there (for example **book.sql**) bypassing any PHP timeouts or maximum upload limits.

Note that the file itself must have permissions that allow the web server to read it.

In most cases, the easiest way is to allow everyone to read the file.

Refreshing the **Import** subpage brings up the following:

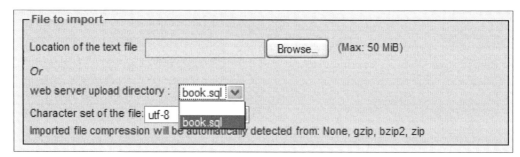

Clicking on **Go** should execute the file.

Automatic decompression is also available for files located in the upload directory. The file names should have extensions such as `.bz2`, `.gz`, `.sql.bz2`, or `.sql.gz`.

 Using the double extensions (`.sql.bz2`) is a better way to indicate that a `.sql` file was produced and then compressed, as we see all of the steps used to generate this file.

Displaying an upload progress bar

Especially when importing a large file, it's interesting to have a visual feedback on the progression of upload. Please note that the progress bar we are discussing here informs us only about the uploading part, which is a subset of the whole import operation.

Having a JavaScript-enabled browser is a requirement for this feature. Moreover, the web server's PHP component must have at least one of the following extensions:

- The well-know `APC` extension (see `http://pecl.php.net/package/APC`), which is highly recommended for its opcode caching benefits
- The `uploadprogress` extension (see `http://pecl.php.net/package/uploadprogress`)

phpMyAdmin uses AJAX techniques to fetch progress information and then displays it as a part of the **File to import** dialog. The number of bytes uploaded, the total number of bytes, and the percentage uploaded are displayed below the bar.

Configuring APC

A few `php.ini` directives play an important role for upload progress. First, the `apc.rfc1867` directive must be set to `On` or `true`, otherwise this extension won't report upload progress to the calling script. When set to `On`, this extension updates an APC user cache entry with the upload status information.

The frequency of the updates can be set via the `apc.rfc1867_freq` directive, which can take the form of a percentage of the total file size (for example `apc.rfc1867_freq = "10%"`), or a size in bytes (suffixes `k` for kilobytes, `m` for megabytes, and `g` for gigabytes are accepted). A value of `0` here indicates update as often as possible, which looks interesting but in reality may slow down the upload.

This very notion of update frequency explains why the bar progresses in chunks rather than continuously when using this mechanism.

Displaying a character set dialog

The `$cfg['AllowAnywhereRecoding']` parameter that we saw in the chapter on exporting also affects importing. When set to `true`, this parameter displays a character set dialog where we can specify which character set the file is encoded in. We must indicate the correct character set to avoid garbled data after the import operation. The default value of the character set for this dialog is drawn from the `$cfg['Import']['charset']` directive.

Summary

This chapter covered:

- Various options in phpMyAdmin that allow us to import data
- The different mechanisms involved in importing files
- The limits that we might hit when performing a transfer, and ways to bypass these limits

The next chapter will explain how to perform single-table searches (including search criteria specification) and how to search in the whole database.

8
Searching Data

In this chapter, we present mechanisms that can be used to find the data we are looking for, instead of just browsing tables page-by-page and sorting them. In **Search** mode, application developers can look for data in ways not expected by the interface they are building—adjusting and sometimes repairing data. This chapter covers single-table searches besides entire database searches. *Chapter 12, Generating Multi-table Queries*, is a complement to this chapter and presents examples of searches involving multiple tables at once.

Using Search page daily

For some users, the main use of phpMyAdmin is the **Search** mode, which is used for finding and updating data. In this regard, the phpMyAdmin team has made it possible to define which subpage is the starting page in Table view. This is accomplished with the `$cfg['DefaultTabTable']` parameter; setting it to `'tbl_select.php'` defines the default subpage to be **Search**.

Single-table searches

This section describes the **Search** subpage where a single-table search is available.

Entering the search subpage

The **Search** subpage can be accessed by clicking on the **Search** link in the Table view. This has been done here for the book table:

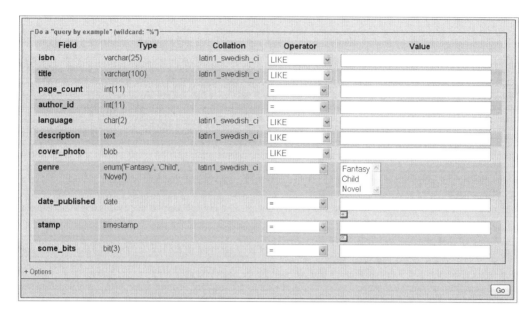

The most commonly-used section of the **Search** interface (the query by example) is the one immediately displayed, whereas other dialogs are hidden in a slider that can be activated by the **Options** link (more on these dialogs later in this chapter).

Searching criteria by field—query by example

The main use of the **Search** panel is to enter criteria for some fields so as to retrieve only the data we are interested in. This is called **query by example** because we give an example of what we are looking for. Our first retrieval will concern finding the book with ISBN **1-234567-89-0**. We simply enter this value in the **isbn** box and choose the **Operator =**:

Clicking on **Go** gives the following results (shown partially in the following screenshot):

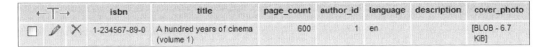

←T→	isbn	title	page_count	author_id	language	description	cover_photo
☐ ✎ ✕	1-234567-89-0	A hundred years of cinema (volume 1)	600	1	en		[BLOB - 6.7 KiB]

This is a standard results page. If the results ran to several pages, we could navigate through them, and edit and delete data for the subset that we have chosen during the process. Another feature of phpMyAdmin is that the fields used as the criteria are highlighted by changing the border color of the columns to better reflect their importance on the results page.

It isn't necessary to specify that the **isbn** column be displayed even though this is the column in which we search. We could have selected only the **title** column for display (see the *Selecting fields to be displayed* section of this chapter) and chosen the **isbn** column as a criterion.

Searching for empty or non-empty values

Two handy operators are present in the operator's list when the column has a character type, such as CHAR, VARCHAR, or TEXT:

    = ' '
    ! = ' '

These are the ones to use when you want to search for an empty (= ' ') or non-empty (! = ' ') value in some field. Normally, entering nothing in a field's **Value** means that this field does not participate in the search process. However, with one of these operators, this field is included in the generated search query.

> Please do not confuse this method with searching for a NULL value, which is quite different. Indeed, a NULL value (refer to http://en.wikipedia.org/wiki/Null_(SQL) for a more complete explanation) is a special value that conveys that some information is missing in this column.

Producing reports with Print view

We can see the **Print view** and **Print view (with full texts)** links on the results page. These links produce a more formal report of the results (without the navigation interface) directly to the printer. In our case, using **Print view** would produce the following:

SQL result

Host: localhost
Database: marc_book
Generation Time: May 19, 2010 at 07:45 AM
Generated by: phpMyAdmin 3.3.2 / MySQL 5.1.45-standard-log
SQL query: SELECT * FROM `book` WHERE `isbn` LIKE '1-234567-89-0' LIMIT 0, 30 ;
Rows: 1

isbn	title	page_count	author_id	language	description	cover_photo	genre	date_published	stamp	some_bits
1-234567-89-0	A hundred years of cinema (volume 1)	600	1	en		[BLOB - 6.7 KiB]	Fantasy	0000-00-00	2010-05-15 08:56:53	101

This report contains information about the server, database, time of generation, version of phpMyAdmin, version of MySQL, and the generated SQL query. The other link, **Print view (with full texts),** would print the contents of the **TEXT** fields in their entirety.

Searching with wildcard characters

Let's assume we are looking for something less precise—all books with "cinema" in their title. First, we go back to the search page. For this type of search, we will use SQL's **LIKE** operator. This operator accepts wildcard characters—the % character (which matches any number of characters) and the underscore (_) character (which matches a single character). Thus we can use **%cinema%** to let phpMyAdmin find any substring that matches the word "cinema". If we left out both wildcard characters, we will get exact matches with only that single word.

This substring matching is easier to access, being part of the **Operator** drop-down list. We only have to enter the word **cinema** and use the operator **LIKE %...%** to perform that match. We should avoid using this form of the **LIKE** operator on big tables (thousands of rows), as MySQL does not use an index for data retrieval in this case, leading to wait times that depend on the server hardware and its current load. This is why this operator is not the default one in the drop-down list, even though this method of search is commonly used on smaller tables.

Here is a screenshot showing how we perform a search on **cinema** with the operator **LIKE %...%**:

 The LIKE operator can be used for other types of wildcard searches, for example History%, which would search for this word at the beginning of a title. As the expression does not start with a wildcard character, MySQL will try to use an index if it finds one that speeds up data retrieval. For more details about MySQL's use of indexes, please refer to http://dev.mysql.com/doc/refman/5.1/en/mysql-indexes.html.

Using either of these methods produces the following results:

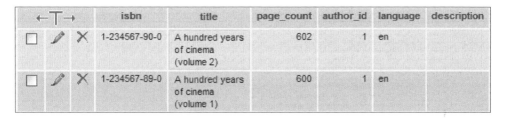

The % and _ wilcard characters may be repeated in a search expression; for example, histo__ (two underscores) would match history whereas histo% would match history and historian. The MySQL manual gives more examples at http://dev.mysql.com/doc/refman/5.1/en/string-comparison-functions.html.

Performing a case-sensitive search

In the previous example, we could have replaced **cinema** with **CINEMA** and achieved similar results. The reason is that the collation of the title column is latin1_swedish_ci. This collation comes from the collation set by default at the time of database creation, unless the server's default collation has been changed (see http://dev.mysql.com/doc/refman/5.1/en/charset-mysql.html). Here, ci means that comparisons are done in a case-insensitive way. Please refer to http://dev.mysql.com/doc/refman/5.1/en/case-sensitivity.html for more details.

Combining criteria

We can use multiple criteria for the same query (for example, to find all the English books of more than 300 pages). There are more comparative choices in **Operator** because the **page_count** field is numeric, as shown in the following screenshot:

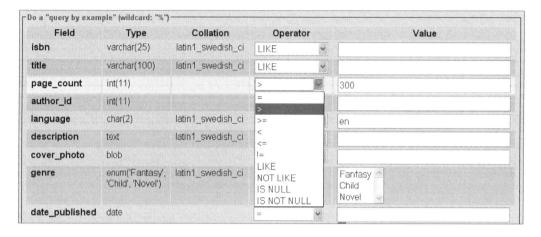

Search options

The **Options** slider reveals additional panels to further refine the search process.

Selecting the fields to be displayed

In the **Options** slider, a **Select fields** panel facilitates selection of the fields to be displayed in the results. All fields are selected by default, but we can *Ctrl* + click other fields to make the necessary selections. Mac users would use *Command* + click to select/unselect the fields.

Here are the fields of interest in this example:

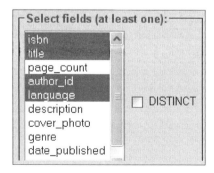

We can also specify the number of rows per page in the textbox next to the field selection. The **Add search conditions** box will be explained in the *Applying a WHERE clause* section, which will follow shortly.

Ordering the results

The **Display order** dialog permits the specification of an initial sorting order for the results to come. In this dialog, a drop-down menu contains all of the table's columns; it's up to us to select the one on which we want to sort. By default, sorting will be in **Ascending** order, but a choice of **Descending** order is also available.

It should be noted that on the results page, we can change the sort order using the techniques explained in *Chapter 4, Taking First Steps*.

Applying a WHERE clause

Sometimes, we may want to enter a search condition that is not offered in the **Function** list of the **query by example** section. The list cannot contain every possible variation in the language. Let's say we want to find all the English or French books using the IN clause. To do this, we can use the **Add search conditions** section:

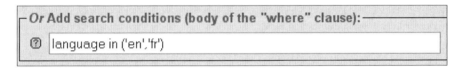

 The complete search expression is generated by combining the search conditions and other criteria (entered in the **query by example** lines) with a logical AND.

We could have a more complex list of search conditions that would be entered in the same textbox, possibly with brackets and operators such as AND or OR.

A **Documentation** link points to the MySQL manual, where we can see a huge choice of available functions. (Each function is applicable to a specific field type.)

Avoiding repeated results

Sometimes, we may want to avoid getting the same results more than once. For example, if we want to know in which cities we have clients, displaying each city name once would be enough. Here, we want to know in which languages our books are written. In the **Select Fields** dialog, we choose just the **language** field, and we check **DISTINCT**, as shown in the following screenshot:

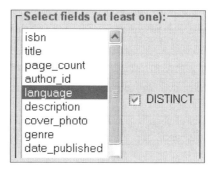

Clicking on **Go** produces the following image:

 Using **DISTINCT**, we see each language only once. Without this option, the row containing **en** would have appeared three times.

If we select more than one column (for example `author_id` and `language`) and mark the `DISTINCT` option, we'll now see two lines in the results because there are two books in English but from different authors. Results are still not repeated.

Performing a complete database search

In the previous examples, searching was limited to one table. This assumes knowledge of the exact table (and columns) where the necessary information might be stored.

When the data is hidden somewhere in the database, or when the same data can be presented in various columns (for example, a **title** column or a **description** column), it's easier to use the database search method.

We enter the **Search** page in the Database view for the `marc_book` database:

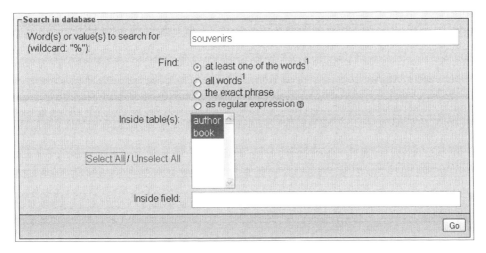

In the **Word(s) or value(s)** section, we enter what we want to find. The % wildcard character can prove useful here—but let's remember the performance advice about wildcard characters given earlier in this chapter. We enter **souvenirs**.

In the **Find** section, we specify how to treat the values entered. We might need to find **at least one of the words** entered, **all words** (in no particular order), or **the exact phrase** (words in the same order, somewhere in a column). Another choice is to use a **regular expression**, which is a more complex way of performing pattern matching. More details are available at `http://dev.mysql.com/doc/refman/5.1/en/regexp.html` and `http://www.regular-expressions.info/`. We will keep the default value—**at least one of the words**.

We can choose specific tables, in order to restrict the search, or we can select all tables. As we only have two (small) tables, we select both.

As the search will be done on each row of every table selected, we might hit some time limits if the number of rows or tables is too big. Thus, this feature can be deactivated by setting `$cfg['UseDbSearch']` to FALSE. (It's set to TRUE by default).

Clicking on **Go** finds the following for us:

Search results for *"souvenirs"* at least one of the words:		
0 match(es) inside table *author*		
1 match(es) inside table *book*	Browse	Delete
Total: *1* match(es)		

This is an overview of the number of matches and the relevant tables. We might get some matches in the tables in which we may not be interested. However, for the matches that look promising, we can **Browse** the results page, or we can **Delete** the unwanted rows.

Restricting the search to a column

Sometimes, a particular column name is part of one (or many) tables, and we want to search only inside this column. For example, suppose that we are looking for "Marc", but this name could also be part of a book's title. So we want to restrict the search to only the "name" column in all of the chosen tables. This can be achieved by entering "name" in the **Inside field** option.

Stopping an errant query

Suppose we launch a complex search and notice that the browser is waiting for the results. This might happen with a database search but could also happen with a single-table search. We can click the stop button in the browser but this will only tell the web server to cease handling our request. However, at this point the MySQL server process is busy, possibly doing a complex join or a full table scan. Here is a method to stop this errant query:

1. We open a different browser (for example, the errant query was launched via Firefox and we open Internet Explorer)

2. We log in via phpMyAdmin to MySQL with the same account

3. On the homepage we click **Processes**

4. At this point, we should see a process identified by **Query** under the **Command** column and containing the errant query (other than SHOW PROCESSLIST which is not the one to kill)

5. We click on **Kill** for this process

6. We immediately click again on **Processes** and the chosen process should now be identified as **Killed** instead of **Query**

Summary

In this chapter, we saw an overview of single table searches with "query by example criteria" and additional criteria specification—selecting displayed values and ordering results. We also saw wildcard searches and full database search.

The next chapter explains how to perform the operations on tables—for example, changing a table's attributes, such as its storage engine. The subjects of repairing and optimizing tables are also covered in the next chapter.

9
Performing Table and Database Operations

In the previous chapters, we dealt mostly with table fields. In this chapter, we will learn how to perform some operations that influence tables or databases as a whole. We will cover table attributes and how to modify them, and will also discuss multi-table operations.

Various links that enable table operations have been put together on the **Operations** subpage of the Table view. Here is an overview of this subpage:

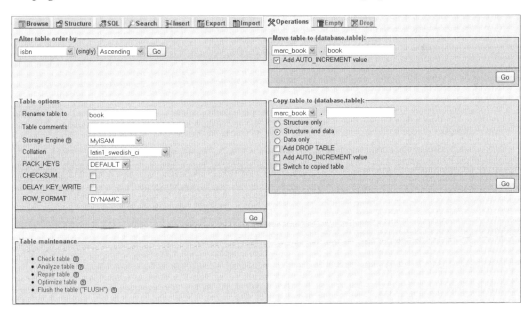

Maintaining a table

During its lifetime, a table repeatedly gets modified and is therefore continually growing and shrinking. In addition, outages may occur on the server, leaving some tables in a damaged state.

Using the **Operations** subpage, we can perform various operations, which are listed next. However, not every operation is available for every storage engine:

- **Check table**: Scans all rows to verify that deleted links are correct. A checksum is also calculated to verify the integrity of the keys. If everything is alright, we will obtain a message stating **OK** or **Table is already up to date**; if any other message shows up, it's time to repair this table (see the third bullet).

- **Analyze table**: Analyzes and stores the key distribution; this will be used on subsequent JOIN operations to determine the order in which the tables should be joined. This operation should be performed periodically (in case data has changed in the table), in order to improve JOIN efficiency.

- **Repair table**: Repairs any corrupted data for tables in the MyISAM and ARCHIVE engines. Note that a table might be so corrupted that we cannot even go into Table view for it! In such a case, refer to the *Multi-table operations* section for the procedure to repair it.

- **Optimize table**: This is useful when the table contains overheads. After massive deletions of rows or length changes for VARCHAR fields, lost bytes remain in the table. phpMyAdmin warns us in various places (for example, in the Structure view) if it feels the table should be optimized. This operation reclaims unused space in the table. In the case of MySQL 5.x, the relevant tables that can be optimized use the MyISAM, InnoDB, and ARCHIVE engines.

- **Flush table**: This must be done when there have been many connection errors and the MySQL server blocks further connections. Flushing will clear some internal caches and allow normal operations to resume.

- **Defragment table**: Random insertions or deletions in an InnoDB table fragment its index. The table should be periodically defragmented for faster data retrieval. This operation causes MySQL to rebuild the table, and only applies to InnoDB.

 The operations are based on the available underlying MySQL queries — phpMyAdmin only calls those queries.

Changing table attributes

Table attributes are the various properties of a table. This section discusses the settings for some of them.

Table storage engine

The first attribute that we can change is called **Storage Engine**.

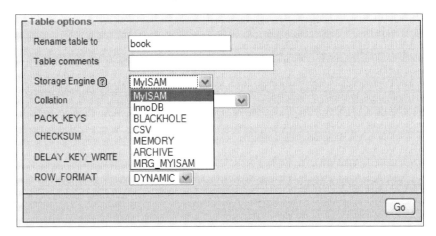

This controls the whole behavior of the table—its location (on-disk or in-memory), the index structure, and whether it supports transactions and foreign keys. The drop-down list varies depending on the storage engines supported by our MySQL server.

 Changing a table's storage engine may be a long operation if the number of rows is large.

Table comments

This allows us to enter comments for the table:

These comments will be shown at appropriate places—for example, in the navigation panel, next to the table name in the Table view, and in the export file. Here is what the navigation panel looks like when the $cfg['ShowTooltip']$ parameter is set to its default value of TRUE:

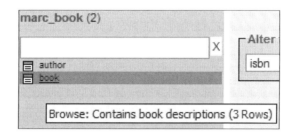

The default value (FALSE) of $cfg['ShowTooltipAliasDB']$ and $cfg['ShowTooltipAliasTB']$ produces the behavior we saw earlier—the true database and table names are displayed in the navigation panel and in the Database view for the **Structure** subpage. Comments appear when the cursor is moved over a table name. If one of these parameters is set to TRUE, the corresponding item (database names for DB and table names for TB) will be shown as a tooltip instead of the names. This time, the mouseover box shows the true name for the item. This is convenient when the real table names are not meaningful.

There is another possibility for $cfg['ShowTooltipAliasTB']$—the 'nested' value. Here is what happens if we use this feature:

- The true table name is displayed in the navigation panel
- The table comment (for example project__) is interpreted as the project name and is displayed as it is (see the *Nested display of tables within a database* section in *Chapter 3, Over Viewing the Interface*)

Table order

When we browse a table, or execute a statement such as SELECT * from book without specifying a sort order, MySQL uses the order in which the rows are physically stored. This table order can be changed with the **Alter table order by** dialog. We can choose any field, and the table will be reordered once on this field.

We choose **author_id** in the example, and after we click on **Go**, the table gets sorted on this field.

Reordering is convenient if we know that we will be retrieving rows in this order most of the time. Moreover, if we use an ORDER BY clause later on, and the table is already physically sorted on this field, the performance should be better.

This default ordering will last as long as there are no changes to the table (no insertions, deletions, or updates). This is why phpMyAdmin shows the **(singly)** warning:

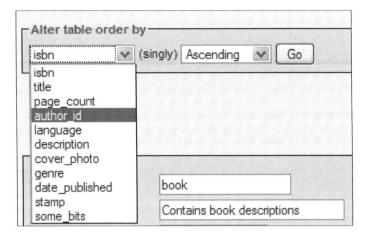

After the sort has been performed on **author_id**, books for author **1** will be displayed first, followed by the books for author **2**, and so on (we are talking about a default browsing of the table without explicit sorting). We can also specify the sort order as **Ascending** or **Descending**.

If we insert another row, describing a new book from author **1**, and then click on **Browse**, the book will not be displayed along with the other books for this author because the sort was done before the insertion.

Table collation

To better see the issues of collation change at various levels, let's first create a new author with a character **é** in his name:

The name column currently has a `latin1_swedish_ci` collation, as can be seen via the **Structure** page. On the **Operations** page, if we change the collation for table `author` from `latin1_swedish_ci` to, say, `utf8_general_ci`, this generates:

```
ALTER TABLE `author` DEFAULT CHARACTER SET utf8 COLLATE
utf8_general_ci
```

Therefore, we only changed the default collation for future columns that will be added to this table.

In an effort to further test collation changes, we can go to the **Structure** page and change the collation of the author's **name** column to `utf8_general_ci` (by clicking on the **Change** icon). Having done that, we browse the `author` table and still see the é character, because MySQL updated the contents of this column on collation change.

Table options

Other attributes that influence the table's behavior may be specified using the **Table options** dialog:

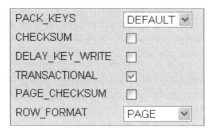

The options are:

- **PACK_KEYS**: Setting this attribute results in a smaller index. The table can be read faster but will take more time to update. It's available for the MyISAM storage engine.

- **CHECKSUM**: This option makes MySQL compute a checksum for each row. This results in slower updates, but finding corrupted tables becomes easier. It's available for MyISAM only.

- **DELAY_KEY_WRITE**: This option instructs MySQL not to write the index updates immediately, but to queue them for writing later. This improves performance but there is a negative trade-off: the index might need to be rebuilt in case of a server failure (see `http://dev.mysql.com/doc/refman/5.1/en/miscellaneous-optimization-tips.html`). It's available for MyISAM only.

- **ROW_FORMAT**: To the storage engines that support this feature (MyISAM, InnoDB, PBXT, and Maria), a choice of row format is presented. The default value being the current state of this table's row format.

- **TRANSACTIONAL, PAGE_CHECKSUM**: This option applies to the Maria storage engine, which will be renamed Aria in a future version. The **TRANSACTIONAL** option marks this table as being transactional; however, the exact meaning of this option varies, as future versions of this storage engine will gain more transactional features. **PAGE_CHECKSUM** computes a checksum on all index pages. This is currently documented at `http://askmonty.org/wiki/Manual:Maria_storage_engine`.

- **auto-increment**: This option changes the auto-increment value. It's shown only if the table's primary key has the auto-increment attribute.

Renaming, moving, and copying tables

The **Rename** operation is the easiest to understand — the table simply changes its name and stays in the same database.

The **Move** operation (shown in the following screenshot) manipulates a table in two ways — it changes the table's name and also the database in which it is stored.

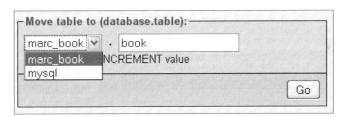

Moving a table is not directly supported by MySQL. So, phpMyAdmin has to create the table in the target database, copy the data, and then finally drop the source table. This could take a long time depending on the table's size.

The **Copy** operation leaves the original table intact and copies its structure or data (or both) to another table, possibly in another database. Here, the **book-copy** table will be an exact copy of the book source table. After the copy, we remain in the Table view for the book table, unless we selected **Switch to copied table** in which case we are moved to the Table view of the newly-created table.

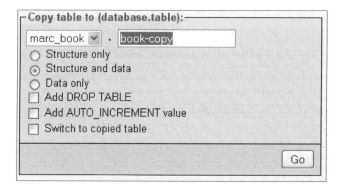

The **Structure only** copy is done to create a test table with the same structure, but without the data.

Appending data to a table

The **Copy** dialog may also be used to append (add) data from one table to another. Both tables must have the same structure. This operation is achieved by entering the table to which we want to copy the data and choosing **Data only**.

For example, book data is coming from various sources (various publishers) in the form of one table per publisher and we want to aggregate all of the data in one place. For MyISAM, a similar result can be obtained by using the Merge storage engine (which is a collection of identical MyISAM tables). However, if the table is InnoDB, we need to rely on phpMyAdmin's **Copy** feature.

Multi-table operations

In the Database view, there is a checkbox next to each table name and a drop-down menu under the table list. This enables us to quickly choose some tables and perform an operation on all those tables at once. Here, we select **book-copy** and **book** tables, and choose the **Check table** operation for the selected tables:

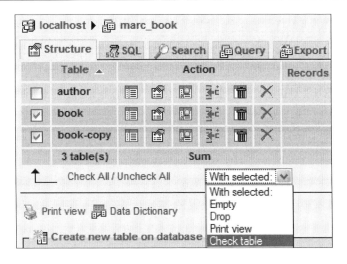

We could also quickly select or deselect all the checkboxes with **Check All / Uncheck All**.

Repairing an "in use" table

The multi-table mode is the only method (unless we know the exact SQL query to type) for repairing a corrupted table. Such tables may be shown with the **in use** flag in the database list. Users seeking help in the support forums for phpMyAdmin often receive this tip from experienced phpMyAdmin users.

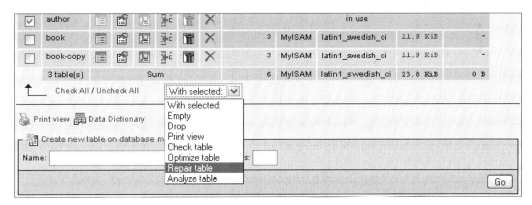

Database operations

The **Operations** tab in the Database view gives access to a panel that enables us to perform operations on a database taken as a whole:

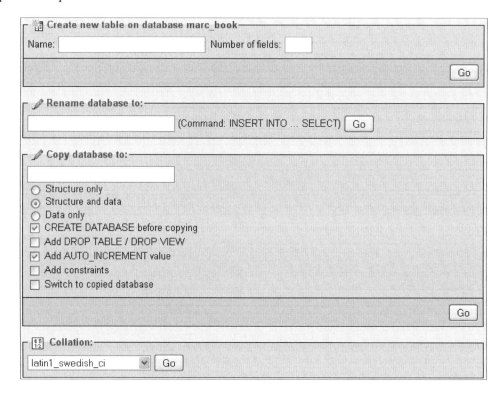

Renaming a database

A **Rename database to** dialog is available. Although this operation is not directly supported by MySQL, phpMyAdmin does it indirectly by creating a new database, renaming each table (thus sending it to the new database), and dropping the original database.

Copying a database

It's also possible to make a complete copy of a database, even if MySQL itself does not support this operation natively. The options are similar to those already explained for the table copy.

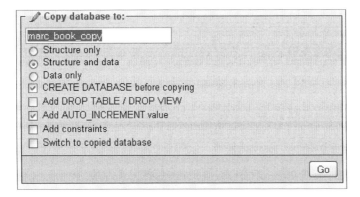

Summary

This chapter covered the operations we can perform on entire tables or databases. It also looked at table maintenance operations for table repair and optimization, changing various table attributes, table movements (including renaming and moving to another database), and multi-table operations.

In the next chapter, we will begin to examine advanced features that rely on the linked-tables infrastructure, such as the relational system.

10
Benefiting from the Relational System

Welcome to the section of the book where we start to cover advanced features. The relational system allows users to work more closely with phpMyAdmin, as we will see in the following chapters. This chapter explains how to define inter-table relations. It also explains how to install the linked-tables infrastructure—a prerequisite for the advanced features.

Relational MySQL

When application developers use PHP and MySQL to build web interfaces or other data-manipulation applications, they usually establish relations between tables using the underlying SQL queries. Examples of this would be queries to: "get an invoice and all its items" and "get all books by an author".

In the early versions of phpMyAdmin, MySQL stored information about which table belonged to which database. However, the relational data structure (how tables relate to each other) was not stored within MySQL. Relations were temporarily made by the applications in order generate meaningful results. In other words, the relations were in our head.

This was considered a shortcoming of MySQL by phpMyAdmin developers and users. Therefore, the team started to build an infrastructure to support relations for MyISAM tables. The infrastructure evolved to support a growing array of special features. We can describe this infrastructure as **metadata**, that is, data about data.

phpMyAdmin 2.2.0 already had the **bookmarks** feature (the ability to recall frequently-used queries — see *Chapter 14, Using Bookmarks*), and version 2.3.0 generalized the metadata system. Subsequent versions were built on this facility. Examples of this would be: the 2.5.x family with its MIME-based **transformations** (as described in *Chapter 16, Transforming Data Using MIME*) and the 2.10.x family with a graphical relation builder called **Designer** (described in this chapter). Finally, the 3.3.x family relies heavily on this metadata to track changes made via phpMyAdmin, as explained in *Chapter 18, Tracking Changes*.

InnoDB and PBXT

InnoDB (`http://www.innodb.com`) is a MySQL storage engine developed by Innobase Oy, a subsidiary of Oracle. As the InnoDB subsystem must be activated by a system administrator, it may not be available on every MySQL server.

The PrimeBase XT storage engine or PBXT (`http://www.primebase.org`) is developed by PrimeBase Technologies. The minimum MySQL version required is 5.1, as this version supports the pluggable storage engine API that is used by PBXT and other third-parties to offer alternative storage engines. This transactional storage engine is newer than InnoDB. It's usually installed after downloading it from the PrimeBase website and then going through a compile step. For some operating systems, a precompiled binary is available — please visit the previously-mentioned website for download and installation instructions.

When considering the relational aspect, here are the benefits of using the InnoDB or PBXT storage engine for a table:

- They support referential integrity that is based on foreign keys, which are the keys in a foreign (or reference) table. By contrast, using only phpMyAdmin's internal relations (discussed later) brings no automatic referential integrity verification.

- The exported structure for InnoDB and PBXT tables contains the defined relations. Therefore, they are easily imported for better cross-server interoperability.

The foreign key feature of these storage engines can effectively replace the part of phpMyAdmin's infrastructure that deals with relations. We will see how phpMyAdmin interfaces with the InnoDB and PBXT foreign key system later in this chapter.

The other parts of phpMyAdmin's infrastructure (for example, bookmarks) have no equivalent in InnoDB, PBXT, or MySQL. Hence, they are still required in order to access the complete phpMyAdmin feature set. However, in MySQL 5.x, views are supported, and have similarities with phpMyAdmin's bookmarks.

Linked-tables infrastructure

The relational system's infrastructure is stored in tables that follow a predetermined structure. The data in these tables is generated and maintained by phpMyAdmin on the basis of our actions in the interface.

Goal of the infrastructure

Metadata tables contain, for all storage engines, information that is used to support special phpMyAdmin features such as bookmarks and transformations. Moreover, for tables in a storage engine that does not support foreign keys, relations between tables are kept in this infrastructure.

Location of the infrastructure

There are two possible places to store these tables:

1. A user's database: To allow every web developer who owns a database to benefit from these features.

2. A dedicated database called pmadb (phpMyAdmin database): In a multi-user installation (discussed later), this database may be accessible to a number of users while keeping the metadata private.

As this infrastructure does not exist by default, and because phpMyAdmin's developers want to promote it, the interface displays the following error message on the home page, and also for every database when on the **Operations** subpage in the Database view:

 The additional features for working with linked tables have been deactivated. To find out why click here.

This message can be disabled with the following parameter (which, by default, is set to FALSE):

```
$cfg['PmaNoRelation_DisableWarning'] = TRUE;
```

 The message is the same regardless of the current database, as the infrastructure is shared for all of our databases and tables (or all users, in a multi-user installation).

Installing the linked-tables infrastructure

The previous error message is displayed even if only a part of the infrastructure is missing. Of course, with a fresh installation, all of the parts are missing—our database has not yet heard of phpMyAdmin and needs to be outfitted with this infrastructure. Following the **here** link in the previous message brings up a panel explaining that the pmadb, and the tables that are supposed to be a part of it, are either missing or undefined.

It's important to realize that the relational system will work only if two conditions are met:

1. Proper definitions are present in config.inc.php
2. The corresponding tables (and maybe the database) are created

To create the necessary structure that matches our current version of phpMyAdmin, a command file called create_tables.sql is available in the scripts subdirectory of the phpMyAdmin installation directory. However, we should not blindly execute this before understanding the possible choices: single-user installation or multi-user installation.

Installing for a single user

Even if we are entitled to only one database by the system administrator, we can still use all of the relational features of phpMyAdmin. In this setup, we will use our normal database (let's assume its name is **marc_book**) to store the metadata tables.

We need to modify a local copy of the scripts/create_tables.sql file in order to populate our database with all of the required tables. They will have the prefix pma_ to make them easily recognizable. We need to remove the following lines:

```
CREATE DATABASE IF NOT EXISTS `phpmyadmin`
   DEFAULT CHARACTER SET utf8 COLLATE utf8_bin;
USE phpmyadmin;
```

This is necessary because we won't be using a `phpmyadmin` database. Next, we should open our **marc_book** database in phpMyAdmin. We are now ready to execute the script. There are two ways of doing this:

1. As we already have the script in our editor, we can just copy the lines and paste them in the query box of the **SQL** subpage.

2. We can use the import technique shown in *Chapter 7, Importing Structure and Data*. We select the `create_tables.sql` script that we just modified.

After the creation, the navigation panel shows us the special **pma_** tables along with our normal tables:

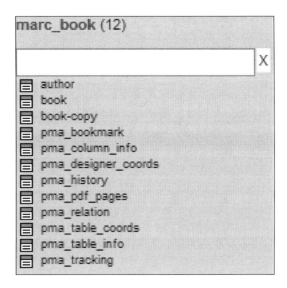

Configuring the infrastructure

It's now time to adjust all the parameters that are related to relational features in the `config.inc.php` file. This can be done easily with the setup script as seen in *Chapter 1, Getting Started with phpMyAdmin*), or by pasting the appropriate lines from the `config.sample.inc.php` file. The database is our own and the table names are the ones that have just been created:

```
$cfg['Servers'][$i]['pmadb']         = 'marc_book';
$cfg['Servers'][$i]['bookmarktable'] = 'pma_bookmark';
$cfg['Servers'][$i]['relation']      = 'pma_relation';
$cfg['Servers'][$i]['table_info']    = 'pma_table_info';
$cfg['Servers'][$i]['table_coords']  = 'pma_table_coords';
$cfg['Servers'][$i]['pdf_pages']     = 'pma_pdf_pages';
$cfg['Servers'][$i]['column_info']   = 'pma_column_info';
```

```
$cfg['Servers'][$i]['history']        = 'pma_history';
$cfg['Servers'][$i]['designer_coords'] = 'pma_designer_coords';
$cfg['Servers'][$i]['tracking']       = 'pma_tracking';
```

> As table names are case sensitive, we must use the same names as the tables created by the installation script. We are free to change the table names (see the right-hand part of the configuration directives listed below) provided we change them accordingly in the database.

The `pmadb` and each table have a specific function, as listed below:

Function	Description	Explained in
pmadb	Defines the database where all of the tables are located	This chapter
bookmarktable	Contains the bookmarks	*Chapter 14, Using Bookmarks*
relation	Defines inter-table relations, as used in many of the phpMyAdmin's features	This chapter
table_info	Contains the display field	This chapter
table_coords and pdf_pages	Contain the metadata necessary for drawing a schema of the relations in a PDF format	*Chapter 15, Documenting the System*
column_info	Used for column-commenting and MIME-based transformations	*Chapter 16, Transforming Data Using MIME*
history	Contains SQL query history information	*Chapter 11, Entering SQL Commands*
designer_coords	Holds the coordinates used by the Designer feature	This chapter
tracking	Contains the metadata and the actual SQL statements related to the tracked tables	*Chapter 18, Tracking Changes*

Between each phpMyAdmin version, the infrastructure may be enhanced—the changes are explained in `Documentation.html`. This is why phpMyAdmin has various checks to ascertain the structure of the tables. If we know that we are using the latest structure, `$cfg['Servers'][$i]['verbose_check']` can be set to FALSE, in order to avoid checks, thereby slightly increasing phpMyAdmin's speed.

Installing for multiple users

In this setup, we will have a distinct database—pmadb—used to store the metadata tables. Our control user (see *Chapter 2, Configuring Authentication and Security*) will have specific rights to this database. Each user will work with his or her login name and password, which will be used to access his or her databases. However, whenever phpMyAdmin itself accesses pmadb to obtain some metadata, it will use the control user's privileges.

 Setting a multi-user installation is possible only for a MySQL system administrator who has the privileges to assign rights to another user (here, the pma user). If you are not in this situation, please refer to the *Installing for a single user* section.

We first ensure that the control user pma has been created and that its definition in config.inc.php is appropriate:

```
$cfg['Servers'][$i]['controluser'] = 'pma';
$cfg['Servers'][$i]['controlpass'] = 'bingo';
```

We then copy the scripts/create_tables.sql file to our local workstation and edit it. We replace the following lines:

```
-- GRANT SELECT, INSERT, DELETE, UPDATE ON `phpmyadmin`.* TO
--      'pma'@localhost;
```

with these:

```
GRANT SELECT, INSERT, DELETE, UPDATE ON `phpmyadmin`.* TO
    'pma'@localhost;
```

We then execute this script by importing it (see *Chapter 7, Importing Structure and Data*). The net effect is to create the phpmyadmin database, assign proper rights to user pma, and populate the database with all of the necessary tables.

The last step is to adjust all of the parameters in config.inc.php that relate to relational features. Please refer to the previous section, except for the database name in the pmadb parameter:

```
$cfg['Servers'][$i]['pmadb'] = 'phpmyadmin;
```

The installation is now complete. We will test the features in the coming sections and chapters. We can perform a quick check by logging out of phpMyAdmin, then logging in and displaying the homepage; the warning message should be gone.

Defining relations with the relation view

After the installation of the linked-tables infrastructure, there are now more options available in the Database view and the Table view. We will now examine a new link —**Relation view**—which can be found in the **Structure** subpage of the Table view.

This view is used to:

- Define the relations of the current table with the other tables
- Choose the display field

Our goal here is to create a relation between the `book` table (which contains the author ID) and the `author` table (which describes each author referenced by an ID). We start at the Table view for the `book` table, go to **Structure**, and then click on the **Relation view** link.

Defining internal relations

As the **book** table is in MyISAM format, we see the following screen (otherwise, the display would be different, as explained in the *Defining foreign key relations* section later):

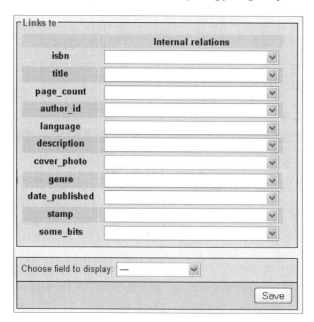

This screen allows us to create **Internal relations** (stored in the `pma_relation` table), because MySQL itself does not have any relational notion for MyISAM tables. The empty drop-down list next to each column indicates that there are no relations (links) to any foreign table.

Defining the relation

We can relate each field of the `book` table to a field in another table (or in the same table, because self-referencing relations are sometimes necessary). The interface finds both the unique and the non-unique keys in all of the tables within the same database, and presents the keys in drop-down lists. (Creating internal relations to other databases from the interface is not currently supported.) The appropriate choice for the **author_id** field is to select the corresponding **author_id** field in the `author` table— this is also called **defining the foreign key**.

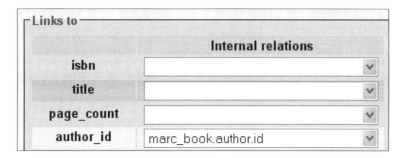

We then click on **Save**, and the definition is saved in phpMyAdmin's infrastructure.

To remove the relation, we would just come back to the same screen, select the empty choice, and click on **Save**.

Defining the display field

The primary key of our `author` table is the `author_id`, which is a unique number that we made up for key purposes. The name field in our table— the `name` — represents the author's name. It would be interesting to see the author's name as a description of each row of the `book` table. This is the purpose of the display field. We should normally define a display field for each table that participates in a relation as a foreign table.

We will see how this information is displayed in the *Benefiting from the defined relations* section. We now go to the **Relation view** for the `author` table (which is the foreign table in this case) and specify the display field. We choose **name** as the display field and click on **Save**:

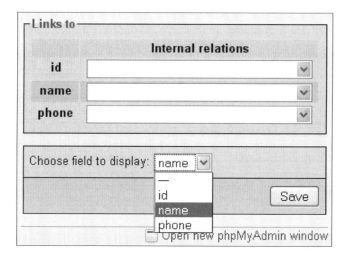

 phpMyAdmin offers the ability to define only one display field for a table, and this field is used in all of the relations where this table is used as a foreign table.

The definition of this relation is now done. Although we did not relate any of the fields in the `author` table to another table, this can also be done. For example, we could have a country code in this table and could create a relation to the country code of a country table.

We will discuss the benefits of having defined this relation in a later section. For now, we will see what happens if our tables are under the control of the InnoDB or PBXT storage engine.

Foreign key relations

The InnoDB and PBXT storage engines offer us a foreign key system.

 At your choice, the exercises in this section can be accomplished with either InnoDB or PBXT. InnoDB has been chosen in the text.

First, we will switch our **book** and **author** tables to the InnoDB storage engine. We can do this from the **Operations** subpage in the Table view. We start by doing this for the **author** table, as shown in the following screenshot:

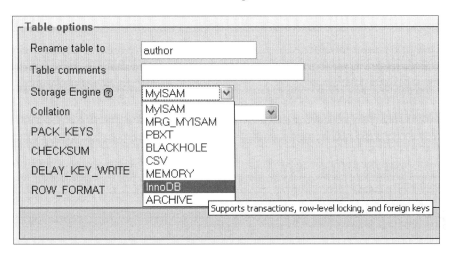

A problem arises when we try to change the storage engine of the **book** table to InnoDB. We have a full-text index in this table, and the InnoDB engine currently does not support this kind of index (PBXT does not support it either):

```
ALTER TABLE `book` ENGINE = InnoDB;
MySQL said:
#1214 - The used table type doesn't support FULLTEXT indexes
```

To get rid of this error message, we go back to the **Structure** for the book table and remove the full-text index on the **description** field, therefore losing the ability to do full-text searches on this column. While we are on this screen, let's also remove the combined index we created on **author_id** and **language**. We will do this because we want to see the consequences of a missing index later in this chapter, when trying to define a foreign key. At this point, we are able to switch the book table to InnoDB.

The foreign key system in InnoDB maintains integrity between the related tables. Hence, we cannot add a non-existent author ID to the book table. In addition, actions are programmable when DELETE or UPDATE operations are performed on the master table (in our case, book).

Opening the book table on its **Structure** subpage and entering the **Relation view** now displays a different page:

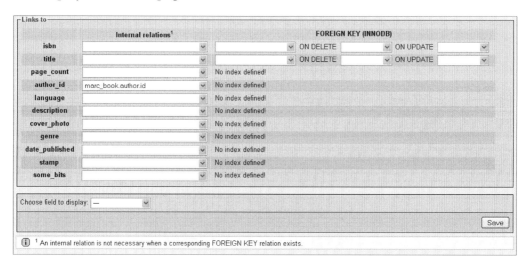

This page tells us:

- There is an internal relation defined for **author_id** to the author table.
- No InnoDB relations are defined yet.
- We will be able to remove the internal relation, when the same relation has been defined in InnoDB. Indeed, phpMyAdmin advises us that: "**An internal relation is not necessary when a corresponding FOREIGN KEY relation exists**". Therefore, it would be better to remove it.
- **ON DELETE** and **ON UPDATE** options are available for InnoDB relations.

In the possible choices for the related key, we see the keys defined in all of the InnoDB tables of the same database. (Creating a cross-database relation is currently not supported in phpMyAdmin.) The keys defined in the current table are also shown, as self-referring relations are possible. Let's remove the internal relation for the **author_id** field and click on **Save**. Our goal is to add an InnoDB-type relation for the **author_id** field, but it's not possible as the **No index defined!** message appears on this line. This is because foreign key definitions in InnoDB or PBXT can be done only if both the fields are defined as indexes.

 Other conditions regarding constraints are explained in the MySQL manual. Please refer to `http://dev.mysql.com/doc/refman/5.1/en/innodb-foreign-key-constraints.html`.

Thus, we come back to the **Structure** page for the book table and add an ordinary (non-unique) index to the **author_id** field, producing:

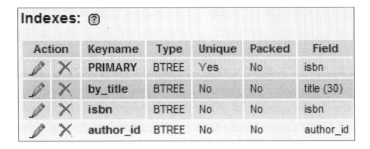

In the **Relation view**, we can try again to add the relation we wanted; it works this time!

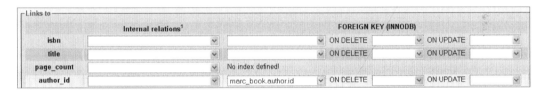

We can also set some actions with the **ON DELETE** and **ON UPDATE** options. For example, **ON DELETE CASCADE** would make MySQL automatically delete all of the rows in the related (foreign) table when the corresponding row is deleted from the parent table. This would be useful, for example, when the parent table is invoices, and the foreign table is invoice-items. These options are supported natively by MySQL, so deleting outside of phpMyAdmin would cause the deletion to cascade.

 If we have not done so already, we should define the display field for the author table, as explained in the *Defining the display field* section.

Foreign keys without linked-tables infrastructure

We see the **Relation View** link on the **Structure** page of the InnoDB or PBXT table, even though the linked-tables infrastructure is not installed. This brings us to a screen where we can define the foreign keys, in this case for the **book** table.

Note that, if we choose this, the display field for the linked table (in this case `author`) cannot be defined, as it belongs to phpMyAdmin's infrastructure. Thus, we would lose the benefit of seeing the associated description of the foreign key.

Defining relations with the Designer

The Ajax-based Designer offers a visually-driven way of managing relations (both internal and foreign key-based), and defining the display field for each table. It can also act as:

- A menu to access the structure of existing tables and to access the table creation page.
- A PDF schema manager, if we want a PDF schema that encompasses all of our tables.

In the Designer workspace, we can work on the relations for all tables on the same panel. On the other hand, the Relation view shows the relations for only a single table at a time.

We access this feature from the Database view by clicking on the **Designer** menu tab.

 If this menu tab does not appear, it's because we have not yet installed the linked-tables infrastructure as described previously in this chapter—especially the `designer_coords` special table.

Over viewing the interface

The Designer page contains the main workspace where the tables can be seen. This workspace will dynamically grow and shrink, depending on the position of our tables. A top menu contains icons whose description is revealed by hovering the mouse over them. Here is a summary of the goals for the top menu's icons:

Icon	Description
Show/Hide left menu	To display or hide the left-hand menu
Save position	Saves the current state of the workspace
Create table	Quits the Designer and enters a dialog to create a table; we should take care to save the position of tables before clicking on this
Create relation	Puts the designer in a relation creating mode
Choose field to display	Specifies which field represents a table
Reload	Refreshes the tables' information in case their structure has changed outside of the Designer
Help	Displays an explanation about selecting the relations
Angular links/Direct links	Specifies the shape of relation links
Snap to grid	Influences the behavior of table movements, relative to an imaginary grid
Small/Big All	Hides or displays the list of columns for every table
Toggle small/big	Reverses the display mode of columns for every table, as this mode can be chosen by the table with its corner icon V or >
Import/Export	Displays a dialog to import from an existing PDF schema definition or to export to it
Move Menu	The top menu can move to the right and back again

The following image demonstrates the Designer interface containing our three tables and the relations between them:

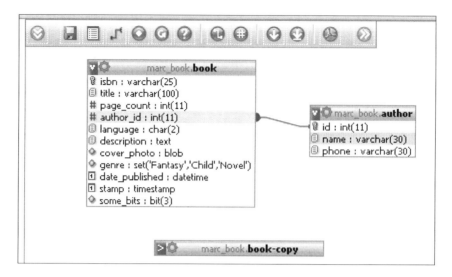

A side menu appears when clicking the **Show/Hide left menu** icon. Its purpose is to present the complete list of tables, so that you can decide which tables appear on the workspace, and to enable access to the **Structure** page of a specific table. In this example, we choose to remove the **book-copy** table from the workspace as shown in the following screenshot:

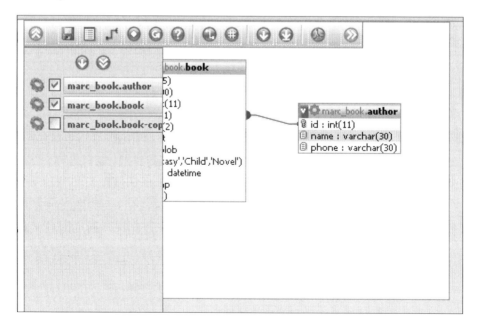

If we want to remove it permanently, we click on the **Save position** top-icon. This icon also saves the current position of our tables on the workspace.

Tables can be moved on the workspace by dragging their title bars, and the list of columns for a table can be made visible/invisible with the help of the upper-left icon on each table. In this list of columns, small icons show us the data type (numeric, text, date), and also tell us whether this column is a primary key.

Defining relations

As we have already defined a relation with the Relation view, we'll first see how to remove it. The Designer does not permit a change in a relation. However, the Designer allows the relation to be removed and re-defined.

The question mark top-icon displays a panel that explains where to click, in order to select a relation for subsequent deletion:

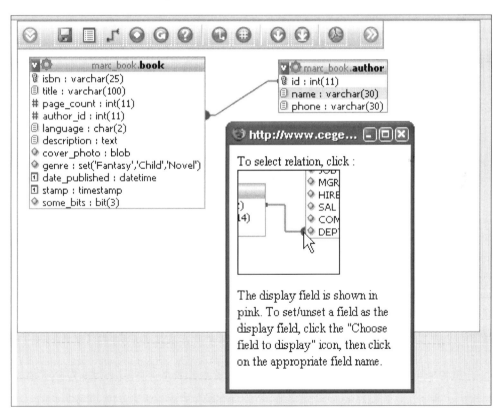

Let's click in the appropriate place to delete this relation. We see a confirmation panel on which we click on **Delete**:

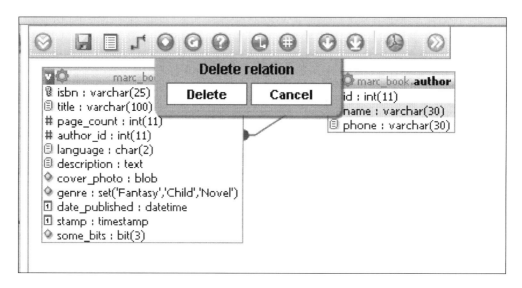

We can then proceed to recreate it. To do this, we start by clicking on the **Create relation** icon:

The cursor then takes the form of a short message saying **Select referenced key**. In our case, the referenced key is the **id** column of the **author** table; so we move the cursor to this column and click on it. A validation is done, ensuring that we chose a primary or unique key.

Next, having changed the cursor to **Select foreign key**, we move it to the author_id column of the book table and click on this. This confirms the creation of the relation. Currently, the interface does not permit the creation of compound keys (having more than one column).

Defining foreign key relations

The procedure to delete or define a relation between InnoDB or PBXT tables is the same as that for internal relations. The only exception is that at the time of creation, a different confirmation panel appears, enabling us to specify the ON DELETE and ON UPDATE actions:

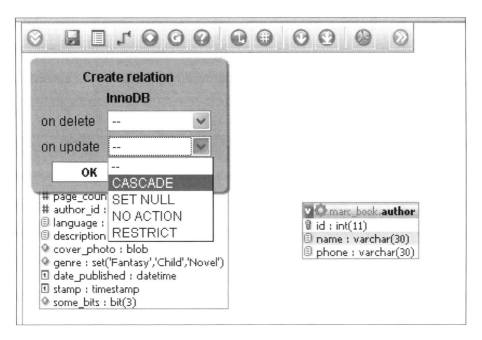

Defining the display field

On the workspace, the name column in the author table has a special background color. This indicates that this column serves as the display field. We can simply click the **Choose field to display** top-icon, and drag the short message **Choose field to display** onto another column—for example, the phone column. This changes the display field to this column. If we were to drag the message to an existing display field column, we would have removed this column from being the display field for the table.

Exporting for PDF schema

In *Chapter 15, Documenting the System*, we'll see how to produce a PDF schema for a subset of our database. We can import the coordinates of tables from such a schema into the Designer's workspace, and conversely export them to the PDF schema. The **Import/export coordinates** top-icon is available for that purpose.

Benefiting from the defined relations

In this section, we will look at the benefits of the defined relations that we can currently test. Other benefits will be described in *Chapter 12, Generating Multi-table Queries* and *Chapter 15, Documenting the System*. Additional benefits of the linked-tables infrastructure will appear in *Chapter 14, Using Bookmarks, Chapter 16, Transforming Data Using MIME*, and *Chapter 18, Tracking Changes*.

These benefits are available for both internal and foreign key relations.

Foreign key information

Let's browse the book table by entering the **Search** subpage and choosing to display the first four columns. We see that the related key (**author_id**) is now a link. Moving the cursor over any **author_id** value reveals the author's name (as defined by the display field of the author table).

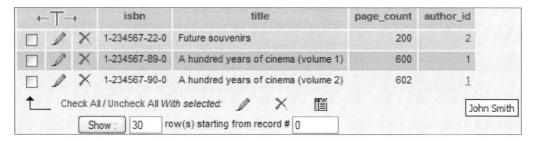

Clicking on the **author_id** brings us to the relevant table—author—for this specific author:

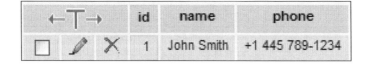

Instead of seeing the keys, we might prefer to see the display field for all of the rows. Going back to the previous search results for the `book` table, we can select the **Relational display field** display option and then click on **Go**. This produces a screen similar to the following screenshot:

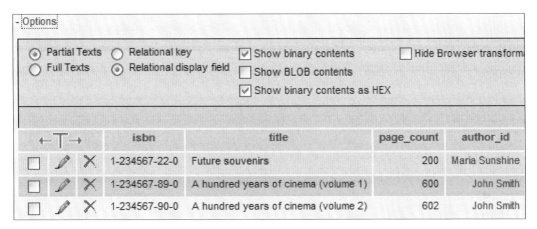

We now switch back to seeing the keys, by selecting **Relational key** and then clicking on **Go**.

The drop-down list of foreign keys

Going back to the `book` table, in **Insert** mode (or in **Edit** mode), there is now a drop-down list of the possible keys for each field that has a defined relation. The list contains the keys and the description (display field) in both orders—key to the display field as well as display field to the key. This enables us to use the keyboard, and type the first letter of either the key or the display field:

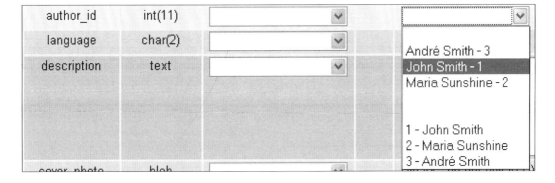

Only the key (in this case **1**) will be stored in the book table. The display field is there only to assist us.

By default, this drop-down list will appear if there are a maximum of 100 rows in the foreign table. This is controlled by the following parameter:

```
$cfg['ForeignKeyMaxLimit'] = 100;
```

For foreign tables with more than 100 rows, a distinct window appears—the foreign-table window (see the next section)—that can be browsed.

We might prefer to see information differently in the drop-down list. Here, **John Smith** is the content and **1** is the ID. The default display is controlled by:

```
$cfg['ForeignKeyDropdownOrder'] = array( 'content-id', 'id-content');
```

We can use one or both of the strings—`content-id` and `id-content`—in the defining array, and in the order that we prefer. Thus, defining `$cfg['ForeignKeyDropdownOrder']` to `array('id-content')` would produce a list with only those choices:

```
1 - John Smith
2 - Maria Sunshine
3 - André Smith
```

The browsable foreign-table window

Our current `author` tables have very few entries. Thus, to illustrate this mechanism, we will set the `$cfg['ForeignKeyMaxLimit']` to an artificially low number, 1. Now, in the **Insert** mode for the `book` table, we see a small table-shaped icon for **author_id**. This icon opens another window, which presents the values of the table `author`, and a **Search** input field. On the left, the values are sorted by key value (here, the **author_id** column), and on the right, they are sorted by description:

Choosing one of the values (by clicking either a key value or a description) closes this window and brings the value back to the **author_id** column.

Referential integrity checks

We discussed the **Operations** subpage, and its **Table maintenance** section, in *Chapter 9, Performing Table and Database Operations*. For this exercise, we suppose that both the `book` and `author` tables are not under the control of the InnoDB or PBXT storage engine. If we have defined an internal relation for the `author` table, a new choice appears for the `book` table—**Check referential integrity**:

A link (**author_id -> author.id**) appears for each defined relation, and clicking it starts the verification. For each row, the presence of the corresponding key in the foreign table is verified and errors, if any, are reported. If the resulting page reports zero rows, it's good news!

This operation exists because, for tables under the storage engines that do not support foreign keys natively, neither MySQL nor phpMyAdmin enforce referential integrity. It's perfectly possible, for example, to import data in the `book` table with invalid values for **author_id**.

Automatic updates of metadata

phpMyAdmin keeps the metadata for internal relations synchronized with every change that is made to the tables via phpMyAdmin. For example, renaming a column that is a part of a relation would make phpMyAdmin rename this column in the metadata for the relation. This guarantees that an internal relation continues to function even after a column's name has been changed. The same thing happens when a column or table is dropped.

> Metadata should be maintained manually, in case a change in the structure is made from outside of phpMyAdmin.

Column-commenting

Prior to MySQL 4.1, the MySQL structure itself did not support the addition of comments to a column. Nevertheless, thanks to phpMyAdmin's metadata, we could comment on columns. However, since MySQL 4.1, native column commenting has been supported. The good news is that for any MySQL version, column commenting in phpMyAdmin is always accessed via the **Structure** page by editing the structure of each field. In the following example, we need to comment on three columns of the book table. Hence, we choose them and click on the pencil icon near the **With selected** choice.

	Field	Type
☑	**isbn**	varchar(25)
☐	**title**	varchar(100)
☑	**page_count**	int(11)
☑	**author_id**	int(11)

To obtain the next panel, as seen here, we are working in vertical mode. This can be achieved by setting $cfg['DefaultPropDisplay'] to 'vertical' or, if we are working with three columns or less, leaving this directive at its default value of 3. We enter the following comments:

- **isbn**: book number
- **page_count**: approximate
- **author_id**: cf author table

This is shown in the following screenshot:

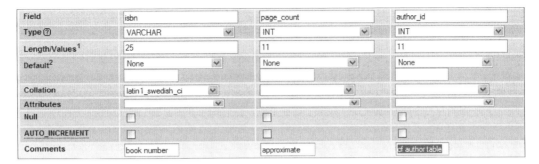

We then click on **Save**.

These comments appear at various places—for example, in the export file (see *Chapter 6, Exporting Structure and Data (Backup)*), on the PDF relational schema (see *Chapter 15, Documenting the System*), and in browse mode, as shown here:

If we do not want the comments to appear in browse mode, we can set `$cfg['ShowBrowseComments']` to FALSE. (It's TRUE by default.)

Column comments also appear as a tool tip in the **Structure** page, and column names are underlined with dashes. To deactivate this behavior, we can set `$cfg['ShowPropertyComments']` to FALSE. (This one is also TRUE by default.)

Automatically migrating column comments

Whenever phpMyAdmin detects that column comments have been stored in its metadata, it automatically migrates these column comments to the native MySQL column comments.

Summary

This chapter covered how to install the necessary infrastructure for keeping special metadata (data about tables), and how to define relations between both InnoDB and non-InnoDB tables. It also examined the modified behavior of phpMyAdmin (when relations are present) and foreign keys. Finally, it covered the Designer feature, column-commenting, and how to obtain information from a table.

The next chapter will cover the means of entering SQL commands, which are useful when the phpMyAdmin's interface is not sufficient to accomplish what we need.

11
Entering SQL Commands

This chapter explains how we can enter our own SQL commands (queries) into phpMyAdmin, and how we can keep a history of these queries.

The SQL query box

phpMyAdmin allows us to accomplish many database operations via its graphical interface. However, there will be times when we have to rely on SQL query input to achieve operations that are not directly supported by the interface. Here are two examples of such queries:

```
SELECT department, AVG(salary) FROM employees GROUP BY department
HAVING years_experience > 10;

SELECT FROM_DAYS(TO_DAYS(CURDATE()) +30);
```

To enter such queries, the SQL query box is available from a number of places within phpMyAdmin.

The Database view

We encounter our first SQL query box when going to the **SQL** menu available in the Database view.

This box is simple—we type in a valid (hopefully) MySQL statement and click on **Go**. Under the query text area, there are bookmark-related choices (explained later in *Chapter 14, Using Bookmarks*). Usually, we don't have to change the standard SQL delimiter, which is a semicolon. However, there is a **Delimiter** dialog in case we need it (see *Chapter 17, Supporting MySQL 5.0 and 5.1*).

For a default query to appear in this box, we can set it with the `$cfg['DefaultQueryDatabase']` configuration directive, which is empty by default. We could enter a query like SHOW TABLES FROM %d in this directive. The %d parameter in this query would be replaced by the current database name, resulting in SHOW TABLES FROM `marc_book` in the query box.

The Table view

A slightly different box is available in the Table view of the book table from the **SQL** menu.

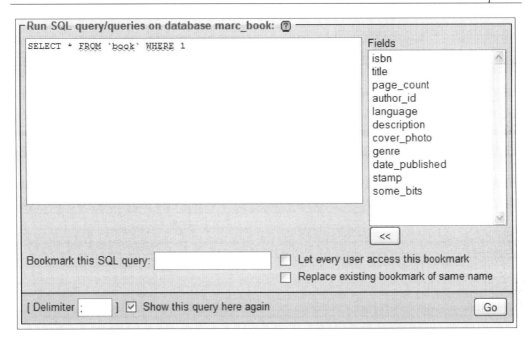

There is a **Fields** selector and an **Insert** button (<<) on the right. The box already has a default query, as seen in the previous screenshot.

This default query is generated from the `$cfg['DefaultQueryTable']` configuration directive, which contains SELECT * FROM %t WHERE 1. Here, the %t is replaced by the current table name. Another placeholder available in `$cfg['DefaultQueryTable']` is %f. This placeholder would be replaced by the complete field list of this table, thus producing the following query:

```
SELECT `isbn`, `title`, `page_count`, `author_id`, `language`,
`description`, `cover_photo`, `genre`, `date_published`, `stamp`,
`some_bits` FROM `book` WHERE 1
```

WHERE 1 is a condition that is always true. Therefore, the query can be executed as it is. We can replace **1** with the condition we want, or we can enter a completely different query.

The Fields selector

The **Fields** selector is a way to speed up query generation. By choosing a field and clicking on the arrows, <<, this field name is copied to the current cursor position in the query box. Here, we select the **author_id** field, remove the digit **1**, and click on <<. Then we add the condition = 2.

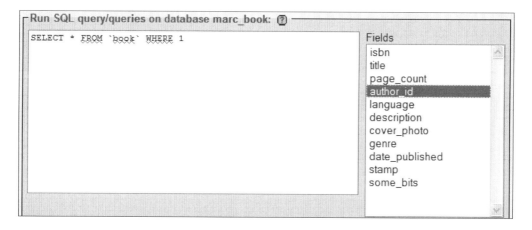

The **Show this query here again** option (checked by default) ensures that the query stays in the box after its execution if we are still on the same page. This can be seen more easily for a query like an UPDATE or DELETE, which affects a table but does not produce a separate results page.

Clicking into the query box

We might want to change the behavior of a click inside the query box with the $cfg['TextareaAutoSelect'] configuration directive. Its default value is FALSE, which means that no automatic selection of the contents is done upon a click. Should you change this directive to TRUE, the first click inside this box will select all of its contents. (This is a way to quickly copy the contents elsewhere, or delete them from the box.) The next click would put the cursor at the click position.

The Query window

In *Chapter 3, Over Viewing the Interface*, we discussed the purpose of the Query window, and the procedure for changing some parameters (like dimensions). This window can easily be opened from the navigation panel using the **SQL** icon or the **Query window** link, and is very convenient for entering a query and testing it.

The following screenshot shows the Query window that appears over the main panel:

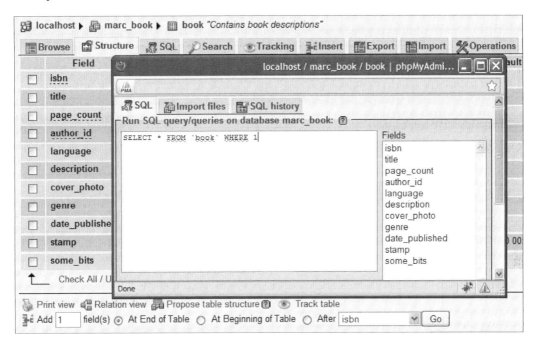

The window seen in the previous screenshot contains the same **Fields** selector and << button as that used in a Table view context. This distinct Query window is a feature supported only on JavaScript-enabled browsers.

Query window options

The **SQL** tab is the default active tab in this window. This comes from the configuration directive $cfg['QueryWindowDefTab'], which contains sql by default.

If we want another tab to be the default active tab, we can replace sql with files or history. Another value, full, shows the contents of all three tabs at once.

In the Query window, we see a checkbox for the **Do not overwrite this query from outside the window** choice. Normally, this is not checked. The changes we make while generating queries are reflected in the Query window. This is called **synchronization**. For example, choosing a different database or table from the navigation or main panel would update the Query window accordingly. However, if we start to type a query directly in this window, the checkbox will be selected in order to protect its contents and remove synchronization. This way, the query composed here will be locked and protected.

Session-based SQL history

The SQL history feature collects all of the successful SQL queries we execute, as PHP session data, and modifies the Query window to make them available. This default type of history is temporary, as $cfg['QueryHistoryDB'] is set to FALSE by default.

Database-based SQL history (permanent)

As we installed the linked-tables infrastructure (see *Chapter 10, Benefiting from the Relational System*), a more powerful history mechanism is available. We can enable this mechanism by setting $cfg['QueryHistoryDB'] to TRUE.

After we try some queries from one of the query boxes, a history is built, visible only from the Query window.

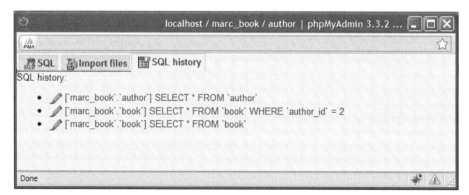

We see (in the reverse order) the last successful queries and the database on which they were made. Queries typed in the query box are kept in this history, along with queries generated by phpMyAdmin (such as those generated by clicking on **Browse**).

These queries are clickable for immediate execution, and the **Edit** icon is available to insert a recorded query into the query box for editing.

The number of queries that will be kept is controlled by $cfg['QueryHistoryMax'], which is set to 25 by default. This limit is not kept for performance reasons, but as a practical limit in order to achieve a visually unencumbered view. Extra queries are eliminated at login time in a process traditionally called **garbage collection**. The queries are stored in the table configured in $cfg['Servers'][$i]['history'].

Editing queries in the query window

On the results page of a successful query, a header containing the executed query appears, as shown in the following screenshot:

Clicking on **Edit** opens the Query window's **SQL** tab, with this query ready to be modified. This happens because of the following default setting for this parameter:

```
$cfg['EditInWindow'] = TRUE;
```

If this parameter is set to FALSE, then a click on **Edit** will not open the Query window; instead, the query will appear inside the query box of the **SQL** subpage.

Multi-statement queries

In PHP and MySQL programming, we can send only one query at a time using the `mysql_query()` function call. phpMyAdmin allows us to send many queries in one transmission, using a semicolon as a separator. Suppose we type the following query in the query box:

```
INSERT INTO author VALUES (100,'Paul Smith','111-2222');
INSERT INTO author VALUES (101,'Melanie Smith','222-3333');
UPDATE author SET phone='444-5555' WHERE name LIKE '%Smith%';
```

We will receive the following results screen:

```
✓   Your SQL query has been executed successfully
INSERT INTO author
VALUES ( 100, 'Paul Smith', '111-2222' ) ;# 1 row(s) affected.
INSERT INTO author
VALUES ( 101, 'Melanie Smith', '222-3333' ) ;# 1 row(s) affected.
UPDATE author SET phone = '444-5555' WHERE name LIKE '%Smith%';# 4 row(s) affected.
                                                    [ Edit ] [ Create PHP Code ]
```

We see the number of affected rows in comments because `$cfg['VerboseMultiSubmit']` is set to TRUE.

Let's send the same list of queries again, and watch the results:

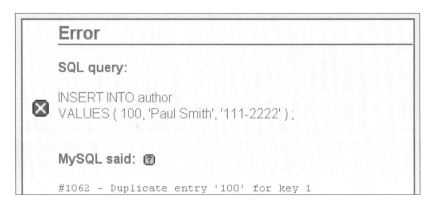

It's normal to receive a **Duplicate entry** error that says the value **100** exists already. We are seeing the results of the first **INSERT** statement; but what happens to the next one? Execution stops at the first error because `$cfg['IgnoreMultiSubmitErrors']` is set to FALSE telling phpMyAdmin not to ignore errors in multiple statements. If it's set to TRUE, the program successively tries all of the statements, and we see two **Duplicate entry** errors.

This feature would not work as expected if we tried more than one SELECT statement. We would see the results of only the last SELECT statement.

Pretty printing (syntax-highlighting)

By default, phpMyAdmin parses and highlights the various elements of any MySQL statement it processes. This is controlled by $cfg['SQP']['fmtType'], which is set to 'html' by default. This mode uses a specific color for each different element (a reserved word, a variable, a comment, and so on), as described in the $cfg['SQP'] ['fmtColor'] array located in the theme-specific layout.inc.php file.

In the previous examples, fmtType was set to 'text' because this mode is more legible in a book. This mode inserts line breaks at logical points inside a MySQL statement, but there is no color used. With fmtType set to 'html', phpMyAdmin would report the SQL statements with syntax highlighting. However, setting fmtType to 'none' removes all formatting, leaving our syntax intact.

> The multi-dimensional arrays used for holding some parameters in the configuration file reflect a programming style adopted by the phpMyAdmin development team. This ensures that parameter names are not very long.

The SQL Validator

Each time phpMyAdmin transmits a query, the MySQL server interprets it and provides feedback. The syntax of the query must follow MySQL rules, which are not the same as the SQL standard. However, conforming to the SQL standard ensures that our queries are usable on other SQL implementations.

A free external service, the Mimer SQL Validator, is available to us, thanks to Mimer Information Technology AB. This validates our query according to the Core SQL-99 rules, and generates a report. The Validator is available directly from phpMyAdmin, and its home page is located at http://developer.mimer.com/validator/index. htm.

> For statistical purposes, this service anonymously stores on its server the queries that it receives. When storing the queries, it replaces database, table, and column names with generic names. Strings and numbers that are part of the query are replaced with generic values so as to protect the original information.

System requirements

This Validator is available as a SOAP service. Our PHP server must have XML, PCRE, and PEAR support. We need some PEAR modules too. The following command (executed on the server by the system administrator) installs the modules we need:

```
pear install Net_Socket Net_URL HTTP_Request Mail_Mime Net_DIME SOAP
```

If we have problems with this command, due to some of the modules being in a beta state, we can execute the following command, which installs SOAP and other dependent modules:

```
pear -d preferred_state=beta install -a SOAP
```

Making the Validator available

Some parameters must be configured in `config.inc.php`. Setting `$cfg['SQLQuery']['Validate']` to TRUE enables the **Validate SQL** link.

We should also enable the Validator itself (as other validators might be available on future phpMyAdmin versions). This is done by setting `$cfg['SQLValidator']['use']` to TRUE.

The Validator is accessed with an anonymous Validator account by default, as configured using the following commands:

```
$cfg['SQLValidator']['username'] = '';
$cfg['SQLValidator']['password'] = '';
```

Instead, if Mimer Information Technology has provided us with an account, we can use that account information here.

Validator results

There are two kinds of reports returned by the Validator—one if the query conforms to the standard, and the other if it does not conform.

Standard-conforming queries

We will try a simple query: SELECT COUNT(*) FROM book. As usual, we enter this query in the query box and send it. On the results page, we now see an additional link—**Validate SQL**.

```
✔ Your SQL query has been executed successfully
SELECT COUNT( * )
FROM book
    ☐ Profiling [ Edit ] [ Explain SQL ] [ Create PHP Code ] [ Refresh ] [ Validate SQL ]
```

Clicking on **Validate SQL** produces the following report:

```
ⓘ Validate SQL
Conforms to Core SQL-99
SQL queries stored anonymously for statistical purposes.
    ☐ Profiling [ Edit ] [ Explain SQL ] [ Create PHP Code ] [ Refresh ] [ Skip Validate SQL ]
```

We have the option of clicking **Skip Validate SQL** to see our original query.

Non-standard-conforming queries

Let's try another query, which works correctly in MySQL: SELECT * FROM book WHERE
language = 'en'. Sending it to the Validator produces the following report:

```
┌SQL query:─────────────────────────────────────────────────
SELECT * FROM book WHERE {error: 1}language = 'en'
{error: 2}LIMIT 0, 30

Errors:

    1. syntax error: language
        expected: ( + - : ? <ascii identifier> <character set identifier>
            <decimal literal> <delimited identifier> <float literal>
            <hex string literal> <identifier> <integer literal>
            <national string literal> <string literal> ANY ARRAY CASE CAST
            CURRENT_DATE CURRENT_DEFAULT_TRANSFORM_GROUP CURRENT_PATH
            CURRENT_ROLE CURRENT_TIME CURRENT_TIMESTAMP
            CURRENT_TRANSFORM_GROUP_FOR_TYPE CURRENT_USER DATE DEREF EXISTS
            FALSE GROUPING INTERVAL LOCALTIME LOCALTIMESTAMP MODULE NEW NOT
            REPEAT ROW SESSION_USER SOME SYSTEM_USER TIME TIMESTAMP TREAT
            TRUE UNIQUE UNKNOWN USER VALUE
        correction: <identifier>
    2. syntax error: LIMIT 0 , 30 <end>
        expected: <end> * + - -> / ; [ || <string literal> AND AT COLLATE DAY
            EXCEPT FOR GROUP HAVING HOUR INTERSECT MINUTE MONTH OR ORDER
            SECOND UNION WINDOW YEAR . IS
        correction: <end>

SQL queries stored anonymously for statistical purposes.
                ☐ Profiling [ Edit ] [ Explain SQL ] [ Create PHP Code ] [ Refresh ] [ Skip Validate SQL ]
```

Each time the Validator finds a problem, it inserts a message, such as {error: 1}, at the point of the error, and adds a footnote to the report. In the example above, the **language** column name is non-standard. Hence, the Validator tells us that it was expecting an identifier at this point. Another non-standard error is reported about the use of a LIMIT clause, which was added to the query by phpMyAdmin.

Another case is that of the backquotes. If we just click on **Browse** for the book table, phpMyAdmin generates SELECT * FROM `book`, enclosing the table name with backquotes. This is MySQL's way of protecting identifiers, which might contain special characters, such as spaces, international characters, or reserved words. However, sending this query to the Validator shows us that the backquotes do not conform to standard SQL. We may even get two errors, one for each backquote.

Summary

This chapter helped us understand the purpose of query boxes and showed us where to find them. It also gave an overview of the Query window options, multi-statement queries, how to use the field selector, how to use the SQL Validator, and finally, how to get a history of typed commands.

The next chapter will explain how to produce multi-table queries without typing much, thanks to phpMyAdmin's query generator.

12

Generating Multi-table Queries

The **Search** pages in the Database or Table view are intended for single-table lookups. This chapter covers the multi-table **Query by example (QBE)** feature available in the Database view.

Many phpMyAdmin users work in the Table view, table by table, and thus tend to overlook the multi-table query generator, which is a wonderful feature for fine-tuning queries. The query generator is useful not only in multi-table situations but also in single table situations. It enables us to specify multiple criteria for a column, a feature that the **Search** page in the Table view does not possess.

 The examples in this chapter assume that a multi-user installation of the linked-tables infrastructure has been made (see *Chapter 10, Benefiting from the Relational System*), and that the book-copy table created during an exercise in *Chapter 9, Performing Table and Database Operations*, is still there in the marc_book database.

To open the page for this feature, we go to the Database view for a specific database (the query generator supports working on only one database at a time) and click on **Query**.

The next screenshot overleaf shows the initial QBE page. It contains the following elements:

- Criteria columns
- An interface to add criteria rows
- An interface to add criteria columns

- A table selector
- The query area
- Buttons to update or execute the query

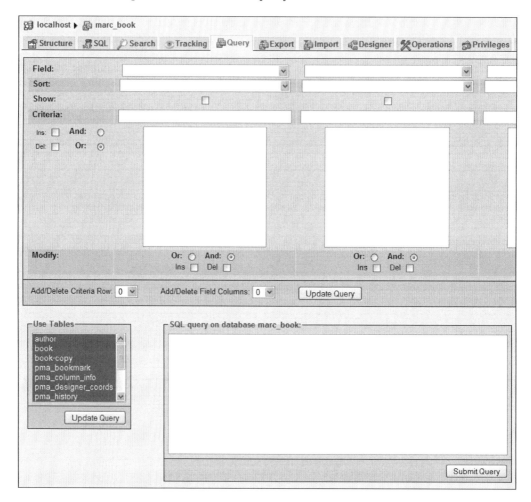

Choosing tables

The initial selection includes all tables in the database. In this example, we assume that the linked-table infrastructure has been installed in the **marc_book** database. (See the section *Installing for a single user* in *Chapter 10, Benefiting from the Relational System*.) Consequently, the **Field** selector contains a great number of fields. For our example, we will work only with the **author** and **book** tables. Hence, we select only these from the **Use Tables** selector.

We then click on **Update Query**. This refreshes the screen and reduces the number of fields available in the **Field** selector. We can always change the selected tables later, using our browser's mechanism for multiple choices in drop-down menus (usually *Ctrl* + click).

Exploring column criteria

Three criteria columns are provided by default. This section discusses the options we have for editing their criteria. These include options for selecting fields, sorting individual columns, entering conditions for individual columns, and so on.

Field selector: Single-column or all columns

The **Field** selector contains all of the individual columns for the selected tables, plus a special choice ending with an asterisk (*) for each table, which means that all of the fields in the table are selected.

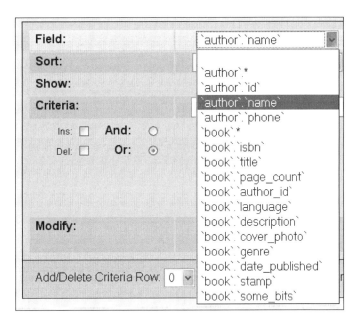

To display all of the fields in the `author` table, we would choose **`author`.*** and select the **Show** checkbox, without entering anything in the **Sort** and the **Criteria** boxes. In our case, we select **`author`.`name`**, as we want to enter some criteria for the author's name.

Sorting columns

For each selected individual column, we can specify a sort (in **Ascending** or **Descending** order), or let this line remain intact (no sorting, which is the default behavior). If we choose more than one sorted column, the sorting will be carried out from left to right.

> When we ask for a column to be sorted, we normally select the **Show** checkbox. However this is not necessary, as we might want to perform just the sorting operation without displaying this column.

Showing a column

We select the **Show** checkbox so that we can see the column in the results. Sometimes we may just want to apply a criterion on a column and not include it in the resulting page. Here, we add the `phone` column, ask for it to be sorted, and choose to show both the name and the phone number. We also choose to sort on the name in ascending order. The sort will be done first by name and then by the phone number, if the names are identical. This is because the name is in a column to the left of the phone column, and thus has a higher priority.

Updating the query

At any point, we can click on the **Update Query** button to see the progress of our generated query. We have to click it at least once before executing the query. For now, let's click it and see the query that is generated in the query area. In the following examples, we will click **Update Query** after each modification:

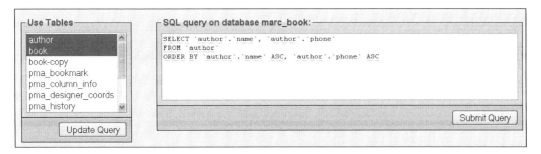

We have selected two tables, but have not yet chosen any column from the **book** table. Hence, this table is not mentioned in the generated query.

Adding conditions to the criteria box

In the **Criteria** box, we can enter a condition (respecting the SQL WHERE clause's syntax) for each of the corresponding columns. By default, we have two criteria rows. To find all of the authors with **Smith** in their names, we use a **LIKE** criterion (LIKE '%SMITH%'), and then click on **Update Query**:

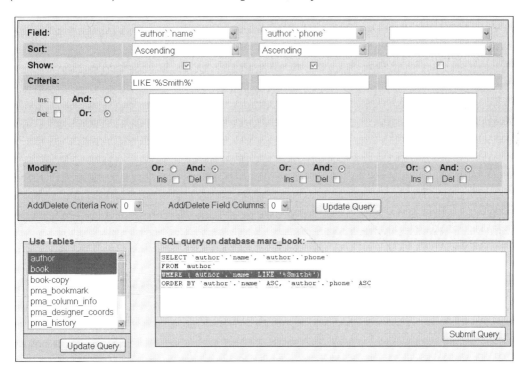

We have another line available, in which we can enter an additional criterion. Let's say we want to find the author **Maria Sunshine** as well. This time, we use an = condition. The two condition rows will be joined by the OR operator, selected by default from the leftmost side of the interface:

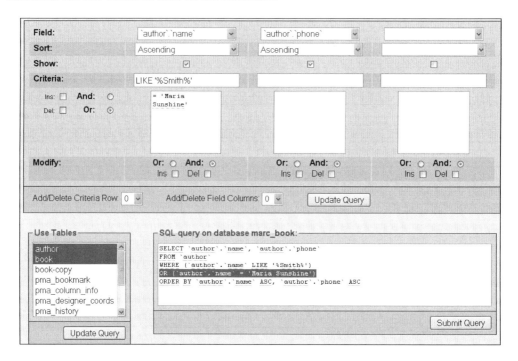

To demonstrate that the OR operator links both the criteria rows better, let's now add a condition, LIKE '%8%', on the phone number:

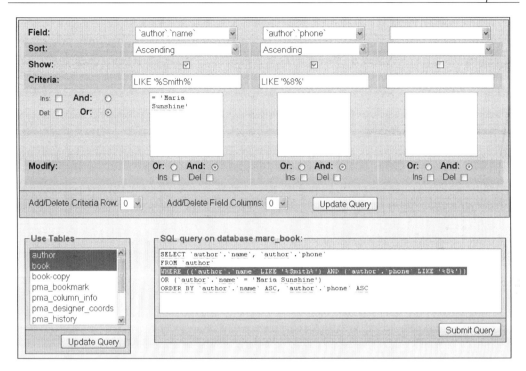

By examining the positioning of the AND and OR operators, we can see that the first row of the conditions is linked by the AND (because AND is chosen under the **name** column) operator, and the second row of conditions is linked to the rest by the OR operator. The condition that we've just added (**LIKE '%8%'**) is not meant to find anyone, because we changed the phone number of all of the authors with the name "Smith" to "444-5555" (in *Chapter 11*, *Entering SQL Commands*).

If we want another criterion on the same column, we just add a criteria row.

Adjusting the number of criteria rows

The number of criteria rows can be changed in two ways. First, we can select the **Ins** checkbox under **Criteria** to add one criteria row (after clicking on **Update Query**). As this checkbox can add only one criteria row at a time, we'll deselect it and use the **Add/Delete Criteria Row** dialog instead. In this dialog, we choose to add two rows.

Another click on the **Update Query** button produces the following screen:

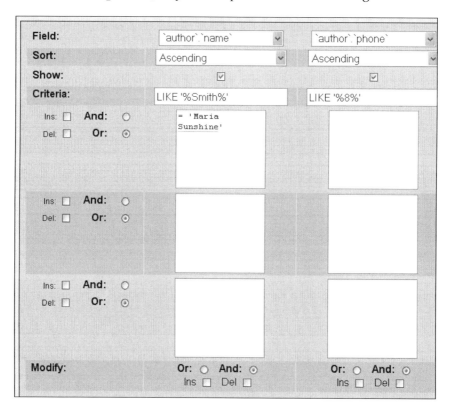

You can see that there are now two additional criteria rows (which are initially empty). We can also remove criteria rows. This can be done by choosing negative numbers in the **Add/Delete Criteria Row** dialog, or by selecting the **Del** checkbox next to the row(s) we want to remove. Let's remove the two rows we've just added, as we don't need them now. The **Update Query** button refreshes the page with the specified adjustment.

Adjusting the number of criteria columns

Using a similar mechanism, we can add or delete columns by selecting the **INS** or **Del** checkboxes under each column, or the **Add/Delete Field Columns** dialog. We already had one unused column (not shown in the previous images, in order to save space). Here, we have added one column using the **Ins** checkbox located under the unused column (this time, we will need it):

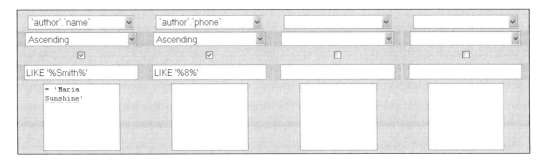

Generating automatic joins

phpMyAdmin can generate the joins between the tables in the query it builds. Let's now populate our two unused columns with the `title` and the `genre` fields from our **book** table, and see what happens when we update the query:

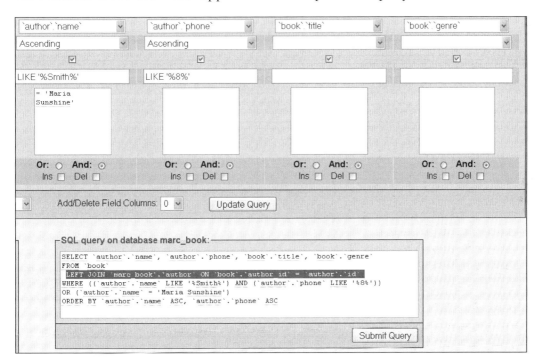

There are now two additional criteria columns, which relate to the `**book**`.`**title**` and the `**book**`.`**genre**` columns respectively. phpMyAdmin used its knowledge of the relations defined between the tables to generate a LEFT JOIN clause (highlighted in the previous screenshot) on the **author_id** key field. A shortcoming of the current version is that only the internal relations, and not the InnoDB relations, are examined.

 There may be more than two tables involved in a join.

Executing the query

Clicking on the **Submit Query** button sends the query for execution. In the following figure, you can see the complete generated query in the upper part of the screen, and the resulting data row in the lower part:

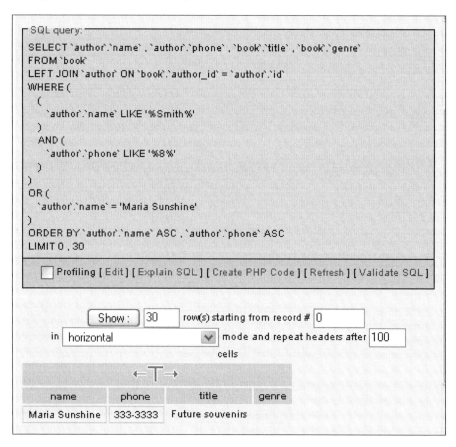

There is no easy way (except by using the browser's **Back** button) to come back to the query generation page once we have submitted the query. *Chapter 14, Using Bookmarks*, discusses how to save the generated query for later execution.

Summary

This chapter covered various aspects of query generation, including opening the query generator, choosing tables, entering column criteria, sorting and showing columns, and altering the number of criteria rows or columns. It also showed us how to use the AND and OR operators to define relations between the rows and columns, and how to use automatic joins between tables.

The next chapter will show you how to synchronize data between servers, and how to manage replication.

13
Synchronizing Data and Supporting Replication

In this chapter, we cover two features that were released in phpMyAdmin 3.3.0. The first feature is the ability to synchronize databases and was asked for by developers who work on more than one server. The second feature permits the management of MySQL replication, which is used in environments where performance and data security are important. These features are somewhat related because we usually need to synchronize the database to a slave server when setting it up in a replication process.

Synchronizing data and structure

In earlier phpMyAdmin versions, it was possible to achieve some synchronization of the structure and data between two databases on the same server or on different servers, but this required manual operations. It was (and still is) possible to export structure and/or data from one database and import in another one. We can even visually compare the structure of two tables and adjust them according to our needs. However, comparing the two databases to ascertain what needs to be imported had to be done with the developer's own eyeballs. Moreover, differences in structure between the databases were not taken into account, possibly resulting in errors when a column was missing in the target table.

The Synchronize feature of phpMyAdmin 3.3 permits much flexibility, by taking care of the initial comparison process and, of course, by performing the synchronization itself. We will first discuss the reasons for synchronizing, and then examine and experiment with all of the steps involved.

 The minimum phpMyAdmin version recommended in order to use the Synchronize feature is version 3.3.4.

Goals of synchronization

Although the reasons for wanting to synchronize two databases may be many, we can group them into the following categories.

Moving between the development and production servers

A sound database development strategy includes performing development and testing on a server that is distinct from the production one. If having a separate development server is not an option, having at least a distinct development database is encouraged. Over time, differences in structure between test and production environments build up, and this is normal. For example, a column may be added in the test version, or character field enlarged. The Synchronize feature permits us to first see the differences and then apply them to production if they make sense.

Moving data sometimes needs to be done the other way around, for example to populate a test database with real production data in order to measure performance.

Collaboration between database designers

Due to the easy manner in which a MySQL test server can be put in place, the situation might arise where each member of a development team has his own server (or his own copy of the database) in which he develops some aspect of a project. When the time comes to reconcile everyone's changes for the same table, the Synchronize feature is invaluable.

Preparing for replication

MySQL supports asynchronous replication between a master server and one or many slave servers. This data replication is termed *asynchronous* because the connection between master and slaves does not need to be permanent. However, to put a replication process in action (and assuming that the master already contains some data), one needs to copy all of the data over to the slaves. A suggestion to accomplish this copy is given in the MySQL manual at `http://dev.mysql.com/doc/refman/5.1/en/replication-howto.html`:

> *If you already have data on your master and you want to use it to synchronize your slave, you will need to create a data snapshot. You can create a snapshot using mysqldump (...)*

However, this requires using a command-line tool, which is not always possible depending on the hosting options. Besides, some parts of the database may already exist on the slave; therefore, the Synchronize feature comes in handy because it's integrated into phpMyAdmin, and because it takes care of the comparison phase.

Over viewing the synchronization process

The initial Synchronize page is displayed via the **Synchronize** menu tab in Server view. Please note that this is the only place where this menu is available.

An important principle to understand is that synchronization is done from a source database to a target database. During this operation, the source database remains unchanged. It's up to us to correctly identify which database is the source and which one is the target (and will be possibly modified).

The whole process is subdivided into steps which can be stopped at any stage:

1. Server and database choice
2. Comparison
3. Full or selective synchronization

We could elect to stop the process for one of the following reasons:

- We don't have the necessary credentials to connect to one of the servers
- We see discrepancies between two databases and are not ready to synchronize because further research needs to be done
- We notice after the comparison phase that the target database is adequately synchronized

Before performing a synchronization, we'll put the necessary elements in place.

Preparing for the synchronization exercise

Because we'll play with only the `author` and `book` tables, this exercise will assume that there are no other tables in the `marc_book` database. Presently there might be some tables prefixed with `pma_`, but we can safely remove them if they are not the active ones, as defined in *Chapter 10, Benefiting from the Relational System*. We start by copying the `marc_book` database to `marc_book_dev` (see *Chapter 9, Performing Table and Database Operations*, for the exact method for doing this).Then we open the `marc_book_dev` database and perform the following actions (*Chapter 5, Changing Data and Structure*, describes how to achieve these):

- Delete the `book` table
- Delete one row of the `author` table
- Change the type of the `name` column from `VARCHAR(30)` to `VARCHAR(29)`
- Delete the `phone` column from the `author` table

Choosing source and target servers and databases

The first panel permits us to connect to servers (if needed) and to pick the correct database, as depicted in the following image:

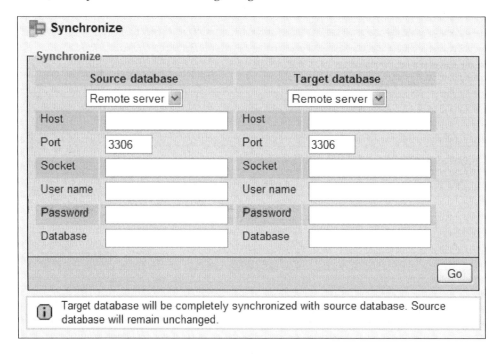

For each database—both source and target—we can select the server location. By default, the selector is placed on **remote server** and we can enter its hostname, port, socket name, and a username, password, and database name. In most cases, the port should be left to the default 3306 and the socket name should be left empty. Notice that we are currently connected to a MySQL server (via the normal login panel) and this panel could permit us to connect to two more servers.

Another choice for server location is **current server**. This refers to the server on which we are connected for normal phpMyAdmin operations; its name is displayed at the top of the main panel. Should we choose this, a JavaScript-enabled browser hides all choices except for the database name (connection credentials are unnecessary in this situation) and a selector becomes available, showing all of the databases to which we have access.

It's perfectly possible to pick the same server (current or remote) on both the source and target sides; however we would at least choose a source database different than the target one in this case. Another common case is to pick the current server and some database as the source, and a remote server with the same database as the target, assuming that the remote server is the production one and that both servers hold a database with the same name.

For this exercise, let's pick **current server** for both source and target servers; we can then choose marc_book as the source database and marc_book_dev as the target one, as shown in the following screenshot:

After clicking on **Go**, phpMyAdmin attempts to connect to the servers if needed; at this point, a connection error message may be displayed. However, the connection should hopefully succeed and the program will start comparing both databases and then show us the results, which we'll interpret in the next section.

Analyzing comparison results

The comparison results panel contains three sections. The first section displays the structure and data differences and contains icons that will be used to initiate a selective synchronization:

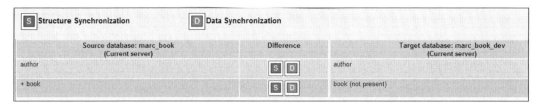

As depicted in the upper part, the red **S** icon triggers structure synchronization, whereas the green **D** icon is for data synchronization. Then, for each table, we get a rundown of the differences. The central **Difference** column would be empty in the case of identical structure and data for the corresponding table. Here we see a red **S** and a green **D** for both tables, but the reason is not the same for each table.

The middle part shows the actions that are scheduled as part of the synchronization process (there are currently none):

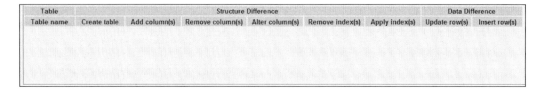

The lower part contains a checkbox (**Would you like to delete all the previous rows from target tables?**), and two action buttons. We will see their purpose in the following sections.

Please note that the book table has a plus sign (+) next to it on the **Source** side, to show that this table is in the source database but not in the target database. We even see a **not present** comment for this table on the **Target** side. If a table was in the target database but not in the source one, it would be marked with a minus sign (-) on the **Target** side.

At this point, we could decide that we are satisfied with the comparison and don't want to proceed further; in this case, we would just have to continue in phpMyAdmin by picking a database and resuming our work. We also have the opportunity of synchronizing the databases in one sweep (complete synchronization) or to make changes in a more granular way (selective synchronization). Let's examine both methods.

Performing a complete synchronization

If we don't want to ask ourselves too many questions and just need a complete synchronization, we click on **Synchronize Databases**. Note that in this case, we don't have to use any red S or green D icons.

If one of the target tables contains some rows that are not present in the corresponding source table, these will remain in the target tables, unless we mark the **Would you like to delete...** option. This is a safety net to avoid unintended loss of data. However, we should select this option if we want an exact synchronization.

After clicking, we obtain the following message: **Target database has been synchronized with source database**. In the lower part of the screen, we see the queries that had to be executed in order to achieve this operation. We also get a visual confirmation that the databases are now synchronized:

Difference	Target database: marc_book_dev (Current server)
	author
	book

Performing a selective synchronization

If we prefer to be more cautious and receive a preliminary feedback on the actions that are about to be done, we can synchronize selected tables. This section assumes that the databases are in the same state as at the end of the *Preparing for the following synchronization exercise* section.

If we click the red S on the line describing the differences for the `author` table, this S icon turns to grey and the middle part of the screen is updated with the actions to be done:

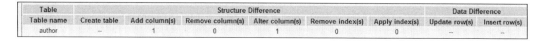

Table			Structure Difference				Data Difference	
Table name	Create table	Add column(s)	Remove column(s)	Alter column(s)	Remove index(s)	Apply index(s)	Update row(s)	Insert row(s)
author	--	1	0	1	0	0	--	--

No real action on the data has been done yet! We still can change our mind by clicking the same icon which would turn red again, removing the proposed changes as depicted in the middle part of the screen.

Now we click the green D and see another line of proposed changes show up:

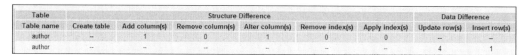

Table			Structure Difference				Data Difference	
Table name	Create table	Add column(s)	Remove column(s)	Alter column(s)	Remove index(s)	Apply index(s)	Update row(s)	Insert row(s)
author	--	1	0	1	0	0	--	--
author	--	--	--	--	--	--	4	1

A row in the `author` table needs to be inserted because there is one less author in the target database. Altogether four rows need to be updated, because we removed the `phone` column in the same table.

We can now click on **Apply Selected Changes**. The **Would you like...** checkbox does not apply to this operation.

We now see that the upper part of the screen proposes fewer changes to make:

We can go on by selecting structure or data changes and then applying them in the order we deem appropriate.

This concludes the section describing the synchronization feature. We continue with coverage of replication support.

Supporting MySQL replication

In the *Preparing for replication* section, we saw an overview of MySQL replication. In this section we cover:

- How we can use phpMyAdmin to configure replication
- How to prepare a test environment containing one master server and two slave servers
- How to send commands to control the servers
- How to obtain information on replication for servers, databases, and tables

phpMyAdmin's interface offers a **Replication** page; however, other pages contain either information about replication or links to control replication actions. We will point to each appropriate location when covering the related subject.

How to use this section depends on how many servers we have at our disposition. If we have at least two servers and want to configure them via phpMyAdmin in a master/slave relationship, we can follow the *Configuring replication* section. If instead we only have one server to play with, then we should take advice from the *Setting up a test environment* section and install many instances of the MySQL server on the same machine.

The Replication menu

In Server view, the **Replication** menu is only shown to privileged users, such as the MySQL root user. When a server is already configured as a master server or a slave server (or both), the replication page is used to display status information and provide links that send commands.

Configuring replication

For this exercise, we assume that the server does not currently occupy the role of master or slave server. phpMyAdmin cannot directly configure all aspects of MySQL replication. The reason is that, contrary to manipulating database structure and data by sending queries to the MySQL server, replication configuration consists (in part) of command lines stored in a MySQL configuration file, often named my.cnf. phpMyAdmin, being a web application, does not have access to this file. This is how the MySQL server's developers intended the configuration to be: at a configuration file level.

The best that phpMyAdmin can do in this situation is to guide us by generating (on screen) the proper command lines in reaction to our preferences; then it's up to us to copy these lines where they need to go and to restart the server(s). phpMyAdmin cannot even read the current replication configuration lines; it can only deduce server status via some SHOW commands.

Let's enter the **Replication** menu and see what happens:

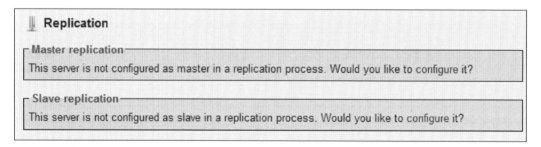

Master server configuration

Now we choose to configure the server as a master by clicking on the appropriate **configure** link. The panel that appears gives us thorough advice:

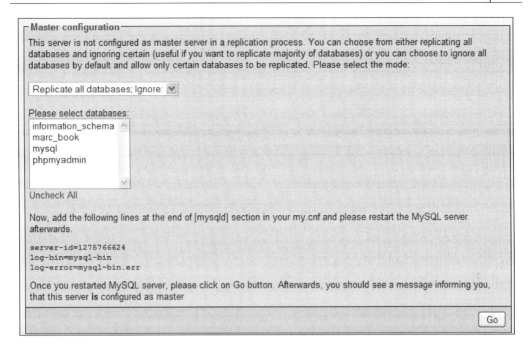

The first paragraph confirms that this server is not configured as a master in a replication process. We want to achieve this configuration, but first we need to think about the kind of replication we want. Should all databases be replicated, except for a few of them? Or do we want the opposite? A convenient drop-down list offers us these choices:

- **Replicate all databases; ignore:**
- **Ignore all databases; replicate:**

The first choice (which is the default) implies that, in general, all databases are replicated; we don't even have to enumerate them in the configuration file. In this case, the databases selector is used to specify which database we want to exclude from the replication process. Let's pick up the `mysql` database and see what happens in our JavaScript-enabled browser:

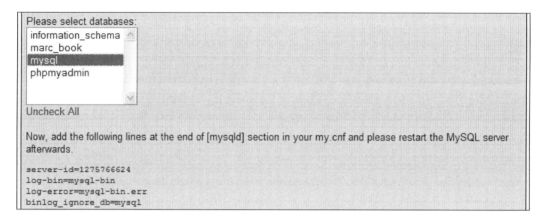

We notice that a line has appeared, stating `binlog_ignore_db=mysql`. This is a MySQL server instruction (not a SQL command) that tells the server to ignore sending transactions about this database, to the binary log. Let's examine the meaning of the other lines. The `server-id` is a unique ID generated by phpMyAdmin; each server that participates in replication must have a unique server ID. Therefore, we either track the server IDs by hand, ensuring their uniqueness, or we simply use the number randomly generated by phpMyAdmin. We also see the `log-bin` and `log-error` instructions; in fact, binary logging is mandatory in order for any replication to occur.

We could add other database names to the list by using *Ctrl*-click or *Command*-click, depending on our workstation's OS. However, all that phpMyAdmin does is to generate syntaxically-valid lines; to make them operational, we still need to follow the given advice and paste these lines at the end of the `[mysqld]` section of our MySQL configuration file. We should then restart the MySQL server process; the way to do this depends on our environment.

After our server has been restarted, we go back to the Replication menu; at this point, we see a different panel regarding the master:

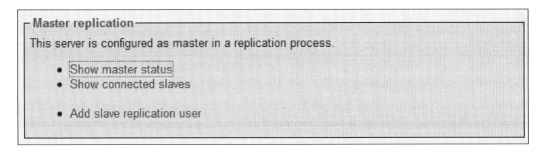

We can use the **Show master status** link to get some information about the master, including the current binary log name and position, and information on which databases to replicate or to ignore, as specified previously.

Show connected slaves would report nothing currently, as no slave is yet connected to this master.

Now would be the time to use **Add slave replication user**, because this master needs to have a separate account dedicated to replication. The slaves will use this account created on the master to connect to it. Clicking on this link displays the following panel, in which a sample user, name, **replic**, is being created:

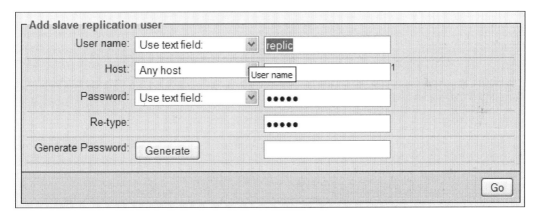

After clicking on **Go**, phpMyAdmin takes care of creating this user with the correct permissions set.

Slave server configuration

Now, on the machine that will act as a slave server in the replication process, we start phpMyAdmin. In the **Replication** menu, we click on **configure** in the following dialog:

```
This server is not configured as slave in a replication process. Would
you like to configure it?
```

The slave server configuration panel appears:

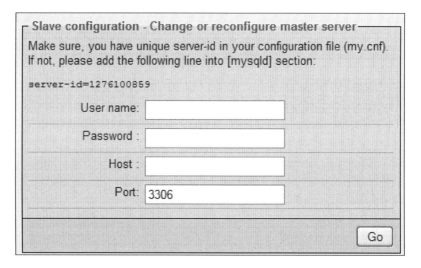

As with the master configuration, we get a suggestion about having a unique server-ID in the configuration file for the slave, and we should follow this advice.

In this panel, we enter the username and password of the dedicated replication account we created on the master. We also have to indicate the hostname and port number corresponding to the master server. After filling this panel and clicking on **Go**, phpMyAdmin sends the appropriate CHANGE MASTER command to the slave, which puts this server in slave mode.

Setting up a test environment

The replication process occurs among at least two instances of the MySQL server. In production, this normally implies a minimum of two physical servers to procure the following benefits:

- Better performance
- Increased redundancy

However, due to MySQL's configurable port number (the default being 3306), data directory, and socket, it's possible to have more than one MySQL instance on the same server. This setup can be configured manually, or via an installation system like the MySQL Sandbox. This is an open source project located at `http://mysqlsandbox.net`. With this tool, we can set up one or many MySQL servers very quickly. By using the powerful `make_replication_sandbox` command, we can install an environment that consists of one master server and two slave servers. Every server can be started or stopped individually.

The following exercises assume that the MySQL Sandbox has been installed on your server and that phpMyAdmin's `config.inc.php` contains a reference to these sandbox servers, as shown in the following code segment (please adjust the socket names to your own environment):

```
$i++;
$cfg['Servers'][$i]['auth_type'] = 'cookie';
$cfg['Servers'][$i]['host'] = 'localhost';
$cfg['Servers'][$i]['socket'] = '/tmp/mysql_sandbox25562.sock';
$cfg['Servers'][$i]['verbose'] = 'master';

$i++;
$cfg['Servers'][$i]['auth_type'] = 'cookie';
$cfg['Servers'][$i]['host'] = 'localhost';
$cfg['Servers'][$i]['socket'] = '/tmp/mysql_sandbox25563.sock';
$cfg['Servers'][$i]['verbose'] = 'slave1';

$i++;
$cfg['Servers'][$i]['auth_type'] = 'cookie';
$cfg['Servers'][$i]['host'] = 'localhost';
$cfg['Servers'][$i]['socket'] = '/tmp/mysql_sandbox25564.sock';
$cfg['Servers'][$i]['verbose'] = 'slave2';
```

Here, we use the `$cfg['Servers'][$i]['verbose']` directive to give a unique name to each instance, as the real server name is `localhost` for all of these instances. Each sandbox server initially contains two databases: `mysql` and `test`.

Controlling a slave server

Here we will assume that the sandbox testing environment has been set. However, the explanations are useful for all situations in which we have a slave server. After connecting to a slave and once again opening the **Replication** menu we see:

```
┌─ Slave replication ─────────────────────────────────────────────────────┐
│ Server is configured as slave in a replication process. Would you like to:│
│                                                                            │
│    • See slave status table                                               │
│    • Control slave:                                                        │
│    • Error management:                                                     │
│    • Change or reconfigure master server                                   │
│                                                                            │
└────────────────────────────────────────────────────────────────────────────┘
```

See slave status table permits us to receive information about all the system variables related to replication for this slave server.

The **Control slave** link reveals more options; some of them can toggle between the stop and start condition:

- **Full stop,** which is used to stop both the IO thread (the part of the MySQL server responsible for receiving updates from the master and writing them to the slave's relay log) and the SQL thread (which reads the updates from the relay log and executes them)

- **Reset slave**, which stops the slave, sends a RESET SLAVE command that causes it to forget its replication position in the master's binary log, and then restarts the slave

- **SQL Thread Stop only** and **IO Thread Stop only** are used to stop only one of these threads

The **Error management** link permits to tell the slave server to skip some of the events (updates) sent from the master. For more details, please visit http://dev.mysql.com/doc/refman/5.1/en/set-global-sql-slave-skip-counter.html.

Finally, **Change or reconfigure master server** could be used to specify that this slave server should now receive updates from a different master.

Obtaining replication information

Apart from the Replication menu, other screens in phpMyAdmin inform us about replication-related items.

Gathering replication status

By entering the **Status** panel in Server view, we first get a brief message, for example:

```
This MySQL server works as master in replication process. For further
information about replication status on the server, please visit the
replication section.
```

There are a few **Replication** links on this page that show us the status variables of either the master or slave servers, and some links to get information about how many slave hosts are connected and the status of replication in general.

Replicated databases

On the master server, having a look at the **Databases** menu in Server view shows us that each database can potentially be replicated, with a green checkmark in the **Master replication** column:

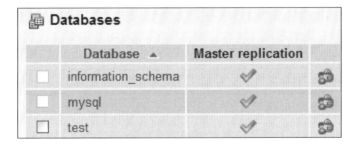

This is because this server is configured with a binary log and these databases are not excluded from replication.

If we had, in the master's configuration file, the following line in the [mysqld] section:

```
binlog_ignore_db=test
```

Then we would exclude from the binary log all transactions that affect the `test` database. Therefore, the output of the **Databases** menu would show a red icon next to the `test` database:

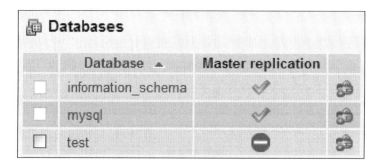

If this is a slave server, a **Server replication** column is shown.

Note that a slave server can itself have a binary log; therefore, in this case both **Master replication** and **Slave replication** columns are shown. This means that this slave could in turn be a master server for another slave server.

Replicated tables

Let's suppose that *on the master*, we create a table named `employee` in the `test` database. At this point, replication does its magic and we can have a look at the `test` database *on a slave server*:

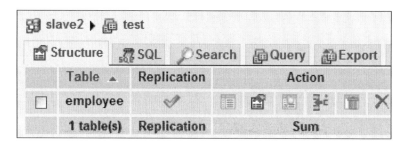

Here, the **Replication** column is shown as a reminder. We should not modify this table on the slave server directly, because its existence is for replication purposes only. If we decide to alter it directly, our changes will be done only in this table, introducing inconsistencies between the master and this slave, which is not a good idea.

Summary

In this chapter, we learnt how to synchronize both the structure and data from one database to another, on the same server or on different servers. We covered the goals of synchronization and how to perform a complete or selective synchronization. We then examined how to use phpMyAdmin to guide us into replication setup, including a master and a slave server; how to prepare a test environment using the MySQL sandbox, and how to control the slave servers.

The next chapter will show you how to keep permanent bookmarks of your queries.

14
Using Bookmarks

This chapter covers query bookmarks—one of the features of the linked-tables infrastructure. Being able to label queries, and recall them by label, can be a real time saver. Bookmarks are queries that are:

- Stored permanently
- Viewable
- Erasable
- Related to one database
- Recorded only as a consequence of a user's action
- Labeled
- Private by default (only available to the user who created them), but possibly public

A bookmark can also have a variable part, as explained in the *Passing a parameter value to a bookmark* section later in this chapter.

There is no bookmark subpage for managing bookmarks. Instead, the various actions for bookmarks are available on specific pages, such as results pages or query box pages.

Comparing bookmark and query history features

In *Chapter 11, Entering SQL Commands*, we learned about the SQL history feature, which automatically stores queries (temporarily or permanently). There are similarities between queries stored in the history and bookmarks. After all, both features are intended to store queries for later execution. However, there are important differences regarding the way the queries are stored and the action that triggers the recording of a query.

There is a configurable limit (see *Chapter 11, Entering SQL Commands*) on the number of queries stored in the permanent history; however, the number of bookmarks is not limited. Also, the history feature presents queries in the reverse order of the time they were sent. However, bookmarks are shown by label (not showing the query text directly). Finally, the storing of queries in the history is automatic, whereas a query is saved as a bookmark via an explicit request from the user.

To summarize, the automatic query history is useful when we neither plan to recall a query, nor wish to remember which queries we typed. This contrasts with the bookmark facility where we intentionally ask the system to remember a query, even giving it a name (label). Therefore, we can do more with bookmarks than with the query history, but both features have their own importance.

Creating bookmarks

There are two instances when it's possible to create a query — after a query is executed (in which case we don't need to plan ahead for its creation), and before sending the query to the MySQL server for execution. Both of these options are explored in the following sections.

Creating a bookmark after a successful query

Initial bookmark creation is made possible by the **Bookmark this SQL query** button. This button appears only after executing a query that generates a result (when at least one row is found); so this method for creating bookmarks only stores SELECT statements. For example, a complex query produced by the multi-table query generator (as seen in *Chapter 12, Generating Multi-table Queries*) could be stored as a bookmark in this way, provided that it finds some results.

Let's see an example. In the **Search** page for the book table, we select the fields that we want in the results, and enter the search values as shown in the following screenshot:

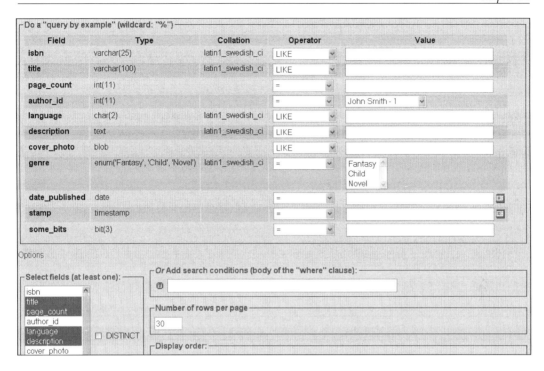

After clicking on **Go**, we see that the results page shows a bookmark dialog. We enter only a label (**books for author 1**) for this bookmark, and then click on **Bookmark this SQL query** to save this query as a bookmark. Bookmarks are saved in the table defined by `$cfg['Servers'][$i]['bookmarktable']`.

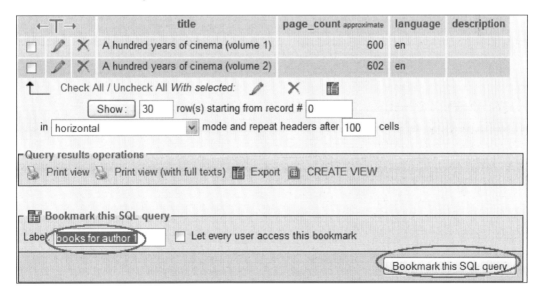

This bookmark dialog can be seen on any page that contains results. As a test, we could just click on **Browse** for a table to get results, and then store this query as a bookmark. However, it does not make much sense to store (in a bookmark) a query that can easily be made with one click.

Storing a bookmark before sending a query

We have seen that it's easy to create a bookmark after the execution of a SELECT statement that generates results. Sometimes, we may want to store a bookmark even if a query does not find any results. This may be the case if the data to which the query refers is not yet present, or if the query is a statement other than SELECT. To achieve this, we have the **Bookmark this SQL query** dialog available in the **SQL** tab of the Database view, Table view, and the query window.

We now go to the **SQL** subpage of the **book** table, enter a query, and directly put the **books in French** bookmark label in the **Bookmark this SQL query** field. If this bookmark label has been used previously, a new bookmark with the same name will be created, unless we select the **Replace existing bookmark of same name** checkbox. Bookmarks carry an internal identifying number, as well as a label chosen by the user.

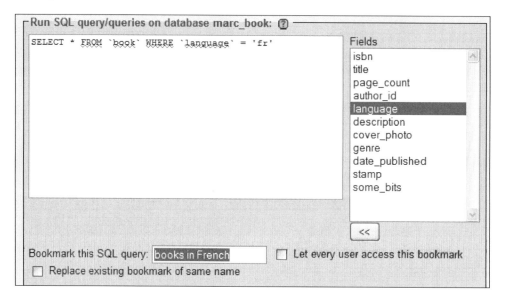

On clicking **Go**, the query is executed and stored as a bookmark. It does not matter if the query does not find anything. This is how we can generate bookmarks for non-SELECT queries such as UPDATE, DELETE, CREATE TABLE, and so on.

This technique can also be used for a SELECT statement that either returns results or does not return results.

Making bookmarks public

All bookmarks we create are private by default. When a bookmark is created, the username using which we are logged in, is stored with the bookmark. Let's suppose that we choose **Let every user access this bookmark** as shown in the following screenshot:

This would have the following effect:

- All users having access to the same database (the current one) will have access to the bookmark

- A user's ability to see meaningful results from the bookmark depends on the privileges they have on the tables referenced in the bookmark

- Any user will be able to delete the bookmark

- Users will be permitted to change the bookmark's query, by storing this bookmark before sending a query and using the **Replace existing bookmark of same name** option

The default initial query for a table

In the previous examples, we chose bookmark labels according to our preferences. However, by convention, if a bookmark has the same name as a table, the query will be executed when **Browse** is clicked for this table. Thus, instead of seeing the normal **Browse** results of this table, we'll see the bookmark's results.

Suppose that we are interested in viewing (by default, in the **Browse** mode) all books with a page count lower than 300. We first generate the appropriate query, which can be done easily from the **Search** page, and then we use **book** as a label on the results page:

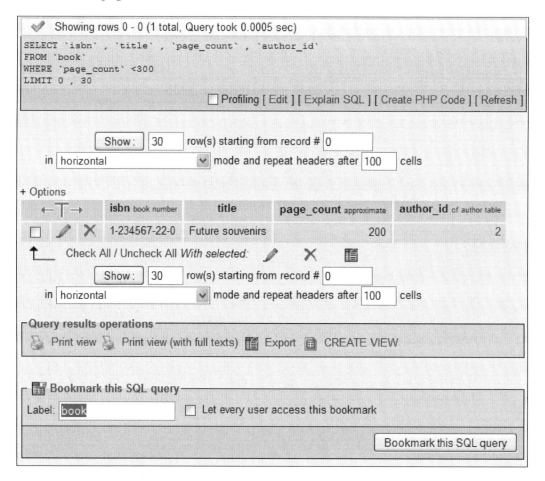

Multi-query bookmarks

A single bookmark can also store more than one query (separated by semicolon). This is mostly useful for non-SELECT queries. As an example, let's assume that we need to clean data about authors by removing an invalid area code from the phone numbers, on a regular basis. This operation would always be followed by a display of the author table.

To accomplish this goal, we store a bookmark (before sending it for execution) that contains these queries:

```
update author set phone = replace(phone,'(123)', '(456)');
select * from author;
```

In the bookmark, we could put many data modification statements such as INSERT, UPDATE, or DELETE, followed optionally by one SELECT statement. Stacking a lot of SELECT statements would not yield the intended result because we would only see the data fetched by the last SELECT statement.

Recalling bookmarks from the bookmarks list

Any created bookmarks can be found on the following pages:

- The Table view: **SQL** subpage of any table from **marc_book**
- The query window: The **SQL-History** tab
- While browsing the **pma_bookmark** table (see the *Executing bookmarks by browsing the pma_bookmark table* section later in this chapter)
- The Database view: **SQL** subpage of the **marc_book** database

Three choices are available when recalling a bookmark: **Submit**, **View only**, and **Delete** (**Submit** being the default).

Executing bookmarks

Choosing the first bookmark and hitting **Go** executes the stored query and displays its results. The page resulting from a bookmark execution does not have another dialog to create a bookmark, as this would be superfluous.

 The results we get are not necessarily the same as when we created the bookmark. They reflect the current contents of the database. Only the query is stored as a bookmark.

Manipulating bookmarks

Sometimes, we may just want to ascertain the contents of a bookmark. This is done by choosing a bookmark and selecting **View only**. Only the query will be displayed. We could then click on **Edit** and rework its contents. By doing so, we would be editing a copy of the original bookmarked query. To keep this new, edited query, we can save it as a bookmark. Again, this will create another bookmark even if we choose the same bookmark label, unless we explicitly ask for the original bookmark to be replaced.

A bookmark can be erased via the **Delete** option. There is no confirmation dialog to confirm the deletion of the bookmark; deletion is followed only by a message stating: **The bookmark has been deleted**.

Bookmark parameters

If we look again at the first bookmark we created (finding all books for **author 1**), we realize that although it's useful, it's limited to finding the same author.

Special query syntax enables the passing of parameters to bookmarks. This syntax uses the fact that SQL comments enclosed within /* and */ are ignored by MySQL. If the /* [VARIABLE] */ construct exists somewhere in the query, it will be expanded at execution time with the value provided when recalling the bookmark.

Creating a parameterized bookmark

Let's say we want to find all the books for a given author when we don't know the author's name. We first enter the following query:

```
SELECT author.name, author.id, book.title
FROM book, author
WHERE book.author_id = author.id
/* AND author.name LIKE '%[VARIABLE]%' */
```

The part between the comments characters (/* */) will be expanded later, and the tags will be removed. We label this query as a bookmark named **find author by name** (before executing it) and then click on **Go**. The first execution of the query just stores the bookmark while retrieving all books by all authors, as this time we haven't passed a parameter to the query.

In this example, we have two conditions in the WHERE clause, of which one contains the special syntax. If our only criterion in the WHERE clause needs a parameter, we can use a syntax such as WHERE 1 /* and author_id = [VARIABLE] */.

Passing a parameter value to a bookmark

To test the bookmark, we recall it as usual and enter a value in the **Variable** field:

When we click on **Go**, we see the expanded query, and the author Smith's books:

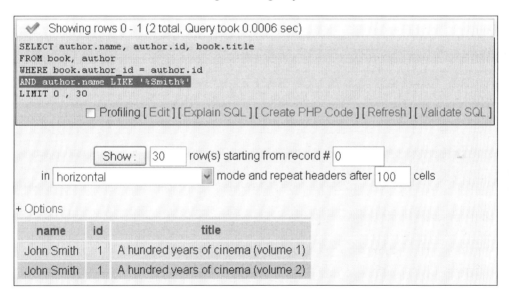

Executing bookmarks by browsing the pma_bookmark table

This feature is available only to users who can directly see the pma_bookmark table. This is the default name given when the linked-tables infrastructure is installed. In a multi-user installation, this table is usually located in a database invisible to unprivileged users. Browsing this table displays a new **Execute bookmarked query** button, which triggers the execution of the query:

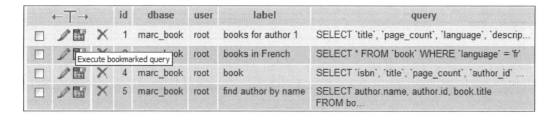

We can now click on the pencil icon to open the **Edit** page for a specific row to see the query's complete text.

Summary

In this chapter, we saw an overview of how to record bookmarks (after or before sending a query), how to manipulate them, and how some bookmarks can be made public. The chapter also introduced us to the default initial query for **Browse** mode. It also covered passing parameters to bookmarks and executing bookmarks directly from the pma_bookmark table.

The next chapter will explain how to produce documentation that explains the structure of your databases via the tools offered by phpMyAdmin.

15
Documenting the System

Producing and maintaining good documentation about data structure is crucial for a project's success, especially when it's a team project. Indeed, being able to show the current data dictionary and proposed column changes to the other team members provides a valuable means of communication. Moreover, a graphical display of the inter-table relations quickly demonstrates the inner workings of the database. Fortunately, phpMyAdmin has documentation features that take care of these things.

Producing structure reports

From the **Structure** subpage of either the Database or the Table view, the **Print view** link is available for producing reports about our database's structure. Moreover, a **Data Dictionary** link in Database view produces a different report. These are detailed in the following sections. In the next major section, the visual relational schema in PDF is explained.

Creating a printable report

When phpMyAdmin generates results, there is always a **Print view** link that can be used to generate a printable report of the data. The **Print view** feature can also be used to produce basic structure documentation. This is done in two steps. The first click on **Print view** displays a report on the screen, with a **Print** button at the end of the page. This **Print** button generates a report formatted for the printer.

The database print view

Clicking **Print view** on the **Structure** subpage for a database generates a list of tables. This list contains the number of records, storage engine, size, comments, the dates of creation, and the last update for each table:

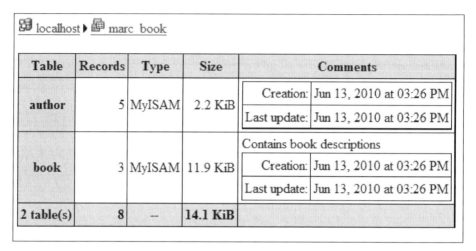

The selective database print view

Sometimes, we prefer to get a report only for certain tables. This can be done from the **Structure** subpage for a database by selecting the tables we want, and then choosing **Print view** from the drop-down menu:

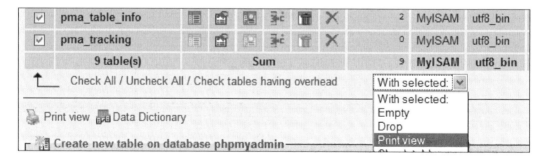

The table print view

There is also a **Print view** link on the **Structure** subpage for each table. Clicking on this link produces information about columns, indexes, space usage, and row statistics for the table, as shown in the following example:

book

Table comments: Contains book descriptions

Field	Type	Null	Default	Links to	Comments	MIME
isbn	varchar(25)	No			book number	
title	varchar(100)	No				
page_count	int(11)	No			approximate	
author_id	int(11)	No		author -> id	cf author table	
language	char(2)	No	en			
description	text	No				
cover_photo	blob	No				
genre	enum('Fantasy', 'Child', 'Novel')	No	Fantasy			
date_published	date	No				
stamp	timestamp	No	0000-00-00 00:00:00			
some_bits	bit(3)	No				

Indexes: ⊚

Keyname	Type	Unique	Packed	Field	Cardinality	Collation	Null	Comment
PRIMARY	BTREE	Yes	No	isbn	3	A		
by_title	BTREE	No	No	title (30)	3	A		
isbn	BTREE	No	No	isbn	3	A		
author_id	BTREE	No	No	author_id	3	A		

Preparing a complete report with the data dictionary

A more complete report about the tables and columns in a database is available from the **Structure** subpage of the Database view. We just have to click on **Data dictionary** to get this report, which is partially shown here:

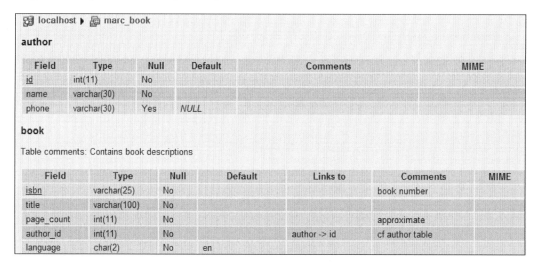

The **MIME** column is empty until we add MIME-related information to some columns (explained in *Chapter 16, Transforming Data Using MIME*).

Generating relational schemas in PDF

In *Chapter 10, Benefiting from the Relational System*, we defined relations between the book and author tables. These relations were used for various foreign key functions (for example, getting a list of possible values in **Insert** mode). We will now examine a feature that enables us to generate a custom-made relational schema for our tables, in the popular PDF format. This feature requires that the linked-tables infrastructure be properly installed and configured, as explained in *Chapter 10, Benefiting from the Relational System*.

Adding a third table to our model

To get a more complete schema, we will now add another table, country, to our database. Here is its export file:

```
CREATE TABLE IF NOT EXISTS `country` (
  `code` char(2) NOT NULL,
  `description` varchar(50) NOT NULL,
  PRIMARY KEY  (`code`)
) ENGINE=MyISAM DEFAULT CHARSET=latin1;

INSERT INTO `country` (`code`, `description`) VALUES
('ca', 'Canada'),
('uk', 'United Kingdom');
```

We will now link this table to the author table. First, in the **Relation view** for the country table, we specify the field that we want to display:

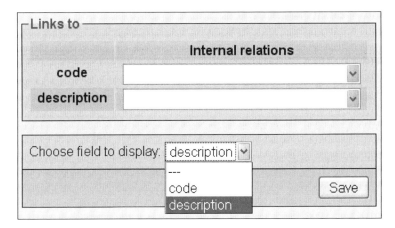

We then add a **country_code** column (same type and size as that of the code column in the country table) to the author table, and in the **Relation view**, we link it to the newly- created country table.

 We must remember to click on **Save** for the relation to be recorded.

For this example, it's not necessary to enter any country data for an author, as we are interested only in the relational schema:

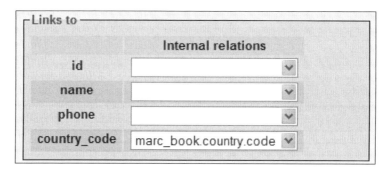

Editing PDF pages

Each relational schema is called a **page**. We can create or edit a page by clicking on **Edit PDF pages** in the **Operations** subpage of the Database view.

Page planning

In the current phpMyAdmin version, a relational schema cannot span multiple databases. But even working with just one database, the number of tables might be large. Representing the various table relations in a clear way could be a challenge. This is why we may use many pages, each showing some tables and their relations.

We must also take into account the dimensions of the final output. Printing on letter-size paper gives us less space to show all of our tables and still have a legible schema.

Creating a new page

As there are no existing pages, we need to create one. Because our most important table is book, we will also name this page, **book**.

We will choose which tables we wish to see in the relational schema. We could choose each table individually. However, for a good start, selecting the appropriate **Automatic layout** checkbox is recommended. Doing this puts all of the related tables from our database into the list of tables to be included in the schema. It then generates appropriate coordinates so that the tables will appear in a spiral layout, starting from the center of the schema. These coordinates are expressed in millimeters, with (0, 0) being located at the upper-left corner. We then click on **Go**:

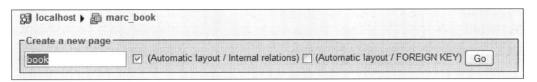

Editing a page

We now get a page with three different sections. The first one is the page menu, where we choose the page on which we want to work (from the drop-down menu). We can also delete the chosen page. We could also eventually create a second schema (page):

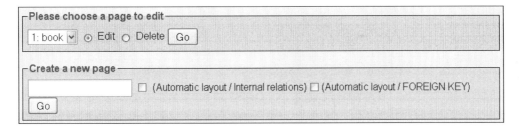

The next section is the table placement portion. We can now see the benefit of the **Automatic layout** feature—we already have our three tables selected, with the (**X**, **Y**) coordinates filled in. We can add a table (on the last line), delete a table (using the checkbox), and change the coordinates (which represent the position of the upper-left corner of each table on the schema):

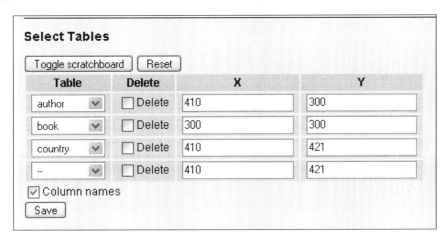

To help set exact coordinates, a visual editor is available for JavaScript-enabled browsers. To control the availability of this editor, the following parameter (which is set to TRUE by default) is available:

```
$cfg['WYSIWYG-PDF'] = TRUE;
```

The editor appears when the **Toggle scratchboard** button is clicked once. It will disappear when this button is clicked again. We can move tables on the scratchboard by using "drag and drop", and the coordinates will change accordingly. The appearance of the tables on the scratchboard provides a rough guide to the final PDF output. Some people prefer to see only the table names (without every column name) on the scratchboard. This can be done by deselecting the **Column names** checkbox and then clicking on **Save**. The following image shows an example of this scratchboard:

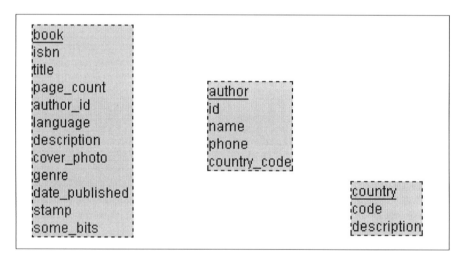

 When we are satisfied with the layout, we must click on **Save**.

Displaying a page

The last section of the screen is the PDF report generation dialog. Now that we have created a page, the **Display PDF schema** is also available from the **Operations** subpage of the Database view. We'll have a look at this dialog from the **Operations** page because the option set is more complete on this page:

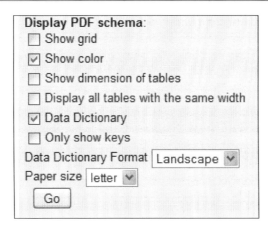

The available options are:

Option	Description
Show grid	The schema will have a grid layer with the coordinates displayed. Useful when designing and testing the schema.
Show color	The links between tables, table names, and special columns (primary keys and display fields) will be in color.
Show dimensions of tables	The visual dimension of each table in the table title (for example, **32x30**) will be displayed. This is useful when designing and testing the schema.
Display all tables with the same width	All tables will be displayed using the same width. (Normally, the width adjusts itself according to the length of the table and column names.)
Data Dictionary	The data dictionary, which was covered earlier in this chapter, will be included at the beginning of the report.
Only show keys	Do not show the columns on which there are no indexes defined.
Data Dictionary Format	Here, we choose the printed orientation of the dictionary.
Paper size	Changing this will influence the schema and scratchboard dimensions.

In `config.inc.php`, the following parameters define the available paper sizes and the default choice:

```
$cfg['PDFPageSizes'] = array('A3', 'A4', 'A5', 'letter', 'legal');
$cfg['PDFDefaultPageSize']  = 'A4';
```

The following screenshot shows the last page of the generated report (the schema page) in PDF format. The first four pages contain the data dictionary along with an additional feature. On each page, the schema can be reached by clicking on the table name, and in the schema, each page in the data dictionary can be reached by clicking on the corresponding table.

Arrows point in the direction of the corresponding foreign table. If **Show color** has been selected, the primary keys are shown in gray and the display fields in black:

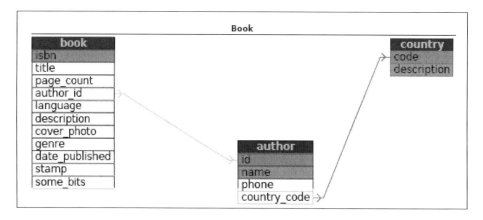

Here is another example generated from the same book table's PDF page definition. This time the grid is shown, but not the colors:

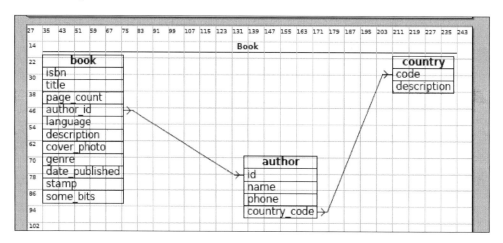

Changing the font in PDF schema

All the text we see in the PDF schema is drawn using a specific font. phpMyAdmin uses the **DejaVuSans** font (`http://dejavu.sourceforge.net`), which covers a wide range of characters.

For actual PDF generation, phpMyAdmin relies on the `tcpdf` library (`http://tcpdf.sourceforge.net`), which itself is an adaptation of the `fpdf` library (`http://www.fpdf.org`). These libraries have two ways of using fonts— embedded and not embedded. Embedding fonts will produce a bigger PDF file because the whole font is included in the PDF file. This is the default option chosen by phpMyAdmin because the library does not depend on the presence of a specific **TrueType** font in the client operating system.

The fonts are located in `libraries/tcpdf/font` under the main `phpMyAdmin` directory.

To use a different font file, we must first add it to the library (tools are present in the original `tcpdf` kit and a tutorial is available on the `http://www.fpdf.org` website) and then modify phpMyAdmin's `pdf_schema.php` source code.

Laying out a PDF schema with the Designer feature

The Designer feature (available in the Database view) offers a more refined way of moving the tables on screen, as the column links follow the table movements. Therefore, an interface exists between the tables' coordinates, as saved by the Designer, and the coordinates for the PDF schema. Let's enter the Designer and click on the small PDF logo.

This brings us to a panel where we can choose the (existing) PDF schema name and the action we want to perform—in our case, to export the Designer coordinates to the PDF schema. We could also use the **Create a new page** dialog, entering a PDF page name, and then clicking on **Go** to create an empty page. From here, we can subsequently export the coordinates saved from the Designer workspace:

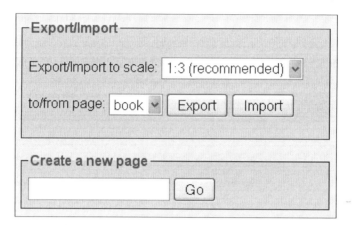

 There is a difference in the span of tables managed by the **Designer** and by the **Edit PDF** feature. The **Designer** manipulates every table of a database, whereas the **Edit PDF** panel offers us a choice of tables enabling us to represent a subset of the relations if there are many tables.

Summary

This chapter covered the documentation features offered by phpMyAdmin—the print view for a database or a table and the data dictionary for a complete column list. The chapter also covered PDF relational schemas. In particular, it focused on how to create and modify a PDF schema page, and how to use the visual editor (scratchboard).

The next chapter will explain how to apply transformations to data, in order to customize the data format at view time.

16
Transforming Data Using MIME

In this chapter, we will cover a powerful phpMyAdmin feature—its ability to transform a column's contents during a table **Browse**, based on certain specific rules called **transformations**. Normally, browsing a table shows only the original data that resides in it. However, MIME-based transformations permit the alteration of the display format.

Browsing data without transformations

Normally, the exact contents of each row are displayed, except that:

- The **TEXT** and **CHARACTER** fields might be truncated, according to `$cfg['LimitChars']`, and depending on whether we have chosen to see **Full Texts** or not

- **BLOB** fields might be replaced by a message such as **[BLOB - 1.5 KB]**

We will use the term **cell** to indicate a specific column of a specific row. The cell containing the cover photograph for the "Future souvenirs" book (a **BLOB** column) is currently displayed as cryptic data such as **‰PNG\r\n\Z\n\0\0\0\rIHDR\0** or as a message stating the **BLOB** field's size. It would be interesting to see a thumbnail (shown in the following screenshot) of the picture directly in phpMyAdmin and possibly the full-size picture itself. This will be made possible with proper transformation.

isbn book number	title	page_count approximate	author_id cfartior table	language	description	cover_photo
1-234567-22-0	Future souvenirs	200	2	en		

Switching display options

In **Browse** mode, the **Options** link reveals a slider that contains, among other choices, a **Hide Browser transformation** checkbox. We can use it whenever we want to switch between seeing the real data of a cell and its transformed version.

Enabling transformations

We define **transformation** as a mechanism by which all of the cells related to a column are transformed at browse time, using the metadata defined for this column. Only the cells visible on the results page are transformed. The transformation logic itself is coded in PHP scripts, stored in `libraries/transformations`, and is called using a plug-in architecture.

The use of this feature is controlled by the `$cfg['BrowseMIME']` directive in `config.inc.php`. The default value of this directive is TRUE, meaning that transformations are enabled. However, the linked-tables infrastructure must be in place (see *Chapter 10, Benefiting from the Relational System*) because the metadata necessary for the transformations is not available in the official MySQL table structure. It's an addition made especially for phpMyAdmin.

In the documentation section on phpMyAdmin's home site (currently at `http://www.phpmyadmin.net/home_page/docs.php`), there is a link pointing to additional information for developers who would like to learn the internal structure of the plug-ins in order to code their own transformations.

Configuring settings for MIME columns

If we go to the Table view of the **Structure** page for the book table and click on the **Change** link for the **cover_photo**, we see three additional attributes for the field (provided the transformations feature is enabled):

- **MIME type**
- **Browser transformation**
- **Transformation options**

This is shown in the following screenshot:

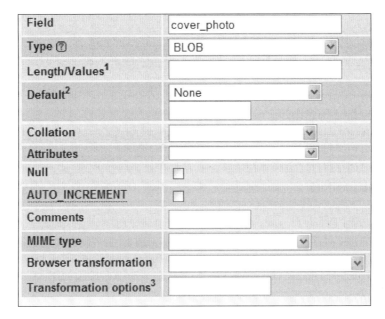

For a specific field, it's possible to indicate only one type of transformation. Here, the field is a **BLOB** field. Hence, it can hold any kind of data. In order for phpMyAdmin to interpret and act correctly on the data, the transformation system must be informed of the data format and the intended results. Accordingly, we have to ensure that we upload data that always follows the same file format.

We will first learn the purpose of these attributes and then try some possibilities in the *Examples of transformations* section, later in this chapter.

Selecting the MIME type

The MIME specification (`http://en.wikipedia.org/wiki/MIME`) has been chosen as a metadata attribute to categorize the kind of data that a column holds. **Multipurpose Internet Mail Extensions (MIME)**, originally designed to extend mail, are now used to describe content types for other protocols as well. In the context of phpMyAdmin, the current possible values are:

- **image/jpeg**
- **image/png**
- **text/plain**
- **application/octetstream**

Support for GIF might be added in a future version.

The **text/plain** type can be chosen for a column containing any kind of text (for example, XHTML or XML text). In the *Examples of transformations* section, you'll see which MIME type you are required to choose in order to achieve a specific effect.

Browser transformations

This is where we set the exact transformation to be done. More than one transformation may be supported per MIME type. For example, for the **image/jpeg** MIME type, we have two transformations available: **image/jpeg: inline** for a clickable thumbnail of the image and **image/jpeg: link** to display just a link.

As we can see in the following image, moving the mouse over each choice in the drop-down menu provides a short explanation of the corresponding transformation. A more complete transformation explanation and a list of the possible options are available on clicking the **transformation descriptions** link:

Browser transformation	
Transformation options[3]	

application/octetstream: download
application/octetstream: hex
image/jpeg: inline
image/jpeg: link

Displays a clickable thumbnail. The options are the maximum width and height in pixels. ...

text/plain: external
text/plain: formatted
text/plain: imagelink
text/plain: link
text/plain: sql
text/plain: substr

[1] If field type is "enum" ... ng this format: 'a','b','c'...
If you ever need to put ... ') amongst those values, precede it with a bac
(for example '\xyz' or 'a'

Assigning values to transformation options

In the *Examples of transformations* section, we will see that some transformations accept options. For example, a transformation that generates an image will need the width and height in pixels. A comma is used to separate the values in the options list, and some options may need to be enclosed within quotes.

Some options have a default value, and we must be careful to respect the documented order for options. For example, if there are two options, and we only want to specify a value for the second option, we can use empty quotes as a placeholder for the first option, to let the system use its default value.

Requirements for image generation

Normal thumbnail generation requires that some components exist on the web server, and that a parameter in `config.inc.php` be correctly configured.

Configuring GD2 library availability verification

phpMyAdmin uses some internal functions to create the thumbnails. These functions need the GD2 library to be present on our PHP server.

phpMyAdmin can detect the presence of the correct GD2 library, but this detection takes some time. It also takes place not once per session, but almost every time an action is taken in phpMyAdmin.

Setting the `$cfg['GD2Available']` parameter in `config.inc.php` to its default value `'auto'` indicates that detection of the library's presence and version is needed.

If we know that the GD2 library is available, setting `$cfg['GD2Available']` to `yes` will make execution quicker. If the GD2 library is not available, you are recommended to set this parameter to `no`.

To find out which GD2 library we have on the server, we can go to phpMyAdmin's homepage and click on **Show PHP information**. If this link is not present, we need to set the `$cfg['ShowPhpInfo']` parameter to `true`. We then look for a section titled **gd** and verify which version is identified. In the following image, all is fine as we can see that the GD version is 2.X with JPEG and PNG support:

gd

GD Support	enabled
GD Version	bundled (2.0.34 compatible)
FreeType Support	enabled
FreeType Linkage	with freetype
FreeType Version	2.3.11
GIF Read Support	enabled
GIF Create Support	enabled
JPEG Support	enabled
libJPEG Version	unknown
PNG Support	enabled
libPNG Version	1.2.40
WBMP Support	enabled
XBM Support	enabled

Directive	Local Value	Master Value
gd.jpeg_ignore_warning	0	0

Asserting support of JPEG and PNG libraries

Our PHP server needs to have support for the JPEG and PNG images if we or our users want to generate thumbnails for these types of images. For more details, please refer to `http://php.net/manual/en/ref.image.php`.

Evaluating the impact of memory limits

On some PHP servers, the default value in `php.ini` for `memory_limit` is 8 MB. This is too low for correct image manipulation, because the GD functions used to produce the final images need some working memory. For example, in one test, a value of 11 MB in `memory_limit` was needed to generate the thumbnail from a 300 KB JPEG image. Also, if multiple rows are viewed at once, more working memory will be needed.

Examples of transformations

We will now discuss a few transformation examples.

Clickable thumbnail (.jpeg or .png)

We will start by changing our **cover_photo** field type from **BLOB** to **LONGBLOB** to ensure that we can upload photographs that are bigger than 65 KB in size. We then enter the following attributes:

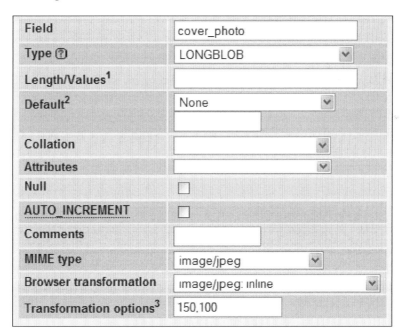

Here, the options are presented in the form of width and height. If we omit the options, the default values are 100 and 100. The thumbnail generation code preserves the original aspect ratio of the image. Therefore, the values entered are the *maximum* width and height of the generated image. We then upload a `.jpeg` file to a cell (by using the instructions provided in *Chapter 5, Changing Data and Structure*). As a result, we get the following in **Browse** mode for this table:

isbn book number	title	page_count approximate	author_id cf author table	language	description	cover_photo
1-234567-22-0	Future souvenirs	200	2	en		

This thumbnail can be clicked to reveal the full-size photograph.

The thumbnail is not stored anywhere in MySQL, but generated each time we go into **Browse** mode for this set of rows. On a double Xeon 3.2GHz server, we commonly experience a generation rate of six JPEG images per second. No caching of these thumbnails is offered by phpMyAdmin.

For a `.png` file, we have to use **image/png** as the MIME type, and **image/png: inline** as the transformation.

Adding links to an image

To provide a link without the thumbnail, we use the **image/jpeg: link** transformation. There are no transformation options. This link can be used to view the photograph (by left-clicking on the link) and then possibly download it (by right-clicking on the photograph itself):

isbn book number	title	page_count approximate	author_id cf author table	language	description	cover_photo	genre
1-234567-22-0	Future souvenirs	200	2	en		[BLOB]	

Date formatting

We have a field named **date_published** in our book table; let's change its type to **DATETIME**. Then, we set its MIME type to **text/plain** and the browser transformation to **text/plain: dateformat**. The next step is to edit the row for the **Future souvenirs** book, and enter **2003-01-01 14:56:00** in the **date_published** field. When we browse the table, we now see the field has been formatted. Moving the mouse over the field reveals the unformatted original contents.

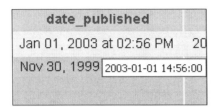

This transformation accepts two options. The first is the number of hours that will be added to the original value, which is zero by default. Adding the number of hours can be useful if we store all times based on **Universal Coordinated Time (UTC)**, but want to display them for a specific zone (for example, UTC+5). The second option is the time format we want to use, specified using any PHP `strftime` parameters. So, if we put **'0','Year: %Y'** in the transformation options we will get the following output:

date_published	stamp
Year: 2003	2006-07-22 09:51:50
Year: 19 2003-01-01 14:56:00 00-00 00:00:00	
Year: 1999	0000-00-00 00:00:00

Links from text

Suppose that we have put a complete URL — `http://domain.com/abc.pdf` — in the **description** field in our book table. The text of the link will be displayed while browsing the table, but we would not be able to click it. We'll now see the use of the **text/plain** MIME type in such a situation.

text/plain: link

If we use a **text/plain** MIME type and a **text/plain: link** browser transformation in the scenario just mentioned, we will still see the text for the link, and it will be clickable:

isbn book number	title	page_count approximate	author_id creation table	language	description
1-234567-22-0	Future souvenirs	200	2	en	http://domain.com/abc.pdf
1-234567-89-0	A hundred years of cinema (volume 1)	600	1	en	

If all of the documents that we want to point to are located at a common URL prefix, we can put this prefix (for example, `http://domain.com/`) in the first transformation option, within the enclosing quotes. Then, we would only need to put the last part of the URL (`abc.pdf`) in each cell.

A second transformation option is available for setting a title. This would be displayed in the **Browse** mode instead of the URL contents, but a click would nonetheless bring us to the intended URL.

 If we use only the second transformation option, we have to put quotes where the first option be entered. It could be done as: `''`, `'this is the title'`.

text/plain: imagelink

This transformation is similar to the previous one, except that in the cell, we place a URL that points to an image. This image will be fetched and displayed in the cell along with the link text. The image could be anywhere on the Web, including our local **server**.

Here we have the following three options available:

- The common URL prefix (like the one for `text/plain: link`)
- The width of the image in pixels (default: 100)
- The height (default: 50)

For our test URL, you should enter these options:

```
'','100','123'
```

If the text for the link is too long, the transformation does not occur. By default, the **Partial Texts** display option is selected:

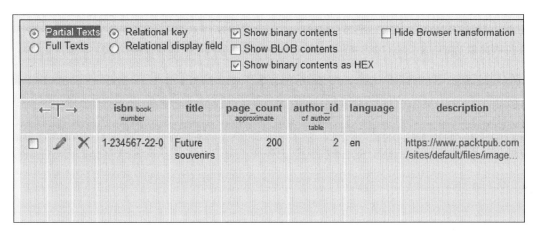

In this case, we can switch to **Full Texts** to reveal the complete link. We can then see the complete image:

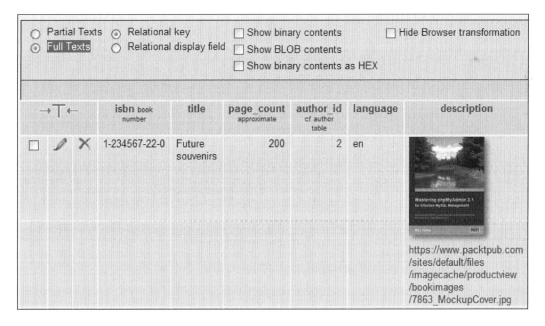

Other transformations, such as `image/jpeg: inline` and `image/png: inline`, specify the exact MIME type of the image. In these cases, phpMyAdmin uses GD2 library functions for the thumbnail generation. However, the link contained in a `text/plain: imagelink` transformation may refer to any browser-supported image type. Therefore, phpMyAdmin just displays a resized image with an HTML `img` tag, and `width` and `height` attributes set according to the size options defined in the transformation. To see the original image, we can click on either the link or the thumbnail.

Preserving the original formatting

Normally, when displaying text, phpMyAdmin helps you get rid of special characters. For example, if we entered **This book is good** in the description field for one book, we would normally see **This book is good** when browsing the table. However, if we used the transformation **text/plain: formatted** for this field, we would get the following while browsing:

In this example, the results are correct. However, other HTML entered in the data field could produce surprising results (including invalid HTML pages). For example, because phpMyAdmin presents results using HTML tables, a non-escaped `</table>` tag in the data field would ruin the output.

Displaying parts of a text

The `text/plain: substr` transformation is available for displaying only a portion of the text. Here are the options:

- First: Where to start in the text (default: 0)
- Second: How many characters (default: all of the remaining text)
- Third: What to display as a suffix in order to show that truncation has occurred; the default is to display ellipses (...)

Remember that `$cfg['LimitChars']` is doing a character truncation for every non-numeric field. Hence, `text/plain: substr` is a mechanism for fine-tuning this, field-by-field.

Displaying a download link

Let's say we want to store a small audio comment about each book inside MySQL. We add a new field to the `book` table, with the name **audio_contents**, and type **MEDIUMBLOB**. We set its **MIME type** to **application/octetstream** and choose the **application/octetstream: download** transformation. In the **Transformation options**, we insert **'comment.wav'**:

MIME type	application/octetstream
Browser transformation	application/octetstream: download
Transformation options[3]	'comment.wav'

This MIME type and extension will inform our browser about the incoming data, and instruct the browser to open the appropriate player. To insert a comment, we first record it in a `.wav` format, and then upload the contents of the file into the **audio_contents** field for one of the books. When browsing our table, we can see a link **comment.wav** for our audio comment.

> The next chapter describes the BLOB streaming technique, which is more appropriate for bigger chunks of data (for example, using phpMyAdmin to watch a movie stored in MySQL!).

Hexadecimal representation

Characters are stored in MySQL (and in computers in general) as numeric data, and converted into something meaningful for the screen or printer. Users sometimes cut and paste data from one application into phpMyAdmin, leading to unexpected results if the characters are not directly supported by MySQL. A case that was reported in phpMyAdmin's help forum involved special quotation marks entered in a Microsoft Word document and pasted to phpMyAdmin. It helps to be able to see the exact hexadecimal codes, and this can be done by using the `application/octetstream: hex` transformation.

In the following example, this transformation will be applied to the **title** field of our `book` table. When browsing the row containing the **Future souvenirs** title, we can see:

As we know which character set this column is encoded with, we can compare its contents with a chart describing each character. For instance, `http://en.wikipedia.org/wiki/Latin1` describes the latin1 character set.

SQL pretty printing

The term **pretty printing** (`http://en.wikipedia.org/wiki/Pretty_printing`) refers to a way of "beautifying" source code. Let's say we are using a table to store the text of a course about SQL. In one column, we might have put some sample SQL statements. If we use the `text/plain: sql` transformation, then these SQL statements will be displayed in color, with syntax highlighting, when the table is browsed.

IP address

An IP (v4) address can be encoded into a long integer (for example, via the PHP `iptolong()` function), and stored into a MySQL `UNSIGNED INT` column. To convert it back to the familiar dotted string (for example, `127.0.0.1`), you can use the `text/plain: longToIpv4` transformation.

Transforming data via external applications

The transformations that have been described previously are implemented directly from within phpMyAdmin. However, some transformations are better executed via existing external applications.

The `text/plain: external` transformation enables us to send a cell's data to another application that will be started on the web server, capture this application's output, and display this output in the cell's position.

 This feature is supported only on a Linux or UNIX server (under Microsoft Windows, output and error redirection cannot be easily captured by the PHP process). Furthermore, PHP should not be running in safe mode. Hence, the feature may not be available on hosted servers.

For security reasons, the exact path and name of the application cannot be set from within phpMyAdmin as a transformation option. The application names are set directly inside one of the phpMyAdmin scripts.

First, in the phpMyAdmin installation directory, we edit the `text_plain__external.inc.php` file in `libraries/transformations/`, and find the following section:

```
$allowed_programs = array();
//$allowed_programs[0] = '/usr/local/bin/tidy';
//$allowed_programs[1] = '/usr/local/bin/validate';
```

No external application is configured by default, and we have to explicitly add our own.

 The names of the transformation scripts are constructed using the following format: the MIME type, a double underscore, and then a part indicating which transformation should take place.

Every program that is allowed, along with its complete path, must be described here, with an index number starting from 0. Then we save the modifications to this script and put it back on the server if needed. The remaining setup is completed from the panel where we chose the options for the other browser transformations.

Of course, we will now choose **text/plain: external** in the transformations menu.

As the first option, we place the application number (for example, 0 would be for the tidy application). The second option holds the parameters we need to pass to this application. If we want phpMyAdmin to apply the `htmlspecialchars()` function to the results, we put **1** as the third parameter—this is the default. We could put a **0** there to avoid protecting the output with `htmlspecialchars()`.

If we want to avoid reformatting the cell's lines, we put **1** as the fourth parameter. This will use the `NOWRAP` modifier, and is done by default.

External application example: In-cell sort

This example shows how to sort the text contents of one a single cell. We start by modifying the `text_plain__external.inc.php` script, as mentioned in the previous section, to add the `sort` program:

```
$allowed_programs[0] = '/bin/sort';
```

Note that our new program bears the index number `0`.

We then add a **TEXT** field whose name is **keywords** to our book table. Finally, we fill in the MIME-related information, entering **'0','-r'** as the transformation options:

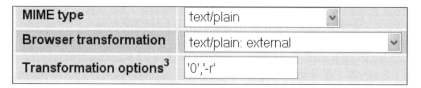

The **'0'** here refers to the index number for sort, and the **'-r'** is a parameter for sort, which makes the program sort in the reverse order.

Next, we **Edit** the row for the book "A hundred years of cinema (volume 1)", entering some keywords in no particular order (as seen in the following screenshot), and hitting **Go** in order to save the changes:

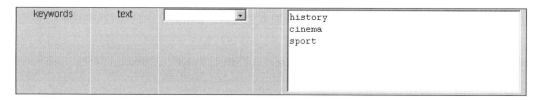

To test the effects of the external program, we browse our table and see the sorted in-cell keywords.

date_published	stamp	keywords
Year: 2003	2006-07-22 10:20:10	
Year: 1999	2006-07-22 10:58:39	sport history cinema

Notice that the keywords are displayed in reverse sorted order.

Summary

In this chapter, we learnt how to improve the browsing experience by transforming data using various methods. This chapter also provided an overview of thumbnail and full-size images for `.jpeg` and `.png` **BLOB** fields, how to generate links, format dates, display only parts of texts, and how to execute external programs in order to reformat cell contents.

The next chapter will cover phpMyAdmin's support for the MySQL features that are new in versions 5.0 and 5.1.

17
Supporting MySQL 5.0 and 5.1

MySQL 5.0 introduced a number of new features that calmed down a number of developers and industry observers who were claiming that MySQL was inferior than competitor products .Views, stored procedures, triggers, a standard INFORMATION_SCHEMA, and (more recently) a profiling mechanism are now present in the MySQL spectrum.

Among the new features of MySQL 5.1, the ones that relate to a web interface (for example, partitioning and events) are supported in phpMyAdmin.

Activating support for views

MySQL 5.0 introduced support for named and updatable views. A view is a derived table (consider it a virtual table) whose definition is stored in the database. A SELECT statement done on one or more tables (or even on views) can be stored as a view and can also be queried.

Views can be used to:

- Limit the visibility of columns (for example, do not show salary information)
- Limit the visibility of rows (for example, do not show data for specific
- world regions)
- Hide a changed table structure (so that legacy applications can continue to work)

Instead of defining cumbersome column-specific privileges on many tables, it's easier to prepare a view containing a limited set of columns from these tables. We can then GRANT permissions on the view as a whole.

To activate support for views on a server after an upgrade from a pre-5.0 version, the administrator has to execute the `mysql_upgrade` program, as described in the MySQL manual (see `http://dev.mysql.com/doc/refman/5.0/en/upgrading-from-previous-series.html`).

 Each user must have the appropriate SHOW_VIEW or CREATE_VIEW privilege to be able to see or manipulate views. These privileges exist at the global (server), database, and table levels.

phpMyAdmin supports two ways of creating a view. We'll explain the manual method first, and then go on with a more visual way.

Manually creating a view

To create a view manually, we use the query box to enter the appropriate statement. Let's enter the following lines, and then click on **Go**:

```
CREATE VIEW book_author AS
SELECT book.isbn, book.title, author.name FROM book
LEFT JOIN author ON author.id = book.author_id
```

 Creating a view implies that the user has privileges on the tables involved, or at least a privilege such as, SELECT or UPDATE on all the columns mentioned in the view.

At this point, the view has been created, and the navigation panel is updated to reflect this fact. If we refresh our browser's page and then access the `marc_book` database, we will see:

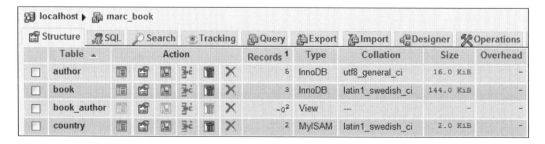

In the navigation panel, there is a different icon next to the **book_author** view, indicating that it's not a regular table. In the main panel, we see the information on the newly-created view. The number of records for the view currently indicates 0 (there is more information on this in the *Performance Hint* section, later in this chapter), and **View** is indicated in the **Type** column. There is no collation or size associated with a view.

This creation step was completed manually. Other operations on views are handled by the phpMyAdmin interface.

Main panel and views

As a view has certain similarities with a table, its name is available in the navigation panel, along with the names of the ordinary tables. On clicking the view name, a panel similar to the one seen for tables is displayed, but with fewer menu tabs than seen in a normal table. Indeed, some operations do not make sense on a view—for example, **Import**. This is because a view does not actually contain data. However, other actions, such as **Browse**, are perfectly acceptable.

Let's browse this view:

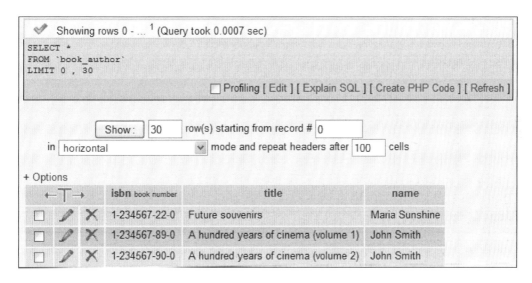

We notice that, in the generated SQL query, we do not see our original CREATE VIEW statement. The reason is that we are selecting from the view using a SELECT statement, hiding the fact that we are pulling data from a view. However, exporting the view's structure would show how MySQL internally stored our view.

```
CREATE ALGORITHM=UNDEFINED DEFINER='marc'@'%' SQL SECURITY DEFINER
VIEW `book_author` AS
```

```
select `book`.`isbn` AS `isbn`,
`book`.`title` AS `title`,
`author`.`name` AS `name`
from (`book` left join `author` on((`book`.`author_id` = `author`.
`id`)));
```

The main panel's menu may look similar to that of a table. However, when necessary, phpMyAdmin generates the appropriate syntax for handling views. For example, clicking on **Drop** would produce:

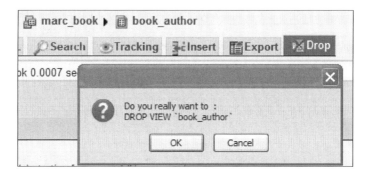

At this point, we can confirm (or not) this view's deletion.

To perform actions on existing views, a user needs to have the appropriate privilege at the view level, but not necessarily any privilege on the tables involved in this view. This is how we can achieve column and table hiding.

Creating a view from results

Creating a complex view may require typing the complete statement into a query box. Another possibility is to take advantage of phpMyAdmin's **Search** (at the table level) or **Query** (at the database level) features to build a rather complex query, execute it, and then easily create a view from the results. We'll see how this is done.

We mentioned that a view can be used to limit the visibility of columns (and, in fact, of tables). Let's say that the number of pages in a book is highly classified information. We open the book table, click **Search**, and choose a subset of the columns (we might have to open the **Options** slider):

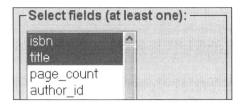

Clicking on **Go** produces a results page, where we see a **CREATE VIEW** link in the **Query results operations** section. We use this link to access the view creation panel, which already has the underlying query in the **AS** box. We need to choose a name for this view (here, we use **book_public_info**), and we can optionally set different column names for it (here, we use **number, title**). The other options can influence the view's behavior, and have been explained in the MySQL manual (see `http://dev.mysql.com/doc/refman/5.1/en/create-view.html`).

Clicking on **Go** generates the view we asked for:

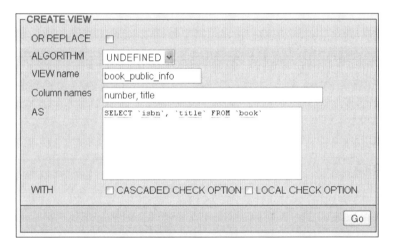

The CHECK OPTION clauses influence the behavior of the updateable views (this is explained in the MySQL manual at the page cited previously).

Renaming a view

phpMyAdmin does not support the renaming of a view directly from the interface. However, as from MySQL 5.0.14, the RENAME TABLE statement can be used (from a phpMyAdmin's query box) as long as we are renaming inside the same database. For example, RENAME TABLE book_public_info TO book_public_info2. It may look curious to use RENAME TABLE for a view but this is the correct way of achieving this result.

Controlling row counting for improved performance

phpMyAdmin has a configuration parameter, $cfg['MaxExactCountViews'], that controls the row counting phase of phpMyAdmin. Sometimes, a view comprises many huge tables, and browsing it would make a large number of virtual rows appear. Therefore, the default value of 0 for this parameter ensures that no row counting happens for views. In this case, we'll see rather strange results when browsing a view: **Showing rows 0 - -1 (0 total, Query took 0.0006 sec)**. But this is more acceptable than slowing down a server.

Nonetheless, if we prefer to see a more exact row count for views, we can put a larger value in this parameter, which acts as an upper limit for the row counting phase.

Supporting routines—stored procedures and functions

It took a while before phpMyAdmin started to include support for stored procedures and functions. The reason is that these features are blocks of code (like a subprogram) that are kept as a part of the database, and phpMyAdmin, being a web interface, is more oriented towards operations that are performed quickly using a mouse.

Nonetheless, phpMyAdmin has a few features that permit a developer to create such routines, save them, recall them to make some modifications, and delete them.

Procedures are accessed by a CALL statement to which we can pass parameters. On the other hand, functions are accessed from SQL statements (for example, SELECT), similar to other MySQL internal functions returning a value.

The CREATE ROUTINE and ALTER ROUTINE privileges are needed to be able to create, see, and delete a stored procedure or function. The EXECUTE privilege is needed to run the routine, although the privilege is normally granted automatically to its creator.

Creating a stored procedure

We'll create a procedure to change the page count for a specific book, by adding a specific number of pages. The book's ISBN and the number of pages to be added will be the input parameters to this procedure. We are using the SQL query box (see *Chapter 11, Entering SQL Commands*) to enter this procedure.

Changing the delimiter

The standard SQL delimiter is the semicolon, and this character will be used inside our procedure to delimit SQL statements. However, the CREATE PROCEDURE statement is by itself an SQL statement; hence, we must come up with a way to indicate to the MySQL parser where this statement ends. The query box has a **Delimiter** input box, which contains a semicolon by default. Therefore, we change it to another string, which, by convention, is a double slash //.

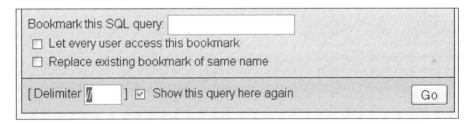

Entering the procedure

We then enter the procedure's code in the main query box:

```
CREATE PROCEDURE `add_page`(IN param_isbn VARCHAR(25),
  IN param_pages INT, OUT param_message VARCHAR(100))
BEGIN
  IF param_pages > 100 THEN
    SET param_message = 'the number of pages is too big';
  ELSE
    UPDATE book SET page_count = page_count + param_pages
    WHERE isbn=param_isbn;
    SET param_message = 'success';
```

```
    END IF;
END
//
```

On clicking **Go**, we get a success message if the syntax is correct. If it is not, well, it's time to revise our typing abilities or debug our syntax. Unfortunately, MySQL does not come with a procedure debugger.

Testing the procedure

Again, in the query box, we test our procedure by entering the following statements. Here, we are using an SQL variable, @message, which will receive the contents of the OUT parameter param_message:

```
call add_page('1-234567-22-0', 4, @message);
SELECT @message;
```

If all went well, we should see that the **@message** variable contains **success**.

We can then verify whether the page count for this book has increased. We also need to test the problematic case:

```
call add_page('1-234567-22-0', 101, @message);
SELECT @message;
```

This procedure is now available for calling (for example) from PHP, using the mysqli extension.

Manipulating procedures and functions

A procedure is stored inside a database, and is not tied to a specific table. Therefore, the interface for manipulating procedures and functions can be found at the database level, on the **Structure** page, under the **Routines** slider:

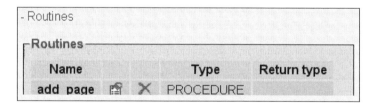

The first icon brings this procedure's text into a query box for editing. The second icon would be used to delete this procedure. When editing the procedure, we notice that the text has been somewhat modified.

```
DROP PROCEDURE `add_page`//
CREATE DEFINER= `marc`@`%` PROCEDURE `add_page`(
  IN param_isbn VARCHAR(25), IN param_pages INT,
  OUT param_message VARCHAR(100))
BEGIN
  IF param_pages > 100 THEN
    SET param_message = 'the number of pages is too big';
  ELSE
    UPDATE book SET page_count = page_count + param_pages
    WHERE isbn=param_isbn;
    SET param_message = 'success';
  END IF;
END
```

First, a DROP PROCEDURE appears. This is normal, because MySQL does not offer a statement that would permit a change to the body of a procedure. Therefore, we have to delete a procedure every time that we want to change it. It's true that the ALTER PROCEDURE statement exists, but it can only change the procedure's characteristics — for example, by adding a comment. Then, a DEFINER clause is shown. It was generated at creation time, and indicates who created this procedure.

At this point, we make any changes we need to make to the code, and click on **Go** to save this procedure.

> It might be tempting to open the book table on its **Structure** page and look for a list of procedures that manipulate this table, such as our add_page() procedure. However, all procedures are stored at the database level, and there is no direct link between the code itself (UPDATE book) and the place where the procedure is stored.

Manually creating a function

Functions are similar to stored procedures. However, a function can return only one value, whereas a stored procedure can have more than one OUT parameter. On the other hand, using a stored function from within a SELECT statement may seem more natural because it avoids the need for an intermediate SQL variable to hold the value of the OUT parameter.

What is the goal of functions? As an example, a function can be used to calculate the total cost of an order, including tax and shipping. Putting this logic inside the database, instead of at the application level, helps to document the application-database interface. It also avoids duplicating business logic in every application that needs to deal with this logic.

We should not confuse MySQL 5.0 functions with UDF (User-Defined Functions), which existed prior to MySQL 5.0. A UDF constitutes code written in C or C++, compiled into a shared object, and referenced via a CREATE FUNCTION statement and the SONAME keyword.

phpMyAdmin's treatment of functions is, in many ways, similar to what we have covered in procedures:

- A query box in which to enter a function
- The use of a delimiter
- A mechanism to manipulate a function that is already defined

Let's define a function that retrieves a country name, based on its code. I prefer to use a param_ prefix to clearly identify the parameters inside the function's definition, and a var_ prefix for local variables. We'll use our trusty SQL query box to enter the function's code, again indicating in this box that we want to use // as the delimiter.

```
CREATE FUNCTION get_country_name(param_country_code CHAR(2))
  RETURNS VARCHAR(50)
BEGIN
  DECLARE var_country_name VARCHAR(50) DEFAULT 'not found';
  SELECT description
    INTO var_country_name
    FROM country
    WHERE code = param_country_code;
  RETURN var_country_name;
END
//
```

We should note that our newly-created function can be seen on the database's Structure page, along with its friend, the add_page procedure:

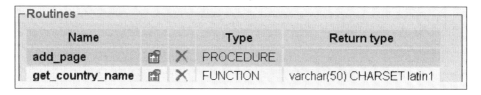

Routines			
Name		Type	Return type
add_page		PROCEDURE	
get_country_name		FUNCTION	varchar(50) CHARSET latin1

Testing the function

To test the function we just created, enter the following query:

```
SELECT CONCAT('ca->', get_country_name('ca'), ', zz->',
   get_country_name('zz')) as test;
```

This will produce the following result:

```
ca->Canada, zz->not found
```

Exporting stored procedures and functions

When exporting a database, procedures and functions do not appear (by default) in an SQL export. A checkbox, **Add CREATE PROCEDURE / FUNCTION / EVENT**, exists in the **Structure** dialog of the **Export** page, and can be selected in order to include procedures and functions in the SQL export file. If we try it, we obtain:

```
DELIMITER $$
--
-- Procedures
--
CREATE DEFINER=`marc`@`%` PROCEDURE `add_page`(
   IN param_isbn VARCHAR(25), IN param_pages INT,
   OUT param_message VARCHAR(100))
BEGIN
   IF param_pages > 100 THEN
      SET param_message = 'the number of pages is too big';
   ELSE
      UPDATE book SET page_count = page_count + param_pages
      WHERE isbn=param_isbn;
      SET param_message = 'success';
   END IF;
END$$


--
-- Functions
--
CREATE DEFINER= `marc`@`%` FUNCTION `get_country_name`
   param_country_code CHAR(2)) RETURNS varchar(50) CHARSET latin1
BEGIN
   DECLARE var_country_name VARCHAR(50) DEFAULT 'not found';
   SELECT description into var_country_name FROM country
   WHERE code = param_country_code;
   RETURN var_country_name;
END$$

DELIMITER ;
```

Executing code with triggers

Triggers are code that we associate with a table to be executed when certain actions occur—for example, after a new INSERT in the table book. The action does not need to take place within phpMyAdmin.

Contrary to routines that are related to an entire database and are visible on the database's **Structure** page, triggers for each table are accessed from *this specific table's* **Structure** page.

 Prior to MySQL 5.1.6, we needed the SUPER privilege to create or delete triggers. In version 5.1.6, a TRIGGER table-level privilege was added to the privilege system. Hence, a user no longer needs the powerful SUPER privilege for these tasks.

In order to perform the following exercise, we'll need a new INT column —total_page_count—in our author table.

The idea here is that every time a new book is created, its page count will be added to the author's total page count. Some people may advocate that it would be better not to keep a separate column for the total here, and instead compute the total every time we need it. In fact, a design decision must be made when dealing with this situation in the real world. Do we need to retrieve the total page count very quickly, for example, for web purposes? And what is the response time to compute this value from a production table with thousands of rows? Anyway, because I need it as an example, the design decision is easy to make here.

Let's not forget that following its addition to the table's structure, the total_page_count column should initially be seeded with the correct total. (However, this is not the purpose of our trigger.)

Manually creating a trigger

The current phpMyAdmin version does not have an interface for trigger creation. Therefore, we enter the trigger definition in a query box, taking special care to enter // in the delimiter box:

```
CREATE TRIGGER after_book_insert AFTER INSERT ON book
FOR EACH ROW
BEGIN
  UPDATE author
  SET total_page_count = total_page_count + NEW.page_count
  WHERE id = NEW.author_id;
END
//
```

Afterwards, the **Structure** page for our book table reveals, under the **Details** slider, a new **Triggers** section that can be used in the same way as routines, to edit or delete a trigger:

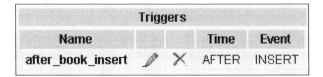

Testing the trigger

Contrary to testing stored procedures or functions, there is neither a CALL sequence nor a function inside a SELECT statement to execute the trigger. Any time the defined operation (a book INSERT) happens, the code will execute (in our case, after the insertion). Therefore, we simply have to insert a new book to see that the author.total_page_count column is updated.

Of course, a completely automatic management of this column would involve creating AFTER UPDATE and AFTER DELETE triggers on the book table.

Using information_schema

In the SQL:2003 standard, access to the data dictionary (or database metadata) is provided by a structure called information_schema. As this is part of the standard, and already exists in other database systems, the decision to implement this feature into MySQL was a very good one.

 MySQL has added some information that is not part of the standard — for example, INFORMATION_SCHEMA.COLUMNS.COLUMN_TYPE. Be aware of the fact that if you plan to use this information in a software project, it has to remain portable to other SQL implementations.

A phpMyAdmin user sees the information_schema as a normal database containing views that describe many aspects of the structure of the databases hosted on the server. Here is a subset of what can be seen (and in fact, the only possible operation on this database is SELECT).

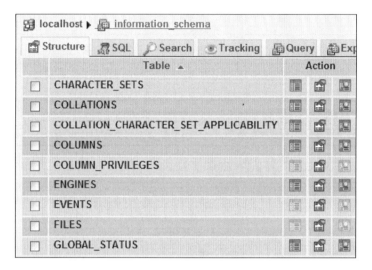

Internally, phpMyAdmin calls the information_schema for some of its operations, instead of the corresponding SHOW statements, in order to retrieve metadata. However, some SELECT operations involving a WHERE clause on information_ schema are really slow (many minutes of wait time) when the server hosts hundreds of databases or tables, and this has yet to be fixed by the MySQL team. Therefore, caution must be exercised when using this feature in our programming projects.

The $cfg['Servers'][$i]['hide_db'] parameter can be used to hide this "database" to users who might be confused by the sudden appearance of a database that they know nothing about. It will probably depend on their level of expertise in MySQL. On a multi-user installation of phpMyAdmin, we cannot please everyone about this parameter's value.

Profiling

Profiling support has been added to MySQL versions 5.0.37 and 5.1.28. We have previously seen the **Profiling** checkbox appear in query results.

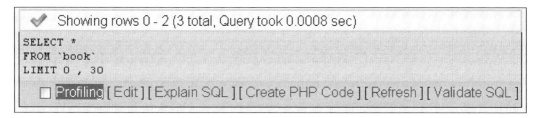

When this box is selected, phpMyAdmin will analyze every query (including the current one), and a report about the execution time of each MySQL internal operation is displayed:

Profiling

Status	Time
starting	0.000046
Opening tables	0.000027
System lock	0.000004
Table lock	0.000006
init	0.000024
optimizing	0.000006
statistics	0.000012
preparing	0.000010
executing	0.000003
Sending data	0.000395
end	0.000004
query end	0.000002
freeing items	0.000192
logging slow query	0.000002
cleaning up	0.000003

Although the profiling system can report additional information about operations (such as the CPU time, and even the internal server's function names), phpMyAdmin currently displays only the name of the operation and its duration.

Partitioning

User-defined partitioning (see `http://dev.mysql.com/doc/refman/5.1/en/ partitioning.html`) is offered in MySQL 5.1. It allows us to "distribute portions of individual tables across a file system according to rules which you can set largely as needed". Using this feature in phpMyAdmin requires knowledge of its syntax because there are many partition types. Also, for each partition type, the number of partitions and the values associated with each partition are too random to be easily represented on a web interface.

Creating a table with partitions

Let's examine this feature by creating a table named `test` with one field. On the table creation panel, if connected to a MySQL 5.1 server, phpMyAdmin shows a **PARTITION definition** dialog:

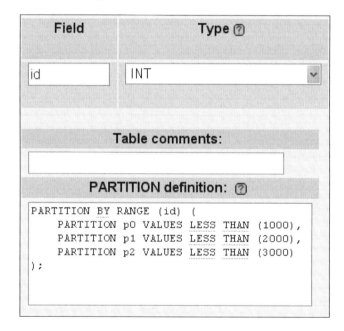

Here, we enter a **PARTITION BY RANGE** clause, which will create partitions on the `id` column.

Maintaining partitions

For a table on which a partition has been defined, the **Operations** subpage displays a **Partition maintenance** dialog where we can:

- Choose a partition and then request an action, such as **Rebuild**, on it
- Remove the partitioning

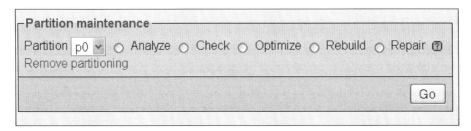

Exporting a partition definition

Finally, exporting this `test` table in SQL mode produces statements with embedded comments that a MySQL 5.1 server would recognize and interpret in order to recreate the same partitions:

```
CREATE TABLE `test` (
  `id` int(11) NOT NULL
) ENGINE=MyISAM DEFAULT CHARSET=latin1
/*!50100 PARTITION BY RANGE (id)
(PARTITION p0 VALUES LESS THAN (1000) ENGINE = MyISAM,
   PARTITION p1 VALUES LESS THAN (2000) ENGINE = MyISAM,
   PARTITION p2 VALUES LESS THAN (3000) ENGINE = MyISAM) */;
```

Exploring the Event Scheduler

The Event Scheduler (see `http://dev.mysql.com/doc/refman/5.1/en/events.html`), another new feature of MySQL 5.1, permits the creation of tasks that will run automatically according to a schedule. The schedule is quite flexible and permits, for example, a statement to be run every ten seconds, starting from midnight, May 18, 2011. These can be one-time events or recurring ones.

Activating the scheduler

We should first verify whether the scheduler is active on our server. If not, we need to activate it. Otherwise, nothing will happen! We start by typing the following statement in the query box:

```
SHOW VARIABLES LIKE 'event%';
```

Next, we look for a variable named `event_scheduler`. If this variable is set to `OFF`, then we need to ask the system administrator (or someone with the `SUPER` privilege) to execute the following statement:

```
SET GLOBAL event_scheduler = ON;
```

Granting EVENT permission

Every user who wants to create or drop an event needs the `EVENT` privilege, either globally or on the database on which he or she plans to add the event. Please refer to the *Chapter 19, Administrating the MySQL Server with phpMyAdmin*, for details about granting such privileges.

Creating an event

The current phpMyAdmin version does not have a web interface on which we could choose the various parts of the `CREATE EVENT` statement. Therefore, the only method left is to use the SQL query box to enter the statement and to understand its syntax! Here, we'll use a totally fictitious example:

```
CREATE EVENT add_page_count
   ON SCHEDULE
      EVERY 1 MINUTE
   DO
      UPDATE author set total_page_count = total_page_count + 1
      WHERE id = 1;
```

You can now get some amusement by browsing the `author` table once in a while, and see the counter incrementing for author 1.

Manipulating events

Events are related to a single database, which is why you see an **Events** slider on the **Structure** page for the `marc_book` database. Activating it reveals the following panel:

Indeed, this is a recurring event. We can use the first icon to edit the event (which will have the effect of deleting and recreating the event), and the **X** icon to remove it.

Exporting

It's possible to generate event-related statements at the end of an SQL database export by selecting the **Add CREATE PROCEDURE / FUNCTION / EVENT** option. Please remember that some events may have an ending moment. Hence, they may have vanished between the time you create them and the time that you attempt to export them!

BLOB streaming

Starting with version 3.1.0, phpMyAdmin supports the Scalable BLOB streaming infrastructure for MySQL. The `http://blobstreaming.org` website explains the goals of this project. Please note that some of its documentation relates to command-line utilities which have little or no use in the context of a web interface such as phpMyAdmin. You should be familiar with BLOB streaming terms, such as repository and field references, before reading further.

In this section, we will use BLOB streaming technology to upload a movie and watch it after streaming from within phpMyAdmin.

System requirements

The chosen method of implementation in phpMyAdmin relies on the following components:

- MySQL 5.1
- PBXT (PrimeBase XT storage engine)
- PBMS (PrimeBase Media Streaming)

PBXT is a streaming-enabled storage engine. Although other non-streaming-enabled storage engines are supported via PBMS UDFs, this mechanism is not implemented in phpMyAdmin.

The presence of the required components can be verified from the phpMyAdmin's home page, by clicking the **Engines** link and looking for the following lines:

```
PBXT / High performance, multi-versioning transactional engine
PBMS / The Media Stream engine for MySQL
```

In case these lines are not present, please follow the instructions on http://www. primebase.org to install PBXT, or on the BLOB Streaming website to install PBMS.

 You won't see PBMS in the storage engine choices of the **Operations** subpage for a table. PBMS is not a storage engine that can be associated with the structure of a table.

Configuring BLOB streaming

Some PBMS system variables have an impact on BLOB streaming behavior, and can be defined in config.inc.php. More details about them on can be found http://blobstreaming.org/documentation/#sysvar. The recommended values to be put in your server's definition are:

```
$cfg['Servers'][$i]['bs_garbage_threshold'] = 50;
$cfg['Servers'][$i]['bs_repository_threshold'] = '32M';
$cfg['Servers'][$i]['bs_temp_blob_timeout'] = 600;
$cfg['Servers'][$i]['bs_temp_log_threshold'] = '32M';
```

Examining implementation limitations in phpMyAdmin

In phpMyAdmin, a few limitations exist with respect to using BLOB streaming. The first limitation has to do with the MySQL server. On a server that has just started, the pbms_field_references global MySQL variable may be set to off. As field references are used extensively for BLOB referencing, phpMyAdmin tries to set this parameter to on, and this can be done only by a user possessing the SUPER privilege. Therefore, such a user must log in once via phpMyAdmin to set this parameter to the appropriate value, and this will have to be repeated on each restart of the MySQL server.

In phpMyAdmin versions 3.1.x to 3.3.x, only PBMS version 0.5.04 is supported.

The second limitation is related to the upload mechanism used to send data to the BLOB repository. The data has to travel first from your workstation to the web server, and then from the web server to the MySQL server. The first travel occurs via a normal HTTP upload. Please refer to the *Limits for the transfer* section of *Chapter 7, Importing Structure and Data*, for more details on the requirements for uploading. To avoid being hindered by this limit, you can use the web server upload directory (also described in *Chapter 7, Importing Structure and Data*).

 An important note about the hostname is due here: In `config.inc.php`, your server name in `$cfg['Servers'][$i]['host']` should be a **fully-qualified domain name (FQDN)**. It should not be something like "localhost"; otherwise, the links used to retrieve streaming data will not work.

Creating the PBMS system tables

If all of the requirements have been met, we can go to the `marc_book` database in the **Operations** subpage. We should see a **BLOB Repository** dialog, a **Status: Disabled** message, and an **Enable** button. We now have to click on **Enable** to create the PBMS system tables inside this database. There are two system tables required by PBMS (`pbms_repository` and `pbms_reference`), and another one (`pbms_custom_content_type`) for phpMyAdmin's internal needs.

After creation, we'll see **Status: Enabled** on the same page, but not the newly-created system tables. Usually, these tables are kept invisible from within phpMyAdmin because a user should not play with them directly.

We also see a **Disable** button. Clicking on this shows the following warning:

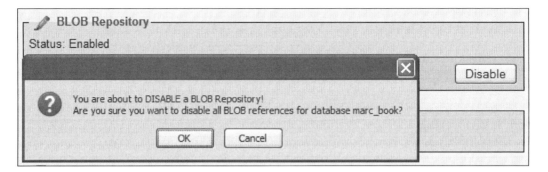

Confirming this warning message would make PBMS forget all of the BLOB references in this database, which would eventually delete all BLOB streaming data previously referenced from this database (if no other reference exists for it from *another* database).

Preparing the table

For this exercise, we'll use the `book.cover_photo` column, and LONGBLOB to hold the BLOB reference (remember that the stream data itself is located in the BLOB repository, and the LONGBLOB column is only there to contain the reference). We ensure that the book table is under the PBXT storage engine, and if this is not the case, we need to go to **Operations** for this table and change the engine, as explained in *Chapter 9, Performing Table and Database Operations*.

Using a LONGBLOB for BLOB reference is currently a PBXT requirement.

Uploading to the BLOB repository

We are finally ready to try our first upload to the repository. In the book table, we access the **Insert** panel (or we edit an existing row). Note the new **Upload to BLOB repository** option in the dialog for the `cover_photo` column:

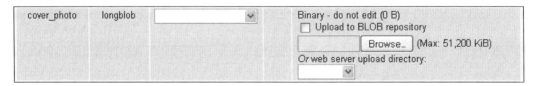

One might ask why this new option is shown. After all, don't we want to upload to the BLOB repository? Maybe! But as this LONGBLOB column may also hold regular data, two possibilities exist:

- Clicking the **Upload to BLOB repository** option, and then browsing for a file or picking one from the web server upload directory. This will send the file to the repository for streaming later.

- Not clicking the option, thereby sending the data directory to this column (not for streaming later).

Obviously, we pick the first choice and upload our favorite movie (we can try a short one first). If the upload works well, we'll see a query similar to this:

```
UPDATE `marc_book`.`book`
SET `cover_photo` = '~*marc_book/~1-150-15591197-0*3907219'
WHERE `book`.`isbn` = '1-234567-22-0' LIMIT 1;
```

Here, cover_photo was updated with the BLOB reference, which is a number generated by the PBMS storage engine.

Streaming the data from the repository

When browsing our table and looking at the row for which we made an upload into the BLOB repository, we see, under the cover_photo column, depending on the data format, one of these messages:

- View image
- Play audio
- View video
- Download file

Clicking on the displayed message starts streaming directly from the server's port 8080 to our browser, sending the appropriate MIME type to inform the browser about which format to expect.

We also see the MIME type of the uploaded data (here, **video/mp4**).

Changing repository data

In case the MIME type for the uploaded data was not interpreted correctly, it's possible to modify it by clicking this link and entering the correct MIME type. Finally, when editing this row, we'll see a **Remove BLOB Repository Reference** option. Selecting this option and then saving the row tells the PBMS engine to forget about this reference, eventually eliminating the BLOB data from the repository.

Summary

MySQL 5.0's new features helped the product to comply with standards. Even though phpMyAdmin has limited support for these features (especially lacking a syntax-oriented editor), it has a basic set of features for working with views, routines, triggers and `information_schema`, and for displaying profiling information. phpMyAdmin also supports MySQL 5.1 partitions and events, the PBXT storage engine, and BLOB streaming.

The next chapter covers the use of the tracking feature that permits the recording of changes made to a MySQL database via phpMyAdmin.

18
Tracking Changes

This chapter will examine how we can use a new feature of phpMyAdmin 3.3—the changes tracking mechanism, how to record structure and data changes done from the phpMyAdmin interface, and how to obtain reports about such changes.

Understanding the goals of the tracking system

This section describes tracking systems that exist in other applications, and compares them to the one offered by phpMyAdmin.

Tracking in other software applications

Having access to historic data that displays all of the changes made to an information system is a feature that is taken for granted in many software products. The *undo* feature of any serious word processing software is an example of being able to go back in time, albeit one step at the time. A more complex example would be the history feature of MediaWiki (the core software of Wikipedia). It enables to go back to any state of a given page, to see the changes between any two versions and even to mark any older version as the current one. Tracking information includes the author (or IP address), the date and time of the change, and a comment.

In MySQL itself, the logging system (binlog) records all changes made to the database; however in this case, the goal is twofold:

- To allow master-slave synchronization
- To enable restoration via the `mysqlbinlog` command-line utility

Tracking in phpMyAdmin

phpMyAdmin's tracking system allows the user to specify which table is going to be tracked, so it can be called an opt-in system. By default, no table is tracked unless a developer elects to do so—and when a developer activates tracking for a table, changes start to be recorded even if performed by someone else. Only the changes done via phpMyAdmin are recorded.

Furthermore, for a given table, we can indicate which statements we are interested in tracking. The list of statements is divided in two groups: data definition and data manipulation.

Suppose that a team is working on a project that involves making changes to the structure of tables. With tracking activated, and assuming that each developer logs in to MySQL with his or her own account, we now have access to historic data, including information about which developer dropped some critical column! Of course, this tracking is not tamper-proof; after all, it's stored in a MySQL table so the security of this tracking information depends on who has access to the tracking table.

Prerequisites

The linked-tables infrastructure stores all of the metadata for the tracking mechanism. If we have implemented this infrastructure a while ago (for a previous phpMyAdmin version, such as 3.1 or older), we can use `scripts/create_tables.sql` from the current phpMyAdmin version to upgrade the infrastructure with the missing tables (in our case, the `pma_tracking` table). The reason for this is that the script creates this table in a prudent way by using the CREATE TABLE IF NOT EXISTS `pma_tracking` statement, thus ensuring that it won't be created if the table is already present.

> In phpMyAdmin 3.3.3, the type of the `data_sql` column in `pma_tracking` was changed from TEXT to LONGTEXT in the `create_tables.sql` script. Therefore it's important to make this change manually, in our own `pma_tracking` table, if we ran this script prior to version 3.3.3.

Configuring a basic tracking mechanism

In `config.inc.php`, for a specific MySQL server's configuration, the `$cfg['Servers'][$i]['tracking']` should contain the name of the tracking table; the suggested name is `pma_tracking` to match the default value inside `scripts/create_tables.sql`.

If this directive is left blank, no tracking is possible on this server (we won't see any **Tracking** menu).

By default, tracking must be activated per table. If we prefer that the tracking mechanism be switched on automatically for all future tables and views, the `$cfg['Servers'][$i]['tracking_version_auto_create']` can be set to TRUE. Please note that this is only for future tables and views—we still need to activate tracking for existing tables.

The advantage of using automatic creation is that we don't have to think about it; tracking is done from the birth of a table. An inconvenient side-effect of this is that we don't have the possibility of choosing which statements will be tracked; these will be taken from the default list (see the *Choosing the statements to be tracked* section later in this chapter).

Other configuration directives will be discussed in the section that relates to them.

Principles

This section defines the important principles on which the tracking mechanism is based: versioning, snapshot, and the archiving issues of tracking information.

Versioning

Using version numbers is something we are familiar with; for example, this book describes phpMyAdmin version 3.3.x. However, at this point we must understand exactly why we use version numbers.

A good reference on software versioning is located in Wikipedia: `http://en.wikipedia.org/wiki/Software_versioning`. This article mentions that version names can be used, but version numbers are more common. More importantly, they state that version numbers "correspond to new developments in the software".

If we apply this principle to database development, the decision that a table is ripe for a new version should be made by the development team when a significant change is about to occur for this table. How significant the change has to be in order to trigger a new version is of course a matter of interpretation within the team. At least one of these decisions is easy to make: version 1 always represents the moment where we switch on the tracking for a particular table.

In the situation where data manipulation statements are tracked, we should also note that the change can be relative to data itself, not necessarily for the structure.

 phpMyAdmin's tracking system uses only positive integers as version numbers; it's not possible to use, for example, version 1.1.

Taking a snapshot of the current structure

Every time we create a new version, the tracking system takes a snapshot of the current structure and indexes of the table, and creates a new row in the tracking system. In this row are stored the database name, table name, version number, date of creation, and the complete structure information.

 This tracking snapshot does not contain a table's data! Therefore, the tracking system is not a backup system.

During the lifespan of this table after the snapshot has been taken, all tracked statements are stored alongside this snapshot. Therefore, a table tracking version consists of the snapshot in addition to all changes made after this snapshot was taken, until a new version is started.

Understanding archiving issues

When a table is dropped, its tracking information survives, unless we decide to suppress it. The impact of this will be discussed below (see the *Deleting tracking information* section).

Initiating tracking for one table

In this section, we will use the Tracking menu in Table view to start collecting the changes that occur for the `author` table. So we open the `author` table and then click on **Tracking**, which produces the following:

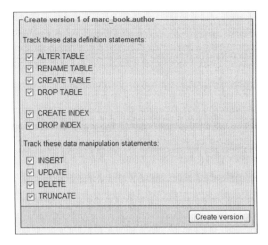

This panel tells us that we are about to create version 1 of the table; this is what we expected. We are offered a choice of data definition and data manipulation statements; for now we will leave all of them marked, and will click on **Create version**. The next section explains how we can specify which statements are to appear in the panel shown above.

After version 1 is created, the following confirmation panel is shown:

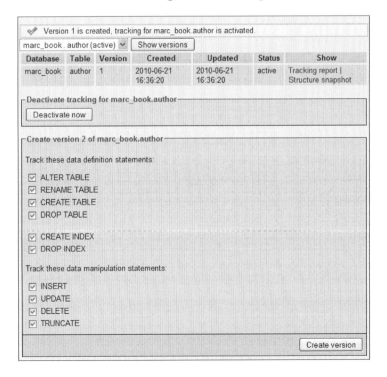

We notice that two distinct actions took place:

- The creation of version 1 itself
- The activation of tracking for this table

Indeed, one or many versions of a table may exist, each one containing a snapshot from some point in time and the changes since this snapshot; but this is independent of the fact that tracking is active for a table and changes are being recorded.

In this panel, we see subpanels that will be covered in the *Choosing the statements to be tracked* and *Deactivating and activating tracking* sections.

Choosing the statements to be tracked

`$cfg['Servers'][$i]['tracking_default_statements']` contains a string that consists of comma-separated statements. These are the ones that are offered in the panel where we can choose which statements we want to track. The default list of statements is defined as follows; please note the dot character that permits the concatenation of strings in PHP:

```
$cfg['Servers'][$i]['tracking_default_statements'] =
    'CREATE TABLE,ALTER TABLE,DROP TABLE,RENAME TABLE,' .
    'CREATE INDEX,DROP INDEX,' .
    'INSERT,UPDATE,DELETE,TRUNCATE,REPLACE,' .
    'CREATE VIEW,ALTER VIEW,DROP VIEW,' .
    'CREATE DATABASE,ALTER DATABASE,DROP DATABASE';
```

Testing the tracking mechanism

We are now ready to verify that this tracking system really works! As the system is supposed to track ALTER TABLE, we will make a slight structure change and see what happens. We go to the **Structure** panel for table **author**, select the **name** column, and increase its size from 30 to 40 characters (refer to *Chapter 5, Changing Data and Structure*, for the detailed steps).

We see the following message:

```
    Table author has been altered successfully

ALTER TABLE `author` CHANGE `name` `name` VARCHAR(40) CHARACTER SET utf8 COLLATE utf8_general_ci NOT NULL

                                                                            [ Edit ] [ Create PH
```

We create another action, this time related to data itself: changing the phone number of author **John Smith** to **111-2222**.

To ensure that these actions were recorded by the tracking system, let's compile a report.

Tracking report

Going back to the **Tracking** panel (still in Table view for **author**), we click on **Tracking report** for version 1, which produces the following report:

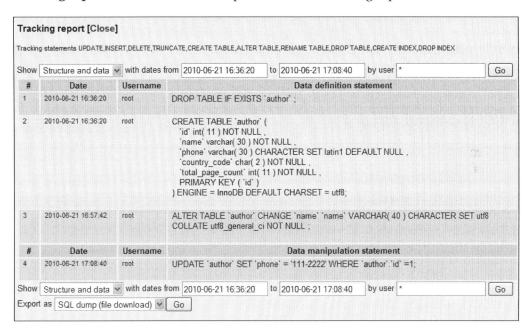

In fact, the report is prefixed to the main tracking information; we could click on **Close** and be back to where we were previously.

We can see that under the **Tracking report** header, a list of the statements that are tracked is shown. Then we have a selector to determine if we want to see on the report the statements corresponding to:

- Structure and data
- Structure only
- Data only

We can also specify the range of dates and times for which we want to produce the report; it's also possible to indicate which users we want to report on (an asterisk represents all users).

The main part of the reports consists of the statements themselves; here we see four statements. The first statement is a DROP TABLE statement, which would be useful for creating this table anew, should we need to export this version and import it back. The second statement contains the snapshot that was taken when version 1 was initiated. Then we see the ALTER TABLE and UPDATE statements that correspond to the actions we performed as a test.

How to export a structure will be covered in the *Exporting a version* section, later in this chapter.

Determining tracking status

Let's cover all of the places in the interface where we can ascertain the tracking activity for a table. Firstly, in Table view, we can see a message positioned under the menu tabs, stating that tracking is activated for this table:

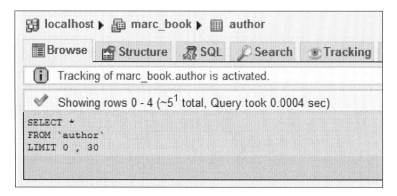

In the **Tracking** panel itself, a **Status** column tells us that tracking is either **active** or **not active** for the latest version. In fact, when we create another version for the table, we'll see that only the most current version can have an active tracking status, as previous versions now only contain historical data.

Database	Table	Version	Created	Updated	Status
marc_book	author	1	2010-06-21 16:36:20	2010-06-21 17:08:40	active

In Database view, each table that is tracked by the tracking system (with an active or not active status) is shown with either the icon of an open eye or a closed (sleeping) one, depending upon its status. In the following example, the eye is open:

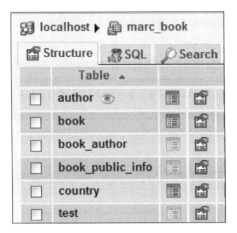

This eye icon is clickable, and brings us to the **Tracking** panel for this specific table.

Finally, in Database view, the **Tracking** menu provides us with an overview of all the tables. First the tracked tables are presented, then the untracked ones. For either category, we have links to see more information, or to start tracking:

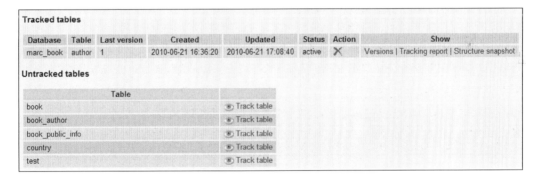

For the tracked tables, here is a breakdown of the information presented, along with the available links:

Title or link	Description
Database	In which database the table is located
Table	Which table is tracked
Last version	The latest tracked version; it's interesting to see how many versions exist for this table
Created	When was this version created
Updated	When was the last tracked statement stored for this table
Status	Active or not active
Action	The red X icon can be used to remove all tracking (see the *Deleting tracking information* section below)
Show Versions	Enters Table view for this table, and displays tracking versions
Show Tracking report	Enters Table view for this table, and displays the tracking report
Show Structure snapshot	Enters Table view for this table, and displays the structure snapshot (see the *Structure snapshot* section later in this chapter)

For the untracked tables, a **Track table** link allows us to enter Table view for this table, directly in the **Tracking** panel, hence creating version 1 in order to start the tracking mechanism.

Deactivating and activating tracking

The **Deactivate now** button (which acts as a toggle, and changes to **Activate now**) is the one to use if we wish to stop (temporarily or permanently) further storing of the tracked statements. Past statements that were stored remain untouched in the tracking data related to the current version.

Structure snapshot

In the **Tracking** panel of Table view, the **Structure snapshot** link displays the past state of the table at the time this version was created. The panel shows both the stored SQL code and a visual representation in the familiar phpMyAdmin **Structure**-panel format:

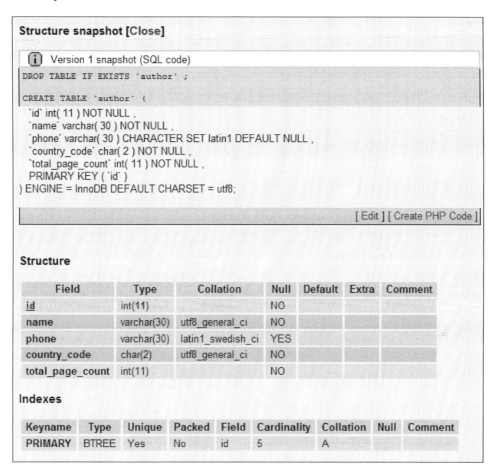

Exporting a version

As the complete SQL code at time of creation for a specific version has been stored, along with all of the tracked statements that occurred since this moment, we might want to reuse them in their executable form. At the bottom of the **Tracking report**, an **Export** dialog is available, offering three variants for exporting. If we choose **SQL dump (file download)**, then all of the statements stored for this version are put in a file that we can save to our workstation. For the author table, this would produce a file containing the following lines:

```
# Tracking report for table `author`
# 2010-06-22 16:33:44

DROP TABLE IF EXISTS `author`;

CREATE TABLE `author` (
  `id` int(11) NOT NULL,
  `name` varchar(30) NOT NULL,
  `phone` varchar(30) CHARACTER SET latin1 DEFAULT NULL,
  `country_code` char(2) NOT NULL,
  `total_page_count` int(11) NOT NULL,
  PRIMARY KEY (`id`)
) ENGINE=InnoDB DEFAULT CHARSET=utf8;
ALTER TABLE `author` CHANGE `name` `name` VARCHAR(40) CHARACTER SET
utf8 COLLATE utf8_general_ci NOT NULL;
UPDATE `author` set `phone` = '111-2222' WHERE `author`.`id` = 1;
```

If, instead, we pick the **SQL dump** choice, the statements appear on screen in a text area; from this point we could cut and paste the SQL code or click on **Go** to run it. As a measure of precaution, extra statements are generated on top of the code; these handle the creation of another database in which the table would be created. Of course, the user must have the rights to create this database.

Finally, the **SQL execution** choice allows us to directly execute the stored statements in the current database. However, a warning message is issued because these statements might reflect an older state of the table; we might not want to revert to this old state. Also, the first statement is, by **default**, a DROP TABLE, **which may or** may not succeed, depending on whether some foreign key constraint blocks the deletion of the table.

Creating a new version

As previously discussed, we can decide to mark a new milestone for a certain table; in other words, we can start a new version. We'll now create a new version as an exercise.

In the **Tracking** panel for the `author` table, we see the dialog for creating **version 2** (because the highest one is currently version 1):

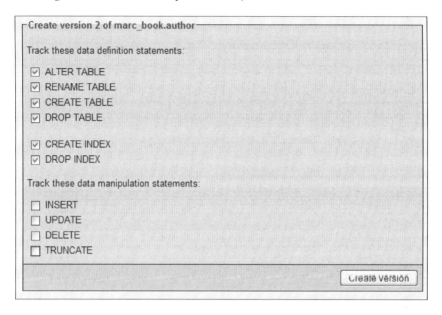

We notice that each version can track its own set of statements—versions are independent from each other in this matter. Here we have decided that version 2 will track only data definition statements. We now see something interesting relative to the status of these versions:

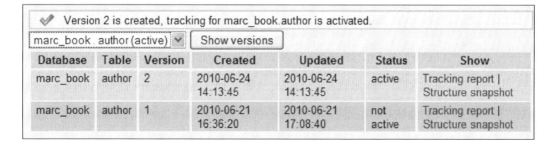

Database	Table	Version	Created	Updated	Status	Show
marc_book	author	2	2010-06-24 14:13:45	2010-06-24 14:13:45	active	Tracking report | Structure snapshot
marc_book	author	1	2010-06-21 16:36:20	2010-06-21 17:08:40	not active	Tracking report | Structure snapshot

Indeed, version 1 was automatically marked as **not active**; it went into some kind of historical status. We can also have a look at version 2's snapshot, which reflects that the name column is a VARCHAR(40).

Quickly accessing tracking information

When we are in the **Tracking** panel for one table, a shortcut dialog allows us to go directly to the **Tracking** panel of any other tracked table.

To explore this feature, let's now create version 1 of the book table. After this is done, we examine the drop-down list next to **Show versions**, and see the following:

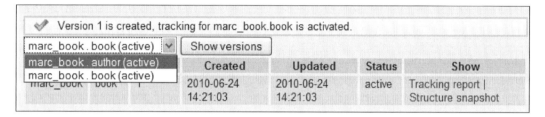

This list is similar to what we would see in the **Tracking** panel for database marc_book when looking at the **Tracked tables** portion, but without the need to go back to this panel.

Deleting tracking information

A feature of the tracking system that might not be evident is that tracking information for all versions of a table—thus for its whole lifespan—is kept when the corresponding table is dropped. The reason for this is to keep the history information intact should we happen to create a table with the same name later on.

Let's create a copy of the author table (refer to *Chapter 9, Performing Table and Database operations*, if needed), named author_copy. We then activate tracking on this new table. The last operation is to drop this table. Even if we no longer see it in the normal list of tables, it's different in the **Tracking** panel for database marc_book:

Tracked tables

Database	Table	Last version	Created	Updated	Status	Action	Show
marc_book	author	2	2010-06-24 14:13:45	2010-06-24 14:13:45	active	✕	Versions | Tracking report | Structure snapshot
marc_book	author_copy	1	2010-06-24 14:39:18	2010-06-24 14:39:39	active	✕	Versions | Tracking report | Structure snapshot
marc_book	book	1	2010-06-24 14:21:03	2010-06-24 14:21:03	active	✕ Delete tracking data for this table	Versions | Tracking report | Structure snapshot

At this point we can go back in time, sort of, and see the tracking report and snapshot for the versions of this deleted table. If we really want to remove all evidence, of the table ever having existed then we can use the red **X** to destroy the tracking data (after clicking on OK in the subsequent confirmation panel).

Summary

In this chapter, we saw an overview of the benefits given by the statements tracking feature, and then we covered all of the panels involved in the creation and maintenance of versions for tables.

The next chapter covers administration of a MySQL server, focusing on the management of user accounts and privileges.

19
Administrating the MySQL Server with phpMyAdmin

This chapter discusses how a system administrator can use the phpMyAdmin server management features for day-to-day user account maintenance, server verification, and server protection. The subject of how non-administrators can obtain server information from phpMyAdmin is also covered.

Server administration is mostly done via the Server view, which is accessed via the menu tabs available on phpMyAdmin's home page.

Managing users and their privileges

The **Privileges** subpage (visible only if we are logged in as a privileged user) contains dialogs to manage MySQL user accounts. It also contains dialogs to manage privileges on the global, database, and table levels. This subpage is hierarchical. For example, when editing a user's privileges, we can see the global privileges as well as the database-specific privileges. We can then go deeper to see the table-specific privileges for this database-user combination.

The user overview

The first page displayed when we enter the **Privileges** subpage is called **User overview**. This shows all user accounts and a summary of their global privileges, as shown in the next screenshot:

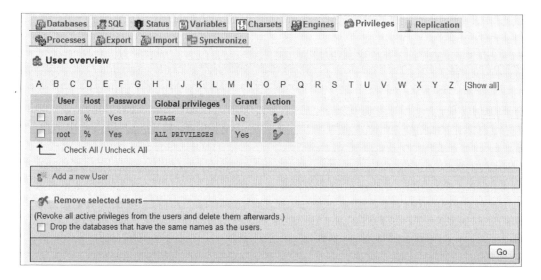

From this page, we can:

- Edit a user's privileges, via the **Edit** link for this user
- Use the checkboxes to remove users, via the **Remove selected users** dialog
- Access the page when the **Add a new User** dialog is available

The displayed users' list has columns with the following characteristics:

Column	Characteristic
User	The user account we are defining.
Host	The machine name, or IP address, from which this user account will be connecting to the MySQL server. A % value here indicates all hosts.
Password	Contains **Yes** if a password is defined and **No** if it isn't. The password itself cannot be seen from phpMyAdmin's interface, or by directly looking at the mysql.user table, as it is encrypted with a one-way hashing algorithm.
Global privileges	A list of the user's global privileges.

Column	Characteristic
Grant	Contains **Yes** if the user can grant his or her privileges to others.
Action	Contains a link to edit this user's privileges.

Privileges reload

At the bottom of **User Overview**, the following message is displayed:

```
Note: phpMyAdmin gets the users' privileges directly from MySQL's
privilege tables. The content of these tables may differ from the
privileges the server uses, if they have been changed manually. In
this case, you should reload the privileges before you continue.
```

Here, the text **reload the privileges** is clickable. The effective privileges (the ones against which the server bases its access decisions) are the privileges that are located in the server's memory. Privilege modifications that are made from the **User overview** page are made both in memory and on disk, in the `mysql` database. Modifications made directly to the `mysql` database do not have immediate effect. The **reload the privileges** operation reads the privileges from the database and makes them effective in memory.

Adding a user

The **Add a new User** link opens a dialog for user account creation. First, we see the panel where we'll describe the account itself:

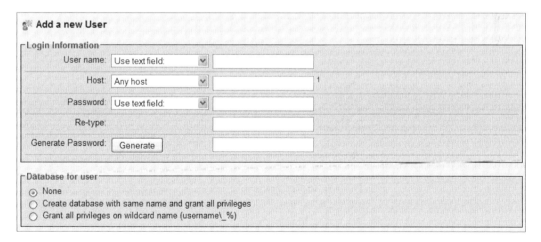

The second part of the **Add a new User** dialog is where we'll specify the user's global privileges, which apply to the server as a whole (see the *Assigning global privileges* section of this chapter).

Entering the username

The **User name** menu offers two choices. Firstly, we can choose **Use text field** and enter a username in the box, or we can choose **Any user** to create an anonymous user (the blank user). Let's choose **Use text field** and enter **bill**.

Assigning a host value

By default, this menu is set to **Any host**, with % as the host value. The **Local** choice means "localhost". The **Use host table** choice (which creates a blank value in the host field) means to look in the `mysql.hosts` table for database-specific privileges. Choosing **Use text field** allows us to enter the exact host value we want. Let's choose **Local**.

Setting passwords

Even though it's possible to create a user without a password (by selecting the **No password** option), it's best to have a password. We have to enter it twice (as we cannot see what is entered) to confirm the intended password. A secure password should have more than eight characters, and should contain a mixture of uppercase and lowercase characters, digits, and special characters. Therefore, it's recommended to have phpMyAdmin generate a password—this is possible in JavaScript-enabled browsers. In the **Generate Password** dialog, clicking on **Generate** enters a random password (in clear text) on the screen and fills the **Password** and **Re-type** input fields with the generated password. At this point, we should note the password so that we can pass it on to the user.

Understanding rights for database creation

A frequent convention is to assign a user the rights to a database having the same name as this user. To accomplish this, the **Database for user** section offers the checkbox **Create database with same name and grant all privileges**. Selecting this checkbox automates the process by creating both the database (if it does not already exist) and the corresponding rights. Please note that, with this method, each user would be limited to one database (user `bill`, database `bill`).

Another possibility is to allow users to create databases that have the same prefix as their usernames. Therefore, the other choice, **Grant all privileges on wildcard name (username_%)**, performs this function by assigning a wildcard privilege. With this in place, user `bill` could create the databases `bill_test`, `bill_2`, `bill_payroll`, and so on; phpMyAdmin does not pre-create the databases in this case.

Assigning global privileges

Global privileges determine the user's access to all databases. Hence, these are sometimes known as "**superuser privileges**". A normal user should not have any of these privileges unless there is a good reason for this.

Of course, if we are really creating a superuser, we will select every global privilege that he or she needs. These privileges are further divided into **Data**, **Structure**, and **Administration** groups.

In our example, **bill** will not have any global privileges.

Limiting the resources used

We can limit the resources used by this user on this server (for example, the maximum queries per hour). Zero means no limit. We will not impose any resource limits on **bill**.

The following screenshot shows the status of the screen just before hitting **Go** to create this user's definition (with the remaining fields being set to default):

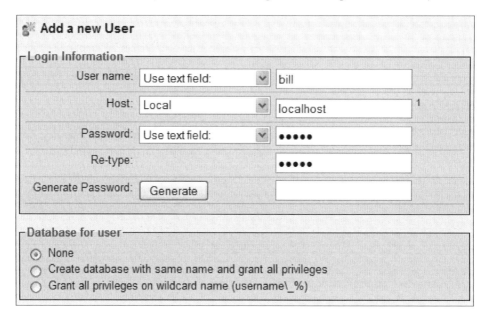

Editing a user profile

The page used to edit a user's profile appears after a user's creation, or whenever we click on **Edit** for a user in the **User overview** page. There are four sections on this page, each with its own **Go** button. Hence, each section is operated independently and has a distinct purpose.

Editing privileges

The section for editing the user's privileges has the same look as the **Add a new User** dialog, and is used to view and change global privileges.

Assigning database-specific privileges

In this section, we define the databases to which our user has access, and his or her exact privileges on these databases.

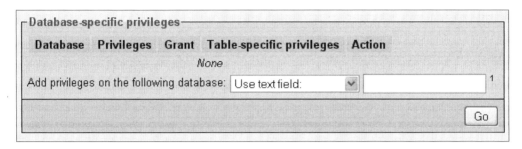

As shown in the previous screenshot, we see **None** because we haven't defined any privileges yet. There are two ways of defining database privileges. First, we can choose one of the existing databases from the drop-down menu:

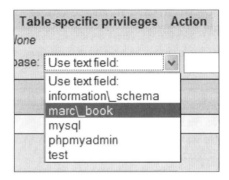

This assigns privileges only for the chosen database. We can also choose **Use text field** and enter a database name. We could enter a non-existent database name, so that the user can create it later (provided that we give him or her the CREATE privilege in the next panel). We can also use special characters, such as the underscore and the percent sign, for wildcards.

For example, entering **bill** here would enable him to create a **bill** database, and entering **bill%** would enable him to create a database with any name that starts with **bill**. For our example, we will enter **bill** and then click on **Go**.

The next screen is used to set **bill**'s privileges on the **bill** database, and create table-specific privileges.

To learn more about the meaning of a specific privilege, we can move the mouse over a privilege name (which is always in English), and an explanation about this privilege appears in the current language. We give **SELECT**, **INSERT**, **UPDATE**, **DELETE**, **CREATE**, **ALTER**, **INDEX**, and **DROP** privileges to **bill** on this database. We then click on **Go**.

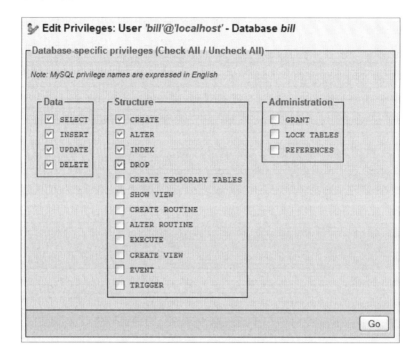

After the privileges have been assigned, the interface stays at the same place, so that we can refine these privileges further. We cannot assign table-specific privileges for the moment, as the database does not yet exist.

To go back to the general privileges page of **bill**, click on the **'bill'@'localhost'** title.

This brings us back to the following, familiar page, except for a change in one section:

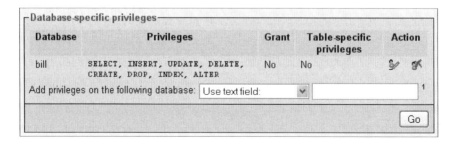

We see the existing privileges (which we can **Edit** or **Revoke**) on the **bill** database for user **bill**, and we can add privileges for **bill** on another database. We can also see that **bill** has no table-specific privileges on the **bill** database.

Changing the password

The Change password dialog is part of the **Edit user** page, and we can use it either to change **bill's** password or to remove it. Removing the password will enable **bill** to login without a password. The dialog offers a choice of password hashing options, and it's recommended to keep the default of **MySQL 4.1+** hashing. For more details about hashing, please visit `http://dev.mysql.com/doc/refman/5.1/en/password-hashing.html`.

Changing login information or copying a user

This dialog can be used to change the user's login information, or to copy his or her login information to a new user. For example, suppose that Bill calls and tells us that he prefers the login name **billy** instead of **bill**. We just have to add a **y** to the username, choose **Local** as the host, and select **delete the old one from the user tables**:

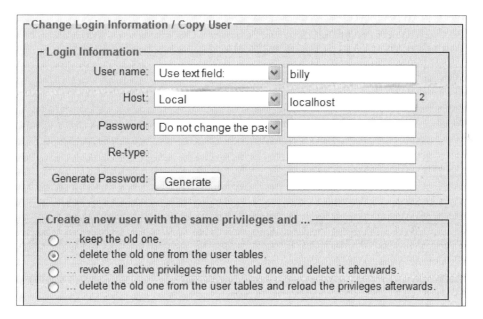

After this operation, **bill** no longer exists in the `mysql` database. Also, all of his privileges, including the privileges on the **bill** database, will have been transferred to the new user—**billy**. But the user definition of **bill** will still exist in memory, and hence it's still effective. If we had chosen the **delete the old one from the user tables and reload the privileges afterwards** option instead, the user definition of **bill** would immediately have ceased to be valid.

Alternatively, we could have created another user based on **bill**, by making use of the **keep the old one** choice. We can transfer the password to the new user by choosing **Do not change the password**, or change it by entering a new password, twice. The **revoke all active privileges...** option immediately terminates the effective current privileges for this user, even if he or she is currently logged in.

Removing a user

Removing a user is done from the **User overview** section of the **Privileges** page. We select the user to be removed. Then (in **Remove selected users**) we can select the **Drop...** option to remove any databases that have the same name as the user we are deleting. A click on **Go** effectively removes the selected users.

Database information

The **Databases** subpage is intended to quickly get privileges information for each database. Optionally, it can also be used to obtain global statistics on these databases, without having to click on each database in the navigation panel. When we enter the **Databases** subpage, we see the list of existing databases:

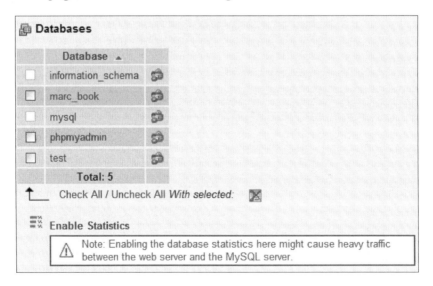

We also see an **Enable Statistics** link. By default, statistics are not enabled because computing the size of data and indexes for all the tables in all of the databases may consume valuable MySQL server resources.

Enabling statistics

If we click on the **Enable Statistics** link, a modified page appears. For each database, we get the default collation for tables in this database, along with the number of tables in the database and the total number of rows for all tables. Next, information about the space used by the data portion of the tables is given, followed by the space taken by all indexes and total space for all tables. Finally, the space that could be reclaimed by optimizing some tables in this database is presented under **Overhead**.

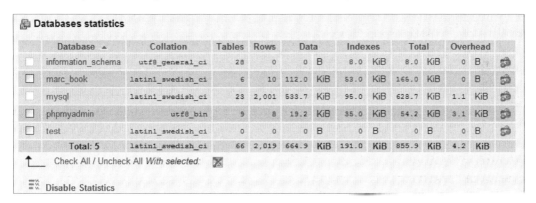

	Database ▲	Collation	Tables	Rows	Data		Indexes		Total		Overhead		
☐	information_schema	utf8_general_ci	28	0	0	B	8.0	KiB	8.0	KiB	0	B	🗐
☐	marc_book	latin1_swedish_ci	6	10	112.0	KiB	53.0	KiB	165.0	KiB	0	B	🗐
☐	mysql	latin1_swedish_ci	23	2,001	533.7	KiB	95.0	KiB	628.7	KiB	1.1	KiB	🗐
☐	phpmyadmin	utf8_bin	9	8	19.2	KiB	35.0	KiB	54.2	KiB	3.1	KiB	🗐
☐	test	latin1_swedish_ci	0	0	0	B	0	B	0	B	0	B	🗐
	Total: 5	latin1_swedish_ci	66	2,019	664.9	KiB	191.0	KiB	855.9	KiB	4.2	KiB	

↑ Check All / Uncheck All *With selected:* 🗙

⠿ Disable Statistics

Sorting statistics

By default, the statistics list is sorted by database name in ascending order. If we need to find the database with the most tables or the database that takes the most space, a simple click on the **Tables** or **Total** column header sorts the list accordingly. A second click reverses the sort order.

Checking the database privileges

Clicking on the **Check Privileges** icon displays all of the privileges on a specific database. A user's global privilege might be shown here, as it gives him or her access to this database as well. We can also see the privileges specific to this database. An **Edit** link takes us to another page, which is used to edit the user's privileges.

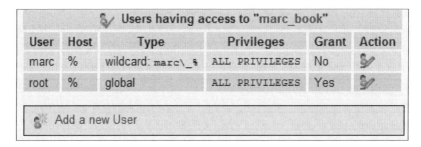

We notice that this panel also contains this link: **Add a new User**. Clicking on this link is a convenient way of creating a user that has privileges to the database we are currently examining. Indeed, after entering the user creation panel from this link, a fourth choice in the database creation or privileges granting dialog is shown and selected by default:

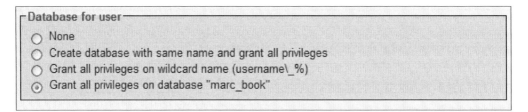

Dropping selected databases

To drop one or more databases, we select the checkboxes next to the names of the databases to be dropped, and then click on the red X next to **With selected**. We then get a confirmation screen. Two of the databases (`mysql` and the virtual `information_schema`) cannot be selected, **the first one to avoid making a big mistake and deleting all of our accounts**, and the second one cannot be selected as this is not a real database.

 This is an operation that should not be taken lightly, and it might be prudent to first export the whole database as a backup.

Server information

The **Status**, **Variables**, and **Processes** menu tabs can be used to get information about the MySQL server, or to act upon specific processes.

Verifying server status

The server status statistics reflect the MySQL server's total activity, including (but not limited to) the activity generated by queries sent from phpMyAdmin.

The general status page

Clicking on the **Status** link produces runtime information about the server. The page has several sections. First, we get information about the elapsed running time and the startup time. Then we get the total and average values for traffic and connections (where the ø means average).

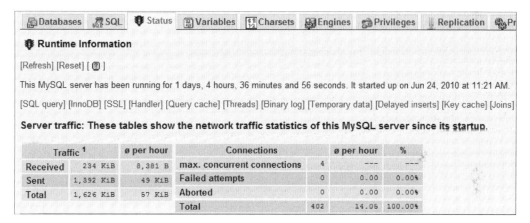

Next, the statistics about the queries are displayed (shown in part here). The average number of queries per hour, minute, and second give a good indication of the server load.

The query statistics are followed by statistics about each MySQL command, including the absolute number of times each command has been executed, hourly average, and the number of times run as a percentage of the total. The presentation order is by descending percentage of utilization: here we see that the SELECT statement is the one most received by this server, with **30.17%**:

Query statistics: Since its startup, 3,276 queries have been sent to the server.

Total	ø per hour	ø per minute	ø per second
3,276	114.48	1.91	0.03

Query type	ø per hour	%	Query type	ø per hour	%
select	867	30.298	30.17%	show slave status	24	0.839	0.84%
set option	832	29.075	28.95%	show keys	20	0.699	0.70%
show tables	310	10.833	10.79%	delete	17	0.594	0.59%
change db	233	8.142	8.11%	show create func	12	0.419	0.42%
show table status	160	5.591	5.57%	show create event	12	0.419	0.42%
show fields	73	2.551	2.54%	show create proc	12	0.419	0.42%
show binlogs	58	2.027	2.02%	show storage engines	8	0.280	0.28%
show databases	58	2.027	2.02%	show charsets	6	0.210	0.21%
show create table	39	1.363	1.36%	grant	6	0.210	0.21%
show variables	34	1.188	1.18%	show collations	6	0.210	0.21%
show triggers	27	0.944	0.94%	show grants	6	0.210	0.21%
show master status	24	0.839	0.84%	drop user	6	0.210	0.21%

Depending on the MySQL version, many other sections containing server information are also displayed.

InnoDB status

On servers supporting InnoDB, a link appears at the end of the **InnoDB** section. When this link is clicked, information about the InnoDB subsystem is displayed, including information about the last InnoDB error that occurred.

Server variables

The **Variables** subpage displays various settings for the MySQL server, which can be defined in, say, the my.cnf MySQL configuration file. These values can't be changed from within phpMyAdmin.

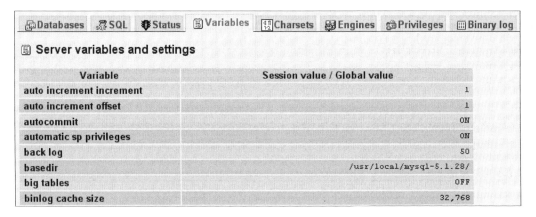

Server processes

The **Processes** subpage is available to both superusers and normal users. A normal user would see only the processes belonging to him or her, whereas a superuser sees all of the processes.

This page lists all active processes on the server. There is a **Kill** link that allows us to terminate a specific process:

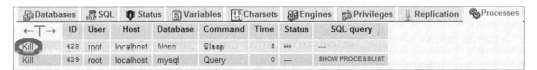

This example has only two running processes— including the one created by the SHOW PROCESSLIST command itself. This process is not killable because it's no longer running when we get to see the page. We would normally see more processes running on a busy server.

Storage engines

Information about the various storage engines is available in a two-level format. First, the **Engines** tab displays an overview of the possible engines for the current MySQL version. The names of the engines that are enabled on this server are clickable:

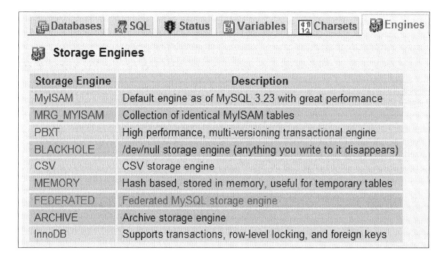

A click on one engine name brings up a detailed panel about its settings. Moving the mouse over the numbers in superscript reveals even more information about a particular setting.

Available character sets and collations

The **Charsets** menu tab on the home page opens the Server view for the **Charsets** subpage, which lists the character sets and collations supported by the MySQL server. The default collation for each character set is shown with a different background color (using the row-marking color defined in `$cfg['BrowseMarkerColor']`).

Examining binary logs

If MySQL's binary log is active on our server, the menu in the Server view changes so that a **Binary log** tab appears. This tab gives access to an interface, through the SHOW BINLOG EVENTS command. This command produces the list of SQL statements that have updated data on our servers. This list could be huge, and currently phpMyAdmin does not limit its display with a pagination technique. Hence, we could hit the browser's memory limits, which depend on the particular browser we are using.

In the following screen, we choose the binary log that we want to examine (unless the server has only one binary log), and the statements are then displayed.

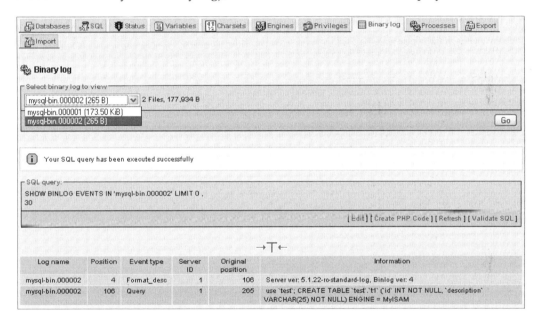

Summary

This chapter covered various features available to system administrators, such as user account management, privileges management, database privileges checks, and server status verification. Appropriate knowledge of the MySQL privileges system is crucial in order to maintain a MySQL server adequately, and this chapter proposes exercises centered around the notion of a user and his or her privileges.

Appendix A, History of phpMyAdmin, is next, which tells the history of the phpMyAdmin project.

The History of phpMyAdmin

This appendix details the birth and evolution of phpMyAdmin over its twelve-year history. A one-person hobby project back in 1998, this software has grown, in terms of both the features and the number of people involved. As a testimony to this growth, the earliest source kit I could find (for version 1.1.0) occupied 9 KB, compared to version 3.3.2's size of 4.5 MB (both sizes taken from the .tar.gz files). Interestingly, early versions displayed **Welcome to phpMySQLAdmin**.

Early events

The first internal version (0.9.0) was programmed by Tobias Ratschiller from Switzerland, and bears the date September 09, 1998. He then released version 1.0.1 on October 26, 1998. The early versions were offered on Tobias's site http://www.phpwizard.net (this site is no longer associated with him). Tobias wrote in the accompanying notes:

> *This work is based on Peter Kuppelwieser's MySQL-Webadmin. It was his idea to create a web-based interface to MySQL using PHP3. Although I have not used any of his source-code, there are some concepts I've borrowed from him. phpMyAdmin was created because Peter told me he wasn't going to further develop his (great) tool.*

Compared to today's version (twelve years after the original version), the first version was somewhat limited in features. Nevertheless it could be used to create databases and tables, edit their structures, and enter and retrieve data. In the following screenshot, you can see that the navigation panel was already in place to list database names (not table names yet), and the main panel was the workspace to manage a database or table. This is how the interface for databases looked like in version 1.3.0:

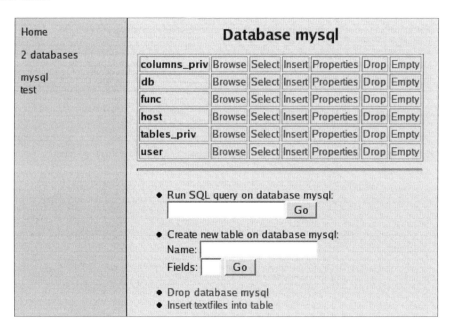

To work on a table, the following screen was available:

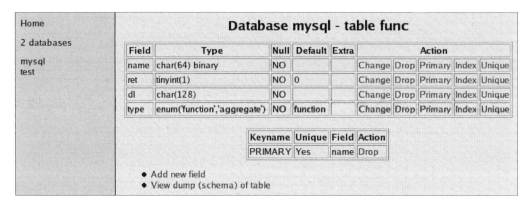

I was using phpMyAdmin from version 1.2.0 (released November 29, 1998), and was immediately hooked to the idea of being able to use a web application to maintain a remote database. However, students at Collège de Sherbrooke, where I work in Québec, Canada, are French speaking folks. Therefore, I contacted Tobias and offered to transform his source code by outsourcing all messages to a message file. He accepted the offer, and I created both the English and French message files. Then, on December 27, 1998, Tobias released version 1.3.1, the first multi-language version. (Meanwhile, he had created the German message file.) This version was the first to display **Welcome to phpMyAdmin**.

In 1999 and the first half of 2000, Tobias, helped by other contributors, improved the navigation system, added features, and merged more language files. His project site maintained a discussion forum allowing new ideas to come along and patches to be discussed. Version 2.1.0 was released on August 06, 2000, and this was the last version released by Tobias, who had no more time to devote to this project.

Project re-launch

However, the user base had already multiplied, and they were asking for more of the product. Patches were floating on the Internet, with no way of coordinating them. A security alert (and fix) had been published by a third-party, but no new version was being released. Finally, on March 31, 2001, Olivier Müller registered the phpMyAdmin project on SourceForge.net, and released a 2.2.0 pre-launch version. This was called the *unofficial* version. This restart of the project attracted some developers, who now had the SourceForge infrastructure (CVS server, forums, bug trackers, and mailing lists) to help speed up the development. I personally re-joined the project in May 2001, and started fixing and improving the code, as my co-developers were also doing.

We became *official* on May 28, 2001, as Tobias accepted our version as the new official one. I remember those months of very intense development effort, with daily improvements and bug fixes, along with new documentation sections. This effort culminated on August 31, 2001, with the release of version 2.2.0.

Here's an excerpt from the announcement file for 2.2.0:

> *After five months, five beta releases, and four release candidate versions, the phpMyAdmin developers are pleased to announce the availability of phpMyAdmin 2.2.0. [...] on March 31, 2001. Olivier Müller (Switzerland), supported by Marc Delisle (Québec), Loïc Chapeaux (France), and a team of eight other developers re-started the phpMyAdmin project on SourceForge.net, with the authorization of the original package maintainer. Now, after five months of patches, bug fixes, new features, and testing, the version 2.2.0 is finally ready.*

This version had security fixes and seven new languages (with dynamic language detection). The code had been reworked to be CSS2 and XHTML 1.0 compliant, and to follow the PEAR coding guidelines. The bookmarks feature appeared in this version, and this came from a separate add-on called "phpMyBookmark".

During the following year, the development continued, with the release of seven minor versions. The last version of the 2.2.x series is 2.2.7-pl1, which is also the last to have been fully tested under PHP 3. We registered `phpmyadmin.net` as the official domain name for the project on April 03, 2002 — the date is worth being noted.

Distributors

The list of distributors for phpMyAdmin would be too long and complex to gather, but here are a few pointers. First, the Downloads page of MySQL's website had a "contrib" section in which phpMyAdmin was mentioned very early after its birth. Also, many, if not all, Linux distributors included phpMyAdmin in their kit. Finally, a number of package builders prepare kits for various platforms. I'll just mention the renowned XAMPP kit from Apache Friends, available at `http://www.xampp.org`. Back in mid-2002, the Apache Friends group (led by Kai Seidler) was already busy integrating Apache, PHP, MySQL, and phpMyAdmin.

Evolution

On August 11, 2002, version 2.3.0 was released. There had been so many new features that the pages were becoming too long. So this version was the "great split version", creating subpages to group together related features, and thereby enhancing the Database and Table views.

The team started a schedule of releasing a new minor version (2.3.1, 2.3.2 ...) every two months. Version 2.4.0, released on February 23, 2003, included a new server/ user management facility. Then came version 2.5.0, on May 11, 2003, to mark the new MIME-type cell transformation system.

Version 2.6.0 — released on September 27, 2004 — added support for the new `mysqli` extension available in PHP 5, for better performance and improved security. The interface for this version was redesigned, including new icons and a theme manager. On April 16, 2005, version 2.6.2 was born, adding basic support for MySQL's views.

In June 2005, the first meeting of phpMyAdmin's development team took place in Karlsruhe, Germany, during LinuxTag 2005. Six members of the team from Switzerland, Germany, Czech Republic, and Canada were present, displaying phpMyAdmin and discussing its features with the event's attendees. We also celebrated PHP's and MySQL's 10th anniversary on the same occasion, along with the respective fathers of these products: Rasmus Lerdorf and Michael "Monty" Widenius. A few weeks before that, at the MySQL Users Conference in Santa Clara, a presentation was titled "PHP 5 + MySQL 5 = A Perfect 10". Indeed, we were aware of what this anniversary meant in terms of the product's maturity.

Version 2.7.0 was released on December 04, 2005. With this version, we ended support for older configuration files—those prior to phpMyAdmin 2.3.0. Also, in 2.7.0, a new plug-in-based import module made its debut.

Version 2.8.0 was made available on March 06, 2006. It included a new web-based setup mechanism. With 2.8.0, the team started a new numbering scheme for version releases. The 2.8 family contains fixes for only those features that are already present in 2.8.0. Here are some examples of the versions, which were expected to follow 2.8.0:

- 2.8.0.1, for anything urgent like a security fix
- 2.8.1, containing normal fixes for the 2.8 family
- 2.9.0, with new features

Version 2.9.0, released on September 20, 2006, added many small improvements such as a font size selector, new export formats, and the possibility of using an external authentication method. Version 2.10.0, released on February 27, 2007, had as its main attraction the Designer—a new graphical Ajax-based relation manager. Version 2.11.0, released on August 21, 2007, offered support for creating views. It also offered support for managing procedures, functions, and triggers. This version is still supported in terms of security updates.

GoPHP5 and the 3.x branch

phpMyAdmin accepted an invitation to become an initial member of the GoPHP5 initiative (see `http://GoPHP5.org`). This initiative promotes the adoption of PHP 5 among web hosts. This means that the new feature releases of phpMyAdmin, after February 05, 2008, require a server that can at least run PHP 5.2.

To better indicate the new PHP requirements, the team switched the major version number to 3. At the same time, it was decided to stop supporting MySQL prior to version 5.0 in the 3.x branch.

Version 3.0 was released on September 27, 2008, with support for MySQL 5.1 features, such as partitioning and the event scheduler. This version also had a new start page, and made use of JavaScript effects. Then, on November 11, 2008, version 3.1 incorporated a new setup script and support for BLOB streaming—the work of two students from the Google Summer of Code (GSoC) 2008. This version also added support for Swekey hardware authentication.

In preparation for GSoC 2009, version 3.2 was released on June 9, 2009. It was time to release this version, which contained many small new features, before merging the upcoming GSoC work. At the end of summer 2009, four students were able to finish their GSoC phpMyAdmin projects, which included new export and import modules, synchronization, change tracking, and replication support. Afterwards, a period of testing and merging occurred for these features.

In February 2010, the second team meeting took place during the Free and Open Source Software Developers' European Meeting (`http://fosdem.org/2010/`) in Brussels, Belgium. Five members from Germany, the Czech Republic, The Netherlands, and Canada discussed the project and decided to switch the localization system to `gettext` and to move the code base to a `git` repository. I gave a talk titled "State of phpMyAdmin" in the MySQL developer room, where I mostly presented the new features for the upcoming new version.

Version 3.3 was released on March 7, 2010 and included the new features of GSoC 2009. Our project was selected by Google for GSoC 2010, this time as a full-fledged participating organization. Six students developed new aspects of phpMyAdmin for the upcoming 3.4 version.

phpMyAdmin continues to be popular. The cumulative downloads, since April 2001, have reached an impressive count of more than twenty million in June 2010, at the time of writing this book.

Awards

phpMyAdmin has won some awards, as can be seen in the "Awards" section of the project's homepage. First, it was awarded "Project of the Month" for December 2002, by the administrators of SourceForge. In the interview-style document that we prepared to put on the SourceForge POTM page, I wrote that I was impressed by the download rate of our product, which was three per minute at that time. (Since then, we have reached ten per minute on peak days.)

phpMyAdmin received 75 percent of the votes from the readers of both the German PHP Magazine and its international version, in the category "Best PHP Application/Tool" for 2003. This award was officially presented to two members of the team at the International PHP Conference, held at Frankfurt in November 2003. The German PHP Magazine hosted the readers' choice again in 2005 and 2006, which phpMyAdmin won both the years.

`SourceForge.net` hosted its "Community Choice Awards" for the first time in 2006, and phpMyAdmin won in two categories—Databases and System Administration. I represented the team at LinuxWorld, Boston, in April for the Awards presentation. The project also won "Best PHP Application of the Year" at the fifth Annual OS/2 World Awards. At the end of 2006, our project won a Silver Trophy at the third "Trophées du Libre" contest; I went to France to receive the trophy.

In 2007, at the `SourceForge.net` "Community Choice Awards" (CCA), phpMyAdmin was nominated in the "Best Tool or Utility for Developers" category, and won the "Best Tool or Utility for SysAdmins" Award.

At the beginning of 2008, MySQL AB was acquired by Sun Microsystems for an amount of $1billion. I assume this gave `SourceForge.net` the idea to propose a new award category: "Most Likely to Be the Next $1B Acquisition". phpMyAdmin won this award too, along with "Best Tool or Utility for SysAdmins". phpMyAdmin was also a finalist for "Best Tool or Utility for Developers".

PhpMyAdmin also won the InfoWorld's "Best of open source platforms and middleware (MySQL administration)" prize for the year 2008. For the 2009 `SourceForge.net` CCA, phpMyAdmin was a finalist for "Best Tool or Utility for Developers" and won "Best Tool or Utility for SysAdmins", which is beginning to look like a habit. More details are available at `http://sourceforge.net/blog/cca09/winners`.

Future phpMyAdmin versions

Here are the points that the development team is considering for future versions:

- Improved support of MySQL's new features
- User preferences in permanent storage
- Interface improvements (usability, AJAXification)
- Internal code improvements

The phpMyAdmin team warmly welcomes new contributors.

B

Troubleshooting and Support

This appendix proposes guidelines for solving some common problems, and provides hints on how to avoid them. It also explains how to interact with the development team for support, bug reports, and contributions.

System requirements

A section at the beginning of the `Documentation.html` file (which is included with phpMyAdmin's software), discusses system requirements for the particular phpMyAdmin version we are using. It's crucial that these requirements be met, and that the environment be properly configured, so that problems are avoided.

Some problems, such as phpMyAdmin bugs, are in fact caused by the server environment. Sometimes, the web server is not configured to interpret `.php` files correctly, or the PHP component inside the web server does not run with the `mysql` or `mysqli` extensions. MySQL accounts may be badly configured. This can happen on home servers as well as on hosted servers.

When we suspect that something is wrong, we can try a simple PHP script, `test.php`, which contains the following, to check if the PHP component answers correctly:

```
<?php
echo 'hello';
?>
```

We should see the **hello** message. If this works, we can try another script:

```
<?php
phpinfo();
?>
```

This script displays information about the PHP component, including the available extensions. We should at least see a section about MySQL (proving that the `mysql` or `mysqli` extension is available), which provides information about the MySQL **Client API version**.

We can also try other PHP scripts that make a connection to MySQL, to see if the problem is more general than just phpMyAdmin not working. As a general rule, we should be running the latest stable versions of every component.

Verifying the base configuration

We should always double-check the way in which we performed the installation, including correct permissions and ownerships. Typos may occur when modifying `config.inc.php`.

Solving common errors

To help solve a problem, we should first pinpoint the origin of the error message. Here are the various components that can generate an error message:

- MySQL server: These messages are relayed by phpMyAdmin, which displays **MySQL said** followed by the message
- PHP component of the web server: For example, **Parser error**
- Web server: The error can be seen from the browser, or in the web server's log files
- Web browser: For example, JavaScript errors

The *Troubleshooting error messages* and *Troubleshooting other problems* sections of this appendix are mostly based on various messages found on phpMyAdmin's help forum and in the FAQ section of `Documentation.html`.

Troubleshooting error messages

This section refers to specific error messages, as displayed by phpMyAdmin.

Cannot load MySQL extension

To connect to a MySQL server, PHP needs the `mysql` extension (the `mysqli` extension is recommended for MySQL 4.1+), which is a set of MySQL functions. This extension may be compiled as a part of the PHP server. This error implies that no other PHP script can make connections to a MySQL server.

The required extension is contained in a file that can be named `mysql.so` or `mysqli.so` on Linux or UNIX, or `mysql.dll` (maybe `mysqli.dll`) on Windows. If our PHP server comes from a software package, we can find and install another software package—probably called `php-mysql` or `php-mysqli`. (The name is distribution dependent.) Otherwise, we can compile our own PHP server with the appropriate extension, as explained in the PHP documentation.

#2003 - Can't connect to MySQL server

This message indicates that the MySQL server is not running, or cannot be reached from the web server. It can also be caused by a socket (Linux/UNIX) or named pipe (Windows) configuration problem.

Socket problem (Linux/UNIX)

This message means that the socket configured in `php.ini` (an example of which is given below) does not correspond to the socket of the running MySQL server:

```
mysql.default_socket = /tmp/mysql.sock
```

As a result, PHP cannot reach MySQL. We can change it to:

```
mysql.default_socket = /var/lib/mysql/mysql.sock
```

However, to be sure, we must find the exact location of this socket.

Named pipe problem (Windows)

This is a problem similar to the one indicated above, but on Windows. It can be solved by adjusting `mysql.default_socket` to the correct named pipe used to connect locally to a MySQL server. For example:

```
mysql.default_socket = MySQL
```

MySQL said: Access denied

This error can be solved when we understand the relevant login parameters.

When using http authentication

We cannot use the web server security mechanism based on a `.htaccess` file and the `http` authentication in `config.inc.php` together. As a workaround, use `cookie` as the authentication type, instead of `http`.

When using http, cookie, or config authentication

The host parameter in `config.inc.php` must match the host defined in the user access privileges. Sometimes, a system administrator may create an account authorizing user `bill` and host `localhost`. If we try to use the `127.0.0.1` host in `config.inc.php`, it will be rejected by MySQL even though it points to the same machine. The same problem can occur if we try the real name of the machine (`mysql.domain.com`) and the definition has been made for `localhost`.

Access denied ... "using password: NO"

If the message ends with **using password: NO**, it means that we are not transmitting a password, and MySQL is rejecting this login attempt. The password value may not have been set in `config.inc.php`.

Access denied ... "using password: YES"

A password has been transmitted, but the host/username/password combination has been rejected by MySQL.

Login without a password is forbidden by configuration

phpMyAdmin wants to promote security; therefore the `$cfg['Servers'][$i]['AllowNoPassword']` directive is set to `false`, blocking attempts to log in with any account but no password. We have to set this to `true` in order to accomplish an initial login, in the case where our account is really without a password.

Warning: cannot add header information

This problem is caused by some characters (such as blank lines or spaces) being present in `config.inc.php`—either before the `<?php` tag at the beginning, or after the `?>` tag at the end. We should remove these with an editor that supports `.php` files (as discussed in *Chapter 1, Getting Started with phpMyAdmin*).

MySQL said: Error 127, Table Must Be Repaired

In the navigation panel, we click on the database name. In the main panel, we select the name of the table for which there is an error (using the relevant checkbox). We then choose **Repair** from the lower drop-down list. More details are available in *Chapter 9, Performing Table and Database Operations*.

BLOB column used in key specification without a key length

MySQL requires that an index set on a **BLOB** column be limited in size. The simple index creation technique available when creating a column does not permit the size to be specified. Therefore, we need to create the column without an index. We then come back to the **Structure** page, and use the **Create an index** dialog to choose the **BLOB** column and then set a size for the index.

IIS: No Input File Specified

This is a permission problem. **Internet Information Server (IIS)** must be able to read our scripts. As the server is running under the user IUSR_machinename, we have to carry out the following steps:

1. Right-click on the folder where we installed phpMyAdmin.

2. Choose **Properties**.

3. Click on **Add** under the **Security** tab, and select the IUSR_machinename user from the list.

4. Ensure that this user has read permission on the directory.

A "404: page not found" error when modifying a row

This happens when the $cfg['PmaAbsoluteUri'] parameter in config.inc.php is not set properly. *Chapter 1, Getting Started with phpMyAdmin*, explains how to take care of this parameter.

Troubleshooting other problems

Here, we cover solutions to problems that do not show up on the screen as a specific error message.

Blank page or weird characters

By default, phpMyAdmin uses output buffering and compression techniques to speed up the transmission of results to the browser. These techniques can interfere with other components of the web server, causing display problems. We can set $cfg['OBGzip'] to FALSE in config.inc.php. This should solve the problem.

Not being able to create a database

No privileges appears next to the **Create database** dialog on the home page, if phpMyAdmin detects that the account used to log in does not have the permissions necessary to create a database. This situation occurs frequently on hosted servers, where the system administrator prefers to create one database for each customer.

If we are not on a hosted server, this message simply reflects the fact that we have neither the global **CREATE** privilege nor any **CREATE** privilege on a wildcard database specification.

Problems importing large files or uploading large BLOB files

Usually, these problems indicate that we have hit a limit during the transfer. *Chapter 8, Searching Data*, explains these limits and the recommended course of action. As a last resort, we might have to split our large text files. (Search the Internet for **file splitters**.)

MySQL root password lost

The MySQL manual explains the general solution at `http://www.mysql.com/doc/en/Resetting_permissions.html`.

The solution involves stopping the MySQL server and restarting it with the special option `skip-grant-tables` (which basically starts the server without security). The way to stop and restart the server depends on the server platform used. We can then connect to the server from phpMyAdmin as a superuser (like root) with any password. The next step is to change the root's password (see *Chapter 19, Administrating the MySQL Server with phpMyAdmin*). We can then stop the MySQL server and restart it using normal procedures. (Security will become active again.)

Duplicate field names when creating a table

Here is a curious symptom. When we try to create a table containing, for example, one field named FIELD1 of type VARCHAR(15), it looks like phpMyAdmin has sent a command to create two identical fields named FIELD1. The problem is not caused by phpMyAdmin, but by the environment. In this case, the Apache web server seems well-configured to run PHP scripts when in fact it is not. However, this bug appears only for some scripts.

The problem occurs when two different (and conflicting) sets of directives are used in the Apache configuration file. The first set of directives are:

```
SetOutputFilter PHP
SetInputFilter PHP
```

The second one is:

```
AddType application/x-httpd-php .php
```

These sets of directives may be in two different Apache configuration files, and hence, difficult to notice. The recommended way is to use `AddType`. Using this, we just need to comment out the other lines (as shown in the following snippet), and then restart Apache:

```
#SetOutputFilter PHP
#SetInputFilter PHP
```

Authentication window displayed more than once

This problem occurs when we try to start phpMyAdmin with a URL other than the one set in `$cfg['PmaAbsoluteUri']`. For example, a server may have more than one name, or we may try to use the IP address instead of the name.

Column size changed by phpMyAdmin

For a more efficient column definition, MySQL itself sometimes decides to change the column type and size. This happens mostly with **CHAR** and **VARCHAR** type fields.

Seeing many databases that are not ours

This problem occurs mostly after an upgrade to MySQL 4. The automatic server upgrade procedure gives the global privileges **CREATE TEMPORARY TABLES**, **SHOW DATABASES**, and **LOCK TABLES** to all users. These privileges also enable users to see the names of all of the databases (but not their tables) until we upgrade the GRANT tables privilege as described in the MySQL manual. If the users do not need these privileges, we can revoke the privileges. The users will then see only those databases to which they have access rights.

Not being able to store a value greater than 127

This is normal if we have defined a column of type TINYINT, as 127 is the maximum value for this column type. Similar problems may arise with other numeric column types. Changing the type to INT expands the available range of values.

Seeking support

The starting point for support is the phpMyAdmin home page, `http://www.phpmyadmin.net`, which has sections on documentation and support. There, you will find links to the discussion forums and to various trackers, such as:

- Bug tracker
- Feature requests tracker
- Translations tracker
- Patches tracker
- Support tracker

FAQs

The `Documentation.html` file, which is a part of the product, contains a lengthy FAQ section with numbered questions and answers. It's recommended to peruse this FAQ section as a source of help.

Help forums

The development team recommends that you use the product's forums to search for the problem encountered, and then start a new forum discussion, before opening a bug report.

Creating a SourceForge account

Creating a (free) SourceForge user account, and using it for posting on forums, is highly recommended. This enables better tracking of questions and answers.

Choosing the thread title

It's important to choose the summary title carefully when you start a new forum thread. Titles such as "Help me!", "Help a newbie!", "Problem", or "phpMyAdmin error!" are difficult to deal with, as the answers are threaded to these titles and further reference becomes problematic. Better titles would be: "Import with UploadDir", "User can't but root can login", or "Server not responding".

Reading the answers

As people will read and, almost always answer, your question(s), giving feedback in the forum about the answers can really help the person who answered, and also help others also help who encounter the same problem.

Using the support tracker

The support tracker is another place to ask for support. Also, if we have submitted a bug report, which is in fact a support request, the report will be moved to the support tracker. If you have a SourceForge user account, you will be notified of this tracker change.

Using the bug tracker

In this tracker, we see bugs that have not yet been fixed, along with the bugs that have been fixed for the next version. (This is to avoid getting duplicate bug reports.)

Environment description

As developers will try to reproduce the problem mentioned, it helps to describe your environment. This description can be short, but should contain the following items:

- phpMyAdmin version (the team, however, expects that it's the current stable version)
- Web server name and version
- PHP version
- MySQL version
- Browser name and version

Usually, it isn't necessary to specify the operating system on which the server or the client is running, unless we notice that the bug pertains to only one OS. For example, FAQ 5.1 describes a problem where the user could not create a table having more than fourteen fields. This happens only in Windows 98.

Bug description

We should give a precise description of what happens (including any error message, the expected results, and the effective results we get). Reports are easily managed if they describe only one problem per bug report (unless the problems are clearly linked).

Sometimes, it might help to attach a short export file to the bug report, to help developers to reproduce the problem. Screenshots are also welcome.

Contributing to the project

Since 1998, hundreds of people have contributed translations, code for new features, suggestions, and bug fixes.

The code base

The development team maintains an evolving code base from which they periodically issue releases. On `http://phpmyadmin.net`, the **Improve** page explains how anyone can contribute, and gives pointers about the project's `git` source code repository. A contribution (translation update, patch, new feature, and so on) will be considered with a higher priority if it refers to the latest code base, and not to an outdated phpMyAdmin version. Another useful page of instructions for using Git—which is used for storing the code base—is located at `http://wiki.phpmyadmin.net/pma/Devel:Git`.

Translation updates

Taking a look at the project's current list of 58 languages, you will notice that they are not equally well maintained. Since the project's move to a `gettext`-based localization system, everyone is encouraged to contribute to translations. For the upcoming 3.4 version and onwards, the project is using a translation server equipped with the Pootle software, located at `https://l10n.cihar.com/projects/phpmyadmin`. It's also possible to use this server to translate phpMyAdmin's `Documentation.html`.

Patches

The development team can manage patches more easily if they are submitted in the form of a `git format-patch` against the current code base, with an explanation of the solved problem or the new feature achieved. Contributors are officially credited in `Documentation.html`, or at least in `ChangeLog`.

Index

R

relational MySQL
  about 189
  InnoDB 190
  PBXT 190
relational schemas, in PDF
  generating 272
  PDF pages, editing 274
  PDF schema, laying out with Designer
    feature 279
  third table, adding to model 273
relations, with Designer
  defining 202-206
  display field, defining 207
  foreign key relations, defining 207
  interface, over-viewing 202-205
  PDF schema, exporting 208
relations, with relational view
  defining 196
  display field, defining 197, 198
  foreign key relations 198-201
  foreign keys, without linked-tables infra-
    structure 201
  internal relations, defining 196
  relation, defining 197
rename operation 183
replication information
  replicated databases 255, 256
  replicated tables 256
  replication status, gathering 255
replication menu, MySQL 248
results, browse mode
  sorting 89

S

"Save as file" subpanel
  about 133
  character set, selecting 134
  compression file 134
  file name template 133
  Kanji support 135
search options, single-table searches
  about 170
  fields to be displayed, selecting 170, 171
  repeated results, avoiding 172
  results, ordering 171

WHERE clause, applying 171
search page
  using daily 165
security, phpMyAdmin
  about 39
  error messages, displaying 40
  levels 39
  logging, accessing 45
  phpMyAdmin, protecting at directory level
    39
  protecting in-transit area 42
  protection with IP-based access control 40
  Swekey authentication 43
selective exports
  about 146
  partial query results, exporting 146
server information
  about 351
  binary logs, examining 355
  character sets and collations 354
  general status page 351
  InnoDB status 352
  server processes 353
  server status, verifying 351
  server variables 352
  storage engines 354
server parameters, phpMyAdmin
  about 24
  connect_type 25
  extension 25
  port 25
  socket 25
set fields, table structure 114, 115
single-table searches
  about 165
  case-sensitive search, performing 169
  criteria by field, searching 166, 167
  criteria, combining 170
  empty / non-empty values, searching 167
  query by example 166
  reports, producing with print view 168
  search options 170
  search subpage, entering 166
  wildcard characters, searching with 168,
    169
slave server configuration, MySQL
    replication 252

Thank you for buying
Mastering phpMyAdmin 3.3.x for Effective MySQL Management

About Packt Publishing

Packt, pronounced 'packed', published its first book "*Mastering phpMyAdmin for Effective MySQL Management*" in April 2004 and subsequently continued to specialize in publishing highly focused books on specific technologies and solutions.

Our books and publications share the experiences of your fellow IT professionals in adapting and customizing today's systems, applications, and frameworks. Our solution based books give you the knowledge and power to customize the software and technologies you're using to get the job done. Packt books are more specific and less general than the IT books you have seen in the past. Our unique business model allows us to bring you more focused information, giving you more of what you need to know, and less of what you don't.

Packt is a modern, yet unique publishing company, which focuses on producing quality, cutting-edge books for communities of developers, administrators, and newbies alike. For more information, please visit our website: www.packtpub.com.

About Packt Open Source

In 2010, Packt launched two new brands, Packt Open Source and Packt Enterprise, in order to continue its focus on specialization. This book is part of the Packt Open Source brand, home to books published on software built around Open Source licences, and offering information to anybody from advanced developers to budding web designers. The Open Source brand also runs Packt's Open Source Royalty Scheme, by which Packt gives a royalty to each Open Source project about whose software a book is sold.

Writing for Packt

We welcome all inquiries from people who are interested in authoring. Book proposals should be sent to author@packtpub.com. If your book idea is still at an early stage and you would like to discuss it first before writing a formal book proposal, contact us; one of our commissioning editors will get in touch with you.

We're not just looking for published authors; if you have strong technical skills but no writing experience, our experienced editors can help you develop a writing career, or simply get some additional reward for your expertise.

Creating your MySQL Database: Practical Design Tips and Techniques

ISBN: 978-1-904811-30-5   Paperback: 108 pages

A short guide for everyone on how to structure your data and set-up your MySQL database tables efficiently and easily.

1. How best to collect, name, group, and structure your data

2. Design your data with future growth in mind

3. Practical examples from initial ideas to final designs

Expert Cube Development with Microsoft SQL Server 2008 Analysis Services

ISBN: 978-1-847197-22-1   Paperback: 360 pages

Design and implement fast, scalable and maintainable cubes

1. A real-world guide to designing cubes with Analysis Services 2008

2. Model dimensions and measure groups in BI Development Studio

3. Implement security, drill-through, and MDX calculations

4. Learn how to deploy, monitor, and performance-tune your cube

Please check **www.PacktPub.com** for information on our titles

2968739R00219

Printed in Great Britain
by Amazon.co.uk, Ltd.,
Marston Gate.